Bob Oblack

Business
to
Business

Direct Marketing

Bernie Goldberg
&
Tracy Emerick

Direct Marketing Publishers, Inc.

DEDICATION

> To all business-to-business direct marketers --
> we hope you can profit and learn
> from each other.

Published by Direct Marketing Publishers, Inc.
92 Presidential Circle

Hampton, NH 03842

Table of Contents

Introduction

If you have been asked to supervise or manage direct marketing activities in your company, you already know that there seems to be more problems than solutions. In a lot of ways, direct marketing is like a decision tree or maze -- the more you get into it...the more difficult it becomes.

The good news is that you're not alone. Almost everyone who starts down the road of using direct mail, telemarketing or direct response advertising has faced the same problem. The bad news is that all of the available instructional materials and texts are geared towards consumer marketing.

As we began to implement business-to-business direct marketing programs, we felt alone and like pioneers. There is very little written on the subject and seminars and programs we attended were not geared to our needs. That's why we developed this book. If you feel like us, this book will give you a basis for understanding and implementing business-to-business direct marketing.

You can become an expert in the direct marketing field if you spend about two years making mistakes. You will still have to learn by your own mistakes even with this book as a guide, but there is no reason not to profit from the same mistakes that have been made by others.

Volumes have been written and are continually being developed on the subject of direct marketing. All spend 90% of the time on how to reach the consumer and may commit one chapter to selling to other businesses. Their approach is to say, "Oh, by the way...".

The focus on consumer direct marketing is well justified. There are about 90 million households and over 240 million people in the United States that businesses are trying to reach through direct marketing. In addition, the concepts initially developed in America are growing at a phenomenal rate in other countries. Meanwhile, the business marketer is looking at a universe of somewhere between 10 and 12 million companies in the United States. Just looking at the numbers a book is doing a reasonable job if it spends 10% on how to market to other businesses ... right?

You can't fault the other books; most are very good. The easy action and opportunity for direct marketing experts is in consumer direct marketing. In addition, marketing to the consumer has a long head start and more documented experience than selling to other businesses. However, all businesses are engaged in direct marketing even though they may call it something different.

The smaller number of businesses employs most of the adult population. It is the complexity of targeting a consumer in their place of business that makes direct marketing to business so difficult. The segmentation techniques used in the consumer world don't work when selling to other businesses. The large universe in the consumer world allows you to make mistakes and still have almost an unlimited group to sell to.

On the other hand, because most businesses only sell to smaller segments of a particular business market, the number of targets is limited. The range of experimentation is reduced and you must develop better measurement and testing techniques to be successful. We were unable to find any book that really dealt with these complex issues. The more we discussed the subject the more we were convinced that a complete text on business-to-business direct marketing really needed to be written.

This book first differentiates consumer direct marketing from business-to-business direct marketing. It focuses on the needs of the business marketer. Business marketing is more difficult to plan and evaluate, especially if you are using a field sales force. Throughout this book, we focus on how to work with a field sales organization and be successful with direct marketing. We have dedicated a whole chapter to lead generation for field sales.

How to create and use a database to effectively control your efforts is also stressed and examined. Given the limited size of the business universe and the higher cost of identifying prospects, database marketing is absolutely critical.

Planning and measurement are the cornerstones to successful direct marketing. You will not only find the techniques and processes to allow you to succeed in these areas but also the actual cases and formula to make these approaches come alive.

Every business is looking at two major growth areas in direct marketing: telemarketing and cataloging. You will find comprehensive chapters devoted to each of these topics. Among many other findings, you will discover whether you are already in the catalog business and don't know it. And, you will also be able to decide whether you are using telesales or telemarketing.

In a recent study of expenditures published by *Business Marketing Magazine* , (© Crain Communications, Inc.) over $93 billion was spent in 1985 for business marketing. Over $30 billion of the total expenditures was spent for direct marketing. At this level of investment, you have an opportunity to improve your return on investment by becoming more skilled in the tactics of direct marketing.

There is strength in numbers.

Advertising...$8,589,371,000
Direct Marketing...............................30,850,000,000
Trade Shows 21,000,000,000
Sales Promotion................................7,616,900,000
Incentives...15,065,871,000
Sales Force Management....................5,920,000,000
Public Relations.................................2,405,300,000
Research...2,190,200,000
Total..$93,637,642,000

Reprinted with permission from
Business Marketing Magazine © Crain
Communications, Inc.
740 Rush Street
Chicago, Illinois 60611

If you gain one idea per chapter, your effectiveness as a manager can improve your overall results and enhance your position within your company. We hope you can learn from all of our mistakes.

Bernie Goldberg & Tracy Emerick

About the Authors

Bernard A. Goldberg

Bernie Goldberg spent ten years at IBM Corporation in marketing and sales of small to medium computer systems. Bernie was one of the top sales people and later a top sales manager for the company. In addition, he spent two years in sales training and marketing planning. In his last position with IBM in 1979, he managed a pioneering facility in direct marketing and telemarketing. Like most of us he started in business-to-business direct marketing with no experience and no prior training. Because of Bernie's prior sales background he has empathy and understanding for the field sales organization.

Prior to IBM, Bernie spent four years in the Army immediately after receiving his Bachelor of Arts degree from C.W. Post College.

After IBM, Bernie's entrepreneurial spirit fostered two different telemarketing companies. He has specialized in all aspects of business-to-business direct marketing. He is a frequent speaker at direct marketing and telemarketing meetings and has written numerous articles on both subjects. He has also served as Vice Chairman and Programming Chairman of the Business-to-Business Council of the Direct Marketing Association.

Bernie is currently president of his own consulting firm, B. A. Goldberg Consulting, in Yardley, Pennsylvania. A native of Amityville, New York, Bernie resides with his wife and three daughters in Yardley, Pennsylvania.

J. Tracy Emerick

Tracy Emerick has spent the last 15 years involved in all phases of direct marketing. His experience includes working in product development and manufacturing of consumer products sold through direct marketing. Tracy also developed a catalog operation for a 3.5 million member organization while maintaining a $40 million business-to-business operation. He became a pioneer in business telemarketing when he took a national sales force off the road 35% of the time and increased their performance by 50%.

Prior to his experience in direct marketing Tracy earned a bachelor's degree from William and Mary College, spent three years in the Army and earned an MBA from Northeastern University.

To keep his mind alert, Tracy teaches business policy and marketing planning at the MBA level. He has also been engaged by the Direct Marketing Association to offer a national training session on catalog management.

Tracy has been the chairman of the Business-to-Business Council for the past two years. Prior to that he served as the Council's programming chairman for five years. Tracy is currently president of Taurus Marketing, Hampton, New Hampshire, a direct marketing and consulting agency he founded in 1981. Tracy has won many awards for successful client work including the DMA's international ECHO award and the coveted Henry Hoke Award.

Raised as an 'Army Brat' Tracy now calls Hampton, NH home. He lives in this lovely New England seacoast town with his wife and two children.

Chapter One - Business-to-Business Direct Marketing

Consumer Vs. Business-to-Business Direct Marketing

Is there really a difference between direct marketing to consumers at home and direct marketing to prospects at their place of business? Let's examine both situations through the best understood method of direct marketing - direct mail advertising - and see whether there is a basic difference.

The consumer receives his or her own mail from a mail box. In most cases, the target or addressed recipient sees each piece of mail and makes a decision whether to open and read the message. Often, this involves a quick sorting between bills and what is perceived to be personal mail in one stack and advertising solicitations of all kinds in another. This process generally takes place where there is a counter and a trash can. All too often from the marketer's point of view, the consumer will toss the advertising mail, unopened, directly into the trash can .

In the consumer area, getting the mail opened and responded to is the major challenge. It is relatively easy to address and reach prospects. With the constant refinement of technology, thousands of lists are available that allow you to target your prospect by first and last name. It isn't necessary to address your message to 'Occupant'. While the rate of change of addresses in the consumer world is estimated at about 15% per year, new postal address change systems are becoming available to consumer marketers in order to keep track of these changes and reduce that number.

Now let's look at the environment for receiving direct mail advertising in the work place. In many businesses, a mail room or mail clerk receives the mail and is responsible for sorting and distributing it to the appropriate parties. In a large company it is likely that a secretary will open the mail. She will evaluate the message you are attempting to deliver and determine if her 'boss' should read it.

Therefore, two potential screens for direct mail solicitations exist in the business world that don't impede the consumer mail marketer. First, the mail room may mis-route or be instructed to throw out advertising mail, especially duplicate copies. Second, the secretarial function is largely to filter out matters considered not essential to her superior's performance. Unsolicited direct mail is often perceived to be a waste of time, so the secretary throws it out.

In addition to these screens, there is another, more fundamental problem facing the business-to-business marketer. As we all know, business is in continuous motion and the only thing constant is change. Your prospect, the target you want to reach, is the individual filling a specific job with responsibilities aligned to your offer. Changing jobs or responsibilities is very common. The rate of change in the job function you're trying to reach can easily be 40% to 50% per year. Therefore, addressing your prospect by name and ensuring that you are really reaching the right person in the right job, is much more difficult in the business arena.

Before defining direct marketing and applying it to the business environment, let's take a quick look at other methods of marketing to businesses and see if they differ from consumer marketing. The process of direct response advertising in magazines, newspapers and other media are similar in both marketplaces. However, the creative approach used in the other media for business-to-business can be substantially different than consumer. We will focus on those areas later in this book.

Telemarketing has additional considerations worth reviewing when contrasting consumer with business-to-business markets. The consumer is normally reachable from 5 to 9 in the evening and on weekends. Usually, you're trying to reach any adult in the household, so if someone answers you can probably get a decision to whatever your offer is. In most cases, you're selling a product so the consumer can simply say 'yes' or 'no' to your offer. Re-scheduling the call to reach the appropriate individual is not necessarily based on a specific time that the individual will be available. A structured re-scheduling approach over a planned number of contacts can be very successful. You don't have to deal with 'on demand re-scheduling' (someone asking you to call back at a specific time on a specific day).

Business-to-business telemarketing introduces the villain 'Bertha Barrier', whose only mission in life is to ensure that no salesperson reaches the other side of her desk. Telemarketing program design has to deal with circumventing 'Bertha' and allowing you to talk to your prospect. Plus you must plan on calling at times when he/she is most likely be in the office and available to talk. In most cases, your target will not be the first person to answer the phone. You'll probably go through two or more individuals prior to reaching your target (switchboard & secretaries). Moreover, due to constant change in responsibilities, often the appropriate decision maker has been mis-identified and you will have to begin anew attempting to contact the correct individual. It is also likely that upon reaching your target directly over the phone, you'll have to re-schedule the call at a specific time and day in order for him or her to agree to hear your message.

Let's put it in perspective: Most of the concepts of direct marketing that work in motivating an individual to respond in the consumer world will also work in the business world. After all, the business person is still the same individual. However, a major difference that should be evaluated relates to whose money he is being asked to spend. In the consumer environment, you're asking the prospect to spend his own funds on your offer. In the business world, the individual is usually being asked to commit corporate funds and not his or her own money.

So the real differences in the two marketplaces involve the accessibility of the prospect and his/her financing or money sources. Obviously the size the two markets is also substantially different. The real challenge we face is to get our message in front of the individual who can make a decision on our offer.

In this this book, we will focus on techniques that have been effective in using direct marketing to sell products or services from one business to another. First, let's get a better understanding of what we mean by direct marketing.

Direct Marketing Defined

There are many definitions for direct marketing. We believe that direct marketing:

Explores, tests and substantiates methods of :

- *Prospecting*
- *Qualifying*
- *Closing*

exclusive of a face-to-face contact by a salesperson.

A more complete explanation of direct marketing can be found in Illustration 1-1. We have simplified the definition into six understandable elements, described in Illustration 1-2. The first element of this definition explains that direct marketing is normally a part of a

DIRECT MARKETING - What is it?

An Aspect of Total Marketing -
Not a fancy term for mail order.

Marketing is the total of activities of moving goods and services from seller to buyer. (See chart). Direct Marketing has the same broad function except that Direct Marketing requires the existence and maintenance of database.

a) to record names of customers, expires and prospects.
b) to provide a vehicle for storing, then measuring, results of advertising, usually direct response advertising.
c) to provide a vehicle for storing, then measuring, purchasing performance.
d) to provide a vehicle for continuing direct communication by mail and/or phone.

Thus

DIRECT MARKETING is interactive, requiring database for controlled activity: By mail, by phone, through other media selected on the basis of previous results.

DIRECT MARKETING makes direct response advertising generally desirable since response (inquiries or purchasing transactions) can be recorded on a database for building the list, providing marketing information.

DIRECT MARKETING plays no favorites in terms of Methods of Selling...and there are only three:
a) Where buyer seeks out seller - retailing, exhibits
b) Where seller seeks out buyer - personal selling
c) Where buyer seeks seller by mail or phone - mail order

DIRECT MARKETING requires that a response or transaction at any location be recorded on cards, mechanical equipment or, preferably, on computer.

DIRECT MARKETING can be embraced by any kind of business as defined by the U.S. Census Standard Industrial Classification System.

DIRECT MARKETING is an interactive system of marketing that uses one or more advertising media to effect a measurable response and/or transaction at any location.

Illustration 1-1.a: Direct Marketing definition from Direct Marketing Magazine.

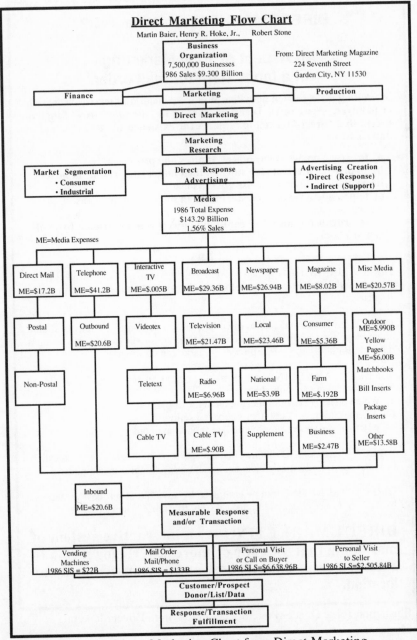

Direct Marketing Flow Chart

Martin Baier, Henry R. Hoke, Jr.,   Robert Stone

Business Organization
7,500,000 Businesses
986 Sales $9.300 Billion

From: Direct Marketing Magazine
224 Seventh Street
Garden City, NY 11530

Finance   **Marketing**   **Production**

Direct Marketing

Marketing Research

Market Segmentation
• Consumer
• Industrial

Direct Response Advertising

Advertising Creation
•Direct (Response)
• Indirect (Support)

Media
1986 Total Expense
$143.29 Billion
1.56% Sales

ME=Media Expenses

Direct Mail	Telephone	Interactive TV	Broadcast	Newspaper	Magazine	Misc Media
ME=$17.2B	ME=$41.2B	ME=$.005B	ME=$29.36B	ME=$26.94B	ME=$8.02B	ME=$20.57B

Postal	Outbound	Videotex	Television	Local	Consumer	Outdoor ME=$.990B
	ME=$20.6B		ME=$21.47B	ME=$23.46B	ME=$5.36B	Yellow Pages ME=$6.00B

Non-Postal		Teletext	Radio	National	Farm	Matchbooks
			ME=$6.96B	ME=$3.9B	ME=$.192B	Bill Inserts

		Cable TV	Cable TV	Supplement	Business	Package Inserts
			ME=$.90B		ME=$2.47B	Other ME=$13.58B

Inbound
ME=$20.6B

Measurable Response and/or Transaction

Vending Machines 1986 SIS = $22B	Mail Order Mail/Phone 1986 SIS = $133B	Personal Visit or Call on Buyer 1986 SLS=$6,638.96B	Personal Visit to Seller 1986 SLS=$2,505.84B

Customer/Prospect Donor/List/Data

Response/Transaction Fulfillment

Illustration 1-1.a: Direct Marketing Chart from Direct Marketing Magazine planned marketing program and will often include a series of contacts.

Direct marketing activity can employ various media forms but it always seeks to produce a lead or an order. <u>Direct marketing will call its identified target to perform some action.</u>

The Definition of Direct Marketing

- **An organized and planned system of contacts**

- **Using a variety of media -- seeking to produce a lead or an order**

- **Developing and maintaining a database**

- **Measurable in cost and results**

- **Works in all methods of selling**

- **Expandable with confidence**

Illustration 1-2:   A simplified definition of Direct marketing.

The creation and maintenance of a database is an integral aspect of direct marketing. "Database" is perhaps the most misunderstood and diversely defined word in business today. Data processing people have one definition, while direct marketers have their own meaning.

As part of the same example displayed in Illustration 1-2, Direct Marketing magazine has established a definition of database that is easy to understand.

The Definition of Direct Marketing with Database Defined

- An organized and planned system of contacts

- Using a variety of media -- seeking to produce a lead or an order

- Developing and maintaining a database
  - **Providing Names of Customers, Prospects**

  - **Vehicle for Storing, Measuring Responses**

  - **Vehicle for Storing, Measuring Purchases**

  - **Vehicle for Continuing Direct Communication**

- Measurable in cost and results

- Works in all methods of selling

- Expandable with confidence

Illustration 1-3: The definition of database

Direct marketing will develop and maintain a database which:

- *provides names of customers or prospects.*
- *is a vehicle for storing and measuring responses.*
- *is a vehicle for storing and measuring purchases.*
- *is a vehicle for continuing direct communication to the prospects, respondents and customers.*

Let's examine each of the elements of this database definition and again differentiate business-to-business from consumer direct marketing implications.

- **Database provides names of customers or prospects.**

  We used to think that buying a mailing list created our own database. The world has become more sophisticated, and technology allows us to do a much better job. The original list is important and becomes a part of the database, but information involving the activity of that list is also essential.

  The U.S. consumer universe consists of over 240 million people in about 90 million households. The business world is not as easily counted. While it is safe to say that there are over 17 million business names in the U.S., each company may have several operating business names. Different company names and abbreviations for the same company alone complicate matters. For example, 3M Corporation has several identities:

     3M
     Three M
     Minnesota Mining and Manufacturing Company
     3M Company
     3M Inc.
     3M Corporation

  These six identities for the same company do not include the seemingly endless name permutations on the divisional and subsidiary level. All of these company name variations make tracking a purchaser or a respondent much more difficult in the business-to-business universe. Addresses, executive names and phone numbers complicate the problem. Plus, list compilers each have different counts for the same type of business lists to be purchased.

  Given this complex web of company divisions and subsidiaries and purchasing decisions delineated in various ways, an extremely sophisticated database capable of tracking and reporting these relationships may be beyond your immediate grasp. But don't be daunted; always capture the information. It is still very difficult to maintain the hierarchy of business and who owns what, but as programming and hardware power advances you may need to do this to target your offer to the appropriate universe. In fact, you're likely to need to reach both the decision makers and the influencers to sell your product or service, and you should start capturing that information immediately.

Business-to-business list management is more difficult than consumer list management. Business addresses may be 4, 5 or 6 lines long including internal 'mail stop' addresses. List selection by title - never a consideration in consumer list selection - can be tricky because an individual's title often carries different weight from company to company. In comparison, a consumer list normally has 3 line addresses and you can almost always count on reaching the decision maker or key influencer.

•   **Database is a vehicle for storing and measuring responses.**

Once you reach the target and get a response to your offer, create a record of that response and whether the prospect has purchased. The database should enable you to track each contact and each response.

Your customers have established a relationship with you and have a lower degree of fear, uncertainty and doubt (FUD). They know who you are, what you sell and the quality of your products. More importantly, they have demonstrated a need for your products or services by purchasing in the past. The best source of additional business is former customers. Many companies forget that prospects who responded, but did not purchase from prior campaigns, are also excellent sources of additional business. They also have established some relationship with you and should not be ignored.

- **Database is a vehicle for storing and measuring purchases.**

  Once prospects respond to a direct marketing program, we want to track these responses to see whether they become buyers.

  Direct marketing programs often use the initial response rate as the sole measurement criteria. Cost per respondent or lead, which is the effective measurement from initial response, is an important first part of the programs measurement criteria. By tracking and measuring the responses, cost per respondent or lead can be established. However, cost per respondent will not help you measure the *profitability* of your program. To evaluate the ultimate success of the program, you should measure the respondent through the entire sales cycle and determine the *cost per order, average order size,* and *lifetime value*.

  When someone initially responds to a direct marketing program, it is referred to as the *front end* of the program. The prospect has responded but whether they will actually purchase the product or service is still unclear: The *back end* of the program refers to the conversion of a respondent to a buyer and a repeat buyer. In direct selling programs, where the response is actually an order, the front end and back end can be the same.

  A program can seem attractive at the front end in terms of cost per respondent. It may be a failure when the cost per order and average order size is reviewed.

- **Database is a vehicle for continuing direct communication to the prospects, respondents and customers.**

  The database should provide a sustained and complete ability to contact:

a) the initial list of prospects
b) the respondents
c) and the buyers.

The need to track the status of each contact while measuring the results of each effort makes this process complicated.

Direct marketing is measurable in both its costs and its results, (see Illustration 1-2). In the consumer universe, a buying decision usually occurs within one contact or call. A business-to-business transaction may have an *influencer* who selects a product but a different person making the actual buying decision. The size of the expenditure can affect the length of time it takes to get a decision. This multilevel decision process often precludes a single contact from generating an order.

In lead generation programs, trying to establish buyers and cost per buyer can be very frustrating (see chapter 3). Several factors affect this:

•   The purchase may occur in the future.
•   The respondent and the buyer may be different people.
•   Tracking the name of the company that actually responds or buys can be even more difficult.

Direct marketing can serve in all methods of selling. In a retail setting, where the buyer seeks the seller, coupons and special offers can drive traffic into the retail center. Or a sales person may use direct marketing as a lead generation vehicle in order to get a face-to-face appointment. Soliciting the prospects to buy through the telephone or mail, similar to the consumer mail order business, is another possibility.

One of the key benefits of direct marketing is that a successful technique can be expanded with confidence. Results should be predictable. If something worked before at a certain volume or rate, we should be able to get similar results, other factors being equal.

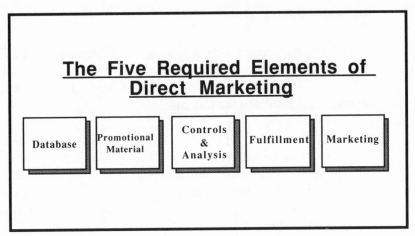

Illustration 1-4: The five elements of Direct Marketing.

Five basic elements are required to perform a successful direct marketing program (Illustration 1-4). They are:

• **Database**

We defined and discussed the elements of the database. A more detailed discussion will follow in chapter 4.

• **Promotional Material**

Specialized promotional material that seeks to produce a response -- either a lead or an order -- is required. We have frequently seen programs in which technical specification material and brochures were redeployed for use in generating sales leads. This material was created as collateral to assist the field sales force; it was not designed to create a response, and is unlikely to do so.

A comment we often hear is, "My business is different. I tried direct marketing, and it didn't work." When the prior attempts are examined, no effort to provide specialized promotional material is evident.

- **Controls and Analysis**

  An effective direct marketing program measures both cost and results. Costs are usually pretty easy to monitor, but in the business-to-business environment it is surprisingly difficult to measure the results of the program.

  - The different company names and abbreviations make tracking difficult. It is not unusual to have a prospect fill out a response device while traveling or away from their office. They may or may not include their company name. If the company name is provided it may be abbreviated or given differently than other names for the same company already on the list.

    In several programs in which we participated, leads were given to the sales people with company name information and the orders were placed with different company names. The orders were actually placed through a leasing company and became impossible to link to the original lead.

  - The decision process frequently extends beyond the one contact and the eventual order may not occur during the original time period designated by the compaign's planners. Lead programs in the high tech area can have selling cycles in months and years. Management wants to measure the success of the lead efforts in weeks, hence the lead programs are never successful.

  - Frequently a company assigns purchasing agents. The respondent and the purchaser may be different people. This creates similar measurement problems we discussed earlier with different company names. Purchasing agents can further complicate the tracking process because on-going direct marketing programs targeted to customers can be aimed at the wrong individual. The purchasing agent is normally told to place the order and may not have the money, authority, need or desire for additional products or services.

- Companies will often have different phone numbers for the corporate offices and the individuals. Phone number as a controlling identifier will not work. In an effort to eliminate duplicate contacts to the same company, using the phone number as a potential key will not work. Many companies use direct-inward-dialing. This service, available from your local phone company, will allow people to have a direct line to their office that can still go through the company switchboard.

- Companies have frequent changes in responsibility and a respondent today may not be the appropriate target tomorrow. This tends to be the most difficult problem in business marketing. It is worthwhile to retain title information on responses to help identify the appropriate target within the company as individuals move around.

- It is possible to receive multiple responses from the same company that only generate one order. This can occur as purchase decisions are centralized and pooled to take advantage of volume discounts. Multiple influencers can also cloud this area.

- **Fulfillment**

Delivering the offer made in the direct marketing promotion is called "fulfillment". The ability to deliver your promise is key to successful direct marketing.

Providing fulfillment includes such simple yet essential steps as ensuring that the 800 number used in the promotion is answered. There have been situations where the advertising department forgot to notify the switchboard, customer service department or outside service that a promotion had been run. You can imagine the way the incoming calls were handled.

Prospects might respond to your promotion and ask for additional information. Responding to this kind of inquiry is another form of fulfillment.

Sending leads to the salesperson and having them follow-up is, again, a form of fulfillment. This seems easy enough, but in our experience, you can never assume anything when planning or instituting a lead generation program for a field sales force. More on this in chapter 3.

Within a true mail order operation, fulfillment involves shipping the product and handling billing, collections, returns and inventory control.

- **Marketing**

  Marketing has two distinct areas that must be addressed to allow direct marketing to succeed.

  The first area to address in marketing is the integration of the direct marketing program in the existing marketing channel. This is the *tactical* use of direct marketing; how you will implement direct marketing with the current approach to selling.

  The *strategic* use of direct marketing relates to the long term efforts and results that will be experienced.

  Both the strategic and tactical ramifications of direct marketing should be evaluated and reviewed prior to beginning a direct marketing project.

A key to the success of the direct marketing effort will be a complete and detailed business plan prior to the start of the project. You can't measure the success of a program if you're not certain of your objectives. This business plan should focus on each of the five elements of direct marketing.

Complete control over each element is required and you must have the ability to react to the changing business environment. In most businesses, the five elements report to different units of the organization and are controlled by managers and executives who are not directly involved in the direct marketing effort.

Look closely at Illustration 1-5 and you'll probably see shades of your own organization. With this 'spaghetti chart' organization you tend to spend more time selling people internally than executing direct marketing. Plan a means to control these five elements of direct marketing prior to implementing a program.

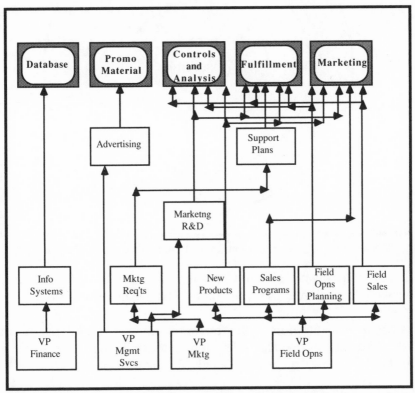

Illustration 1-5: A typical company and the organization that relates to the five elements of Direct Marketing.

The Universe

There are many definitions for the targets we are trying to reach with the direct marketing effort. Let's review the universe concept as it is pictured in Illustration 1-6.

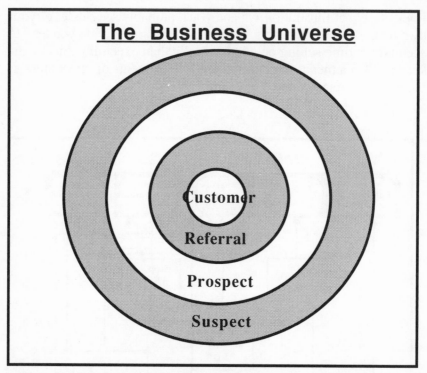

Illustration 1-6: A conceptual view of the business-to-business universe

Imagine the business-to-business universe as a funnel that you are viewing from above. The entire funnel is made up of suspects.

A *Suspect* is no more than a business name. We understand that many businesses operate under more than one name; even an abbreviation of a name can be considered a different suspect.

Prospects comprise the next ring inside the funnel. A prospect is a suspect that meets your predetermined qualification criteria. You might want to include them in an ongoing marketing program. You probably only want to reach each establishment once although it may do business under many different names. Your qualification criteria may also be specific to a certain decision maker or individual within the prospect business.

Referrals are prospects of such high quality that you want to refer them to someone for immediate action. They form the next ring. You may send the referral to a salesperson for disposition or try to generate an order immediately. In the past, we've found that the term 'lead' was used synonymously with referral. The referral term should not be confused with one prospect or customer referring you to another prospect or customer.

The *Customer* is contained in the inner most ring and is the smallest group of the universe. This term describes individuals who have purchased products or services from you.

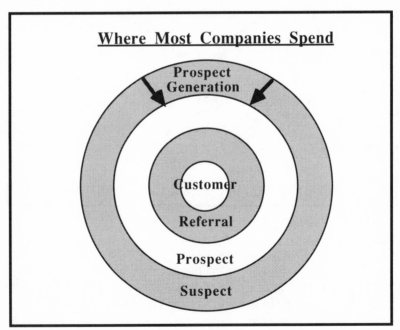

Illustration 1-7: Where most businesses spend resource.

Most businesses spend a great deal of their resources attempting to locate prospects in the suspect universe (Illustration 1-7). In reality, each company should spend as little effort as possible on suspects and focus attention on:

1) customers
2) referrals
3) prospects.

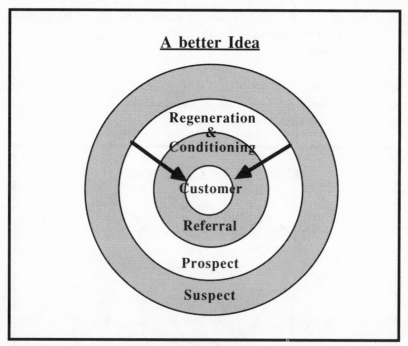

Illustration 1-8: Another way to generate customers.

An interesting point has been raised by some of our clients. Frequently, the individual responsible for implementing a direct marketing program has been instructed to eliminate customers and known referrals from the list. In the business-to-business arena, no computer program can eliminate all customers and active referrals from any list, due to the abbreviation and different name problem. Some duplication and mistaken contacts are unavoidable.

We have graphically looked at the business-to-business universe as a funnel. As you know, as the neck of the funnel narrows, the pressure increases. It is impossible not to get the rings towards the center of the funnel wet.

In other words, when designing a selective direct marketing program, anticipate that everyone will hear of your offer, not just a few. A program that could have a negative effect on your customers and active referrals should be carefully evaluated. Direct marketing should generate a lead or an order, not hurt business.

When you attempt to eliminate certain names because of the impact direct marketing will have on selected groups, you're trying to avoid their getting wet. You can restrict the offer to certain prospects or customers easier than trying to eliminate their names. You should be able to explain or justify an offer that does not include your customers; it is not unusual to have special terms and conditions that apply to an offer in unique situations.

The Objective

Targets can fall into one of four categories (Illustration 1-9).

1) Prospects or suspects who are not qualified and not interested are relatively easy to eliminate from further activity. They will not respond to direct marketing contacts or advertising and require no further action at this time.

2) The not qualified yet interested group can be a terrible drain on resources if you are doing a lead generation program and sending the leads to a sales force for follow-up. These prospects tend to ask many questions with no intention to purchase the product or service you are offering. One of a sales manager's most difficult tasks is to ensure that sales people don't spend their time with this group. A salesperson has to deal with rejection all day long. This type of prospect is a

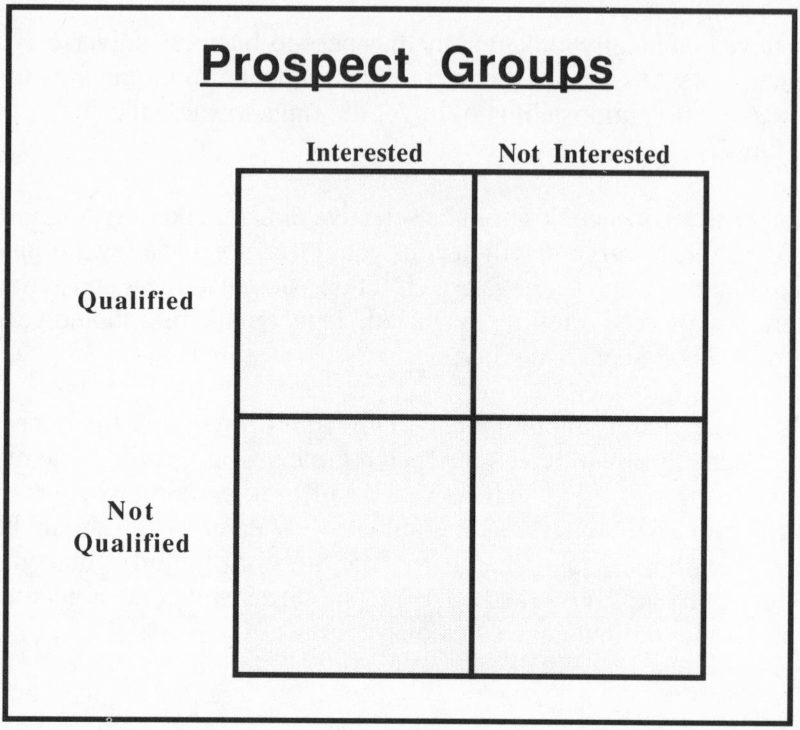

Prospect Groups

Interested   Not Interested

Qualified

Not
Qualified

Illustration 1-9: Another way of looking at the business-to-business universe

false oasis in the desert of rejection. The prospect will talk to
the salesperson and ask lots of questions, but rarely buy anything.

3) The not interested yet qualified prospect can be another big
drain on resources. We often hear sales people say they have
found a great prospect. Which is a better place to spend time?

a) Convincing a prospect who is interested in our product or
service that he can actually use it; that is taking the interested prospect and making him qualified.

Or

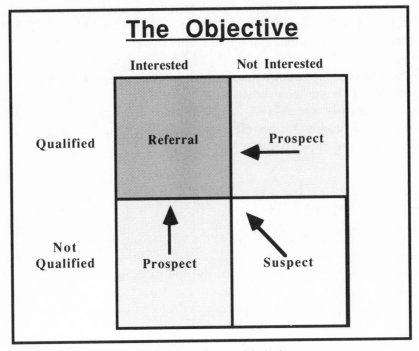

Illustration 1-10: The real objective of Direct Marketing.

    b) Convincing the prospect who is qualified that he should
       be interested in our product or service.

Either situation is difficult and time consuming.

4) The group you need to work on is both qualified and interest-
    ed in your product or service. We are all trying to find the
    qualified and interested prospect, the referral. You can overlay
    our definitions over the four categories of prospects
    (Illustration 1-10).

The ideal situation is to expend our most expensive resource, sales
people, on the group in the upper left corner of the grid; the qualified
and interested group. The interested and not qualified group and the
not interested and qualified group should be cultivated with various

direct response promotional efforts that are less costly than a sales force. A conditioning and regeneration program should be developed to move this group along through the sales cycle.

When a prospect becomes a referral, interested and qualified, the name should be turned over to the sales organization. The objective is to provide only referrals to the sales force. Bear in mind the other groups will provide future referrals. Your direct marketing program should convert these prospects into referrals.

The Buying Decision

People go through a number of steps when they decide to buy anything. Sometimes the buying decision is made very quickly and the prospect doesn't really understand the entire decision process. Focus on each element of the process to ensure you are creating an environment that will encourage the prospect or referral to decide to purchase the product or service offered.

The buying decision can be visualized as a pyramid (Illustration 1-11). One of the cornerstones of the structure is Need. Need can be defined as a problem that a prospect has to address. For example, a prospect having difficulty generating invoices in a timely manner has a need for an invoicing system. The need is not for a particular product, but for a solution to a problem.

The other cornerstone of the buying decision is desire. Again, the desire is not for your product, but for a solution to the problem or to meet the need discussed earlier. The prospect wants to find a better way to invoice.

Once need and desire are established, the prospect must justify making a change to address the need. Justification is not always financial; emotion plays a very important role in the buying decision. The prospect has to be assured that making a change is going to be worthwhile.

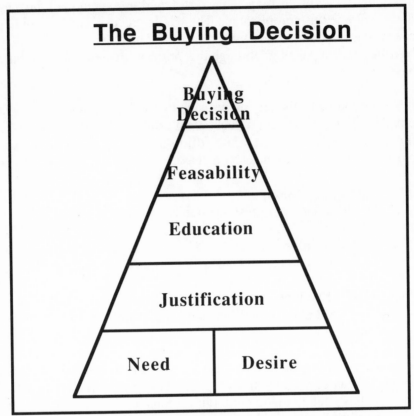

Illustration 1-11: The buying decision as created in the mind of the prospect.

The prospect will study various ways for meeting his need by examining solutions or appropriate approaches. Thus far into the buying decision, the project has still not involved a specific vendor but has centered on how to solve a specific problem.

After understanding the desire to fill a need, and having justified a change, and educating ourselves on the alternatives, the next step in the buying decision is to prove that making a change to meet the needs is feasible within the environment. Will the change to meet the need adversely affect the company? Will the cure kill the patient?

Once the prospect has evaluated each element, he is prepared to make a buying decision. It may seem farfetched to expect each buying decision to be this complicated. The whole process may take only a few moments in the mind of our prospect. The order of activity may be different, but we all go through this process whenever we purchase anything.

It is after you make the buying decision that you select a vendor and a product. You may select product before vendor, but you always make the buying decision first. The following defines a process that prospects go through to make a purchase:

- **Buying Decision**
  Need and interest must be established.

- **Select Vendor**
  Awareness, liking and preference must be established

- **Select Product**
  The need must be fulfilled and justified with the best possible solution

Some direct marketing programs seem to be aimed at the vendor and product areas of the buying process. The assumption is that the prospect has already made the buying decision. In fact, most of the time, the material used in the direct marketing effort is all product oriented and wasn't designed to produce a lead or an order. This is especially true in the technology product arena.

We believe it is always worthwhile to create or affirm the buying decision in all contacts. Need and desire are the cornerstones of the ultimate sale. Evaluate your existing mail pieces and advertising. See which of these areas you're addressing. You may be missing an important opportunity by not focusing on the buying decision.

Business-to-Business Overview Summarized

So far we have reviewed the major distinctions between consumer and business direct marketing. Throughout the remainder of this book we will frequently contrast specific differences in marketing to these two universes. The fundamental differences in the two marketplaces are the accessibility of the prospect and his/her financing or money sources.

Some definitions and concepts in direct marketing have also been established. Direct marketing has five basic elements and you must control all to succeed. The five elements -- database, promotional material, controls and analysis, fulfillment, and marketing -- were described in detail and will be covered at length throughout this book.

The business universe was defined and consists of four major groups:

- suspects
- prospects
- referrals
- customers.

We defined these major groups and then explained the objectives of direct marketing.

The buying decision was explained - how prospects evaluate and ultimately decide on purchasing products. Central to this discussion is our belief that communications to the business universe should address the buying decision as well as selecting vendor and product.

Through out the remainder of this book, the focus will be on practical concepts that you can implement immediately. We'll use actual examples and case studies to illustrate our point. This chapter is our way of establishing common ground and definitions that will act as a foundation for other concepts and techniques.

All good direct marketing has to start with a complete and well documented business plan. So let's examine business planning next.

Chapter Two - Direct Marketing Planning

Why Plan?

To execute effective direct marketing, the most important element is the development of a business plan before starting the program. The business plan is the definition of your objectives and the method of measuring the success of your activities. Throughout this chapter, we will define and display all of the elements in your business plan, including the essential tools you can use to create your own: outlines, flowcharts, budget sheets and the formula for determining them.

Too many books on marketing, advertising and direct marketing contain an obligatory chapter on business planning. Typical presentations on this subject tend to be about as exciting as watching paint dry. However, don't let past dull resuscitations on abstract business theory lessen your zeal to master the business plan. No subject is more vital in determining the success or failure of a marketing effort. Let us show you a practical guide on how to develop and execute a business plan for business-to-business direct marketing. At the end of this chapter, we conclude with an actual business plan.

The best direct marketing business plans can be read and understood by someone who doesn't know a thing about your business. Perhaps the most difficult part of developing the plan is keeping it simple enough for your spouse or child to understand.

Writing a detailed business plan may not seem like the best use of your time because you probably already think that you know everything about your business. Business planning is putting on paper all the facts you have at your disposal.

In many instances, in order to implement your strategy and tactics you'll need outside help. The aid of an agency, consultant or list broker may be required. The business plan can be a tool to quickly and inexpensively bring these people up to speed on the specifics of your business.

There are many purposes for a business plan. Internal support will have to be briefed on your plans and assumptions. You can use it to remind you of your original objectives after the project is complete.

Your management should be given the completed plan prior to starting any activity. By ensuring that everyone has the same understanding and expectations, your project will have a higher chance of success.

The business plan will contain several major sections that can be categorized into the following areas:

- Company Background
- Organization Charts
- Current Costs and Budgets for Sales
- Why use Direct Marketing
- Strategy
- Measurement
- Tactics

Company Background

The background of the business encompasses many areas. The plan should start with a brief history of your company and explain the key reasons for its success. Remember, you're trying to write a plan for someone who doesn't know anything about your company.

You'll be tempted to avoid writing the history of your company. You may think this subject is too basic and superfluous. We have found that by forcing a review of the past, you can build a better foundation for activity in the future. Founders of businesses had great ideas and products. As time goes by, many companies may stray from the things that made them successful in the past. Reviewing the past history of the business may open doors that were accidentally shut.

A review of the products or services offered by your company should follow the history section of the plan. Try to address product evolution and how you obtained your current product mix. If your business has product areas or groups, review the major areas as well as the specific types of products. Don't try to address the marketplace or current marketing strategy. Focus on the product, product features and product benefits offered to your customers. We will focus on the marketplace and marketing strategy later. Again, keep in mind that whoever is reading your plan may not know your company, your industry or the problem that the product is designed to solve.

If you ask your spouse or a close friend to read this section of the plan, pay close attention to the questions you're asked. If the products are not clear, try redefining them again.

Don't try to describe every item of inventory. Focus on the major product categories and what these do for your customers.

Try to present the sales mix and percentage of sales that each major product group is responsible for. Real dollars and percentages of the total are very helpful. A comparison of the last few years of activity

Outline of Business Background

1) Background
   A) History of the company

   B) Product overview
      1) Type of products
      2) Product mix
      3) Revenue by product

   C) Marketplace
      1) The market
      2) Target individuals by product
         a) Decision makers
         c) Influencers
      3) Revenue by market segment

   D) Competition

   E) Current and prior channels of distribution
      1) Current channels by product
      2) Sales people overview
         a) Type of sales organizations
         b) Reporting structures
         c) Personalities
      3) Prior experience with direct marketing
      4) Pricing per channel
         a) Discounts allowed
         b) Pricing and strategy overview
      5) Revenue by channel of distribution

Illustration 2-1: Outline of Business Background

can help to show product trends. The average order size and number of orders by product group are important data to analyze in establishing strategy.

Now that we've examined the products and share of revenue, we should review the market and marketplace. A thorough study of the market is helpful in evaluating strategy and objectives. Review the markets for your products and product groups without focusing on your current marketing strategy. As we tried to avoid strategy discussions in the product review, you should also focus on the market and marketplace separately. Focus on the potential customer for your products; how they think and act; and how they make buying decisions.

The purpose of the market section is to explain the size and composition of your marketing opportunity. You want to review the size of the market and opportunity for you to sell your product. Business counts by Standard Industry Classifications (SIC), geography, and business size are important. List brokers can be very helpful in quantifying your marketing opportunity.

Within the marketplace overview, a section should identify the individuals you're trying to reach. Each product group's target individuals should be identified.

A description of each major decision maker, including personality similarities and organization reporting structures, will be very helpful. As discussed in Chapter one, a unique characteristic of the business market is the multiple levels involved in the purchasing decision.

In your review of the individuals involved in the buying process, focus on influencers as well as decision makers. If selling your products involve both decision makers and influencers, try to describe both of their functions and their interaction. A description of how these players fit into the organization and their interaction in the buying decision can be very helpful. The general personalities of all of these individuals can help in evaluating new or existing strategies.

Keep in mind that different product groups may have different buying decision structures.

A similar kind of analysis should be done for your market and market distribution. Total revenue by market segment and percentages of revenue from market segments should be included. Comparative information over several years can show trends in the marketplace.

The revenue analysis by market may not always be appropriate. Some companies have an unusual distribution of where business is derived. For example, if 25% of your sales comes from one or two accounts, your marketplace is different than a traditional company. This non-typical distribution will distort any analysis and will not be helpful in directing future marketing efforts. However, you should try to identify the unique characteristics of your offering that has caused the unusual distribution. There maybe a special benefit that can allow you to expand your business substantially.

Try to review the average volume of a customer in both dollars sold and number of orders. Later, when we review the need for direct marketing, the customer volume data could become very important.

Competitive products and services can affect your ability to generate sales. A detailed1 analysis of competition should be included within the business plan. If possible, try to evaluate why the competition is succeeding or failing. Competitive pricing and offers can be key ingredients in the direct marketing program you develop. The competitive analysis should focus on the various product and market segments. If your competitors differ by region, be sure to review how this will affect your ability to sell in each area.

Now that you've examined the product and the market, evaluate the strategy and channels you've used to sell your products to that market. This section should review your current and past approaches to selling to the market.

Relate how the current approach and channels of distribution have evolved. Each channel of distribution should be reviewed and explained. The current sales process and channels of distribution are critical to the success of your direct marketing efforts. How the current process works will be critical to any new programs you try.

If sales people are involved, whether your own or other distributors, they can affect direct marketing. The sales forces' personalities, compensation and motivation are important elements to consider when you involve direct marketing.

Describe the reporting structure of the sales organization. The way they are managed is critical to how you'll introduce and manage your direct marketing program. If you or your company has had a prior experience with direct marketing, document the program and results. Sales people are like elephants, they never forget. More importantly, they never forgive. Chapter three reviews how to implement direct marketing with the sales force.

An important and integral part of your business plan deals with introducing the direct marketing plan to the current channels of distribution. Things can't be done in a vacuum. Prior activities can dramatically influence the reception of your current program.

As you discuss the different channels of distribution, review the pricing, discounts offered, and gross revenue by channel. Comparative information for several years will help to identify any trends. Average revenue per order and number of orders is useful information.

If pricing differs by channel of distribution, explain why. The different pricing structure can be an indication of how different offers may be received by your market. You should understand why different customers are paying different prices for the same products.

If selling strategies differ by channel, that is also an important consideration. These different strategies can indicate strategies to test within an integrated direct marketing program.

Organization Charts

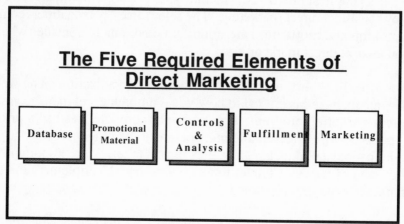

Illustration 2-2: The five required elements of Direct Marketing

After you've reviewed the background of the business, an explanation of the organization should be included in the business plan.

Develop a current organization chart that identifies your functions and where you fit into the company. More importantly, focus on the organization as it controls the five elements necessary for direct marketing. The five elements were presented in Chapter one and are restated in Illustration 2-2.

Direct marketing will frequently report to multiple areas of a company. As you may recall from Chapter one, Illustration 2-3 shows how complicated the reporting structure can make implementing direct marketing. You may not be able to change the structure, but you should certainly be aware of it.

You'll have to coordinate support for all the functions prior to starting the direct marketing project. Frequently, we have seen direct marketing managers spend precious time trying to internally "sell" or gain

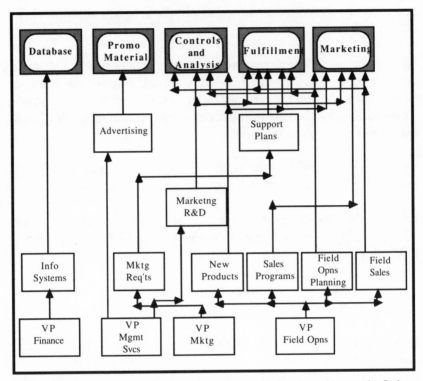

Illustration 2-3: A typical company and the organization that relates to the 5 elements of Direct Marketing.

the proper support from others in the company after the project has started. Measurement and implementation will become very difficult without data processing and controls and analysis support.

Current Costs and Budgets for Sales

So far, most of the information that you have been documenting should be easily available within your company. In fact, there may already be a business plan that you've been able to use. The budgets for the current sales approaches are also pretty easy to establish. Get as much detail as possible on this subject. The key measurement to the success of direct marketing is profitability. If you can produce an order for less than the current approach, the program will probably be considered successful.

Most companies do not measure sales costs on a cost per order or cost per item basis. On the other hand, direct marketing is measurable and normally focuses on the cost per order or cost per item sold. Striking a comparison to measure the success of your program against historical information can be difficult.

Once you've established the selling budget for the year, some simple math will help you establish the overall cost per order or cost per item.

From the first background section you already know the total number of items sold for the last year. In reviewing the budget, you know the total sales expense.

> Sales Expense ÷ Number of Orders = Sales Cost per Order

By dividing the sales expense dollars by the number of orders, you can determine the overall cost per order. This is a good place to start. However, it can be seriously distorted with more expensive products.

> Sales Expense ÷ Total Revenue = % of Revenue used for Sales Expense

Establish the percentage of revenue that is used for sales expense. This is done by dividing the sales expense by the total revenue. Again, reviewing both the product and market sections, you can establish the actual dollars of sales expense per order and per item sold. You'll probably be surprised how expensive generating orders has become.

As we mentioned earlier, comparative results over several years can show interesting trends. Over time, you'll begin to get a better sense as to what has been happening to selling expense.

We have always found that the less expensive products and smaller customers are allocated sales expenses that are not realistic. That is to say, you may find only fractions of a dollar allocated to certain products for sales expense. Certain customers may be allocated sales expenses that amount to less than the cost of one phone contact per year.

This exercise in establishing the cost of the order or the cost of the item often focuses attention on where you need direct marketing support. You will learn where costs have escalated to a point where profitable selling has become prohibitive. A program to save money and reduce costs is easy to get top level management to commit to.

If you're using a sales force to sell, try to establish the cost of the order, average order size and cost per sales call. This is difficult to do and will require you to convince management to agree with certain assumptions. If you can establish the cost per sales call, your direct marketing objectives will be easier to establish.

The advent of personal computers and spread sheets has made life a lot easier. We can model and change assumptions with ease and examine the impact of our changes. There are a number of ways to establish the cost per sales call, we'll examine one from which you may want to create a spread sheet model. This approach is an example that you can expand or contract based on your own requirements.

First, establish the total revenue and marketing costs for the period you will use to establish the cost per sales call. Try to use a 12 month period so you'll have to plan your results on an annual basis. Next identify the total number of sales people you have in your company. Do not include management or field support personnel. These and other 'overhead' costs will be included within the total marketing costs.

Total Marketing Costs ÷ Number of Sales People = Cost
    per Salesperson

By dividing the total marketing costs by the number of sales people, you'll establish the cost per salesperson per year. We have frequently encountered sales executives who maintain that they're paying their sales forces strictly on a commission basis, therefore the commissions are the only cost for the sales people. This ignores the other costs involved in promoting and supporting the products.

If you're only using a sales force, the only time you have an opportunity to sell is when the salesperson makes contact with your customers or prospects. All marketing expense should be apportioned to all of the sales people, since this will give you a much better indication of your true selling costs.

From the background section, you know the total number of orders generated. With the order information you can establish the average order size by dividing the total revenue by the number of orders.

Next, determine the average revenue and orders per salesperson. This is done by dividing the revenue by the number of sales people to determine the average revenue per salesperson. The same technique is used to determine the average number of orders per salesperson.

So far the data we've been creating has been based on numbers you can easily verify. We haven't made any assumptions, except that all marketing expenses should be used to determine the cost per salesperson per year. If your management is uncomfortable with this approach, ask them to give you the average earnings per year per salesperson. If you double this figure, to allow for support, expenses, fringe benefits and general and administrative costs, it may be easier to develop your plan. This approach isn't as accurate as the first method, but will still give you a basis to work from. Remember to document how you arrived at the cost per salesperson per year.

Now that you know the average cost per salesperson, the average number of orders per salesperson and the average revenue per order, you can begin to establish cost per sales call.

Much of the information you will generate on the cost per sales call will be based on assumptions that are difficult to verify. You should try to be as conservative as possible. Use multiple sources for your data and be sure to document how and why you made a certain assumption. Review your assumptions with management and be flexible enough to change based on their suggestions.

You should establish the average number of face-to-face sales calls made per business day. Most companies average between three and four face-to-face sales calls per day. Sales people have to travel to and from the call, require a certain amount of pre-call planning and have to spend some time creating call reports and orders. When you consider all the other activities required of the salesperson, three to four calls per day may be overly optimistic.

The actual number of selling days per year is an interesting and sometimes very depressing aspect of business. There are 365 days per year. 104 are weekends (52x2). This leaves 261 available selling days. When you subtract vacations (average 10 days) and holidays (average 10 days) and personal days (average 6 days) you'll have only 235 potential selling days per year.

This 235 days equals only 19.6 selling days per month. Now estimate the number of days taken from selling time for meetings, administrative work in the office, training and recognition events and you'll probably approach 200 to 220 days available for selling per year. 220 days of selling per year equals 18.3 selling days per month.

Using an average of three sales calls per day, the average salesperson is making 660 sales calls per year. four sales calls per day would be 880 sales calls per year. Although this number is usually far below what management thought was really happening, it is probably overstated. Averaging three or four calls per day doesn't recognize the independence of the sales force and their tendency to play golf, tennis and socially spend time with their customers.

The worksheet in Illustration 2-4 gives a simple format for establishing the cost per order and cost per sales call. Whatever the result of

Salesperson Cost Worksheet

A) Total annual revenue   _____

B) Total annual marketing expenses   _____

C) Total number of orders   _____

D) Total number of salespeople   _____

E) Revenue per salesperson per year   _____
    (A ÷ D = E)
F) Cost per salesperson per year   _____
    (B ÷ D = F)
G) Average order size   _____
    (A ÷ C = G)
H) Average orders per salesperson   _____
    (C ÷ D = H)
I) Average sales calls per day   _____
    (Based on assumption)
J) Number of business days per year   _____
    per salesperson (Normally 200-220)
K) Number of sales calls per year per   _____
    salesperson (J x I = K)
L) Cost per sales call   _____
    (F ÷ K = L)
M) Sales calls per order   _____
    (K ÷ H = M)
N) Closing rate   _____
    (H ÷ K = N)

Illustration 2-4: Salesperson cost worksheet

your sales calls per year assumption, we can use the information to establish the cost per sales call and the closing rate. Dividing the average cost per salesperson per year by the average number of sales calls, establishes the average cost per sales call. Dividing the number of sales calls per year by the number of orders per year will establish the number of sales calls per order. Finally dividing the number of orders by the number of sales calls will establish the closing rate. (Closing rate is the percentage of sales calls that result in an order.)

The cost per sales call may surprise you and your management. As we mentioned in Chapter one, the average cost of an industrial sales call across most industries is over $250. In our experience this cost has frequently been substantially higher. The awareness of how expensive it has become to make a sales call can help you establish where direct marketing can most help your company.

If the average cost of a sales call is $250 and your allowable sales expense was 20% of revenue, you would have to generate a $1250 order for each 5 sales calls. This is arrived at by dividing the cost per sales call by the allowable percentage of revenue for selling expense. Hence, the $250 ÷ 20% = $1250 revenue per order requirement. This would assume that you're experiencing a 100% closing rate. This is an impossible objective. Therefore, you will probably determine that there are certain products and market segments that you can no longer sell to using the traditional salesperson.

Knowing the facts -- the costs and the budgets -- can help you establish a better direction for your program. You'll also establish some measurement criteria that can be helpful in evaluating the success of the program.

Why use Direct Marketing

This section of the business plan is a direct result of the prior sections. The product, market and marketing strategy sections of the business background sections establish what and who you're selling. The budgets and cost section establishes your current costs and will probably highlight the areas that need support.

Describe in clear terms what you plan to do with direct marketing and why. If you're planning a lead generation program, describe why and what you're planning to do.

Make sure you describe the universe you're trying to reach (prospects) and the group that you want to respond (referrals) and finally who will buy (customers). List brokers and list sales people can be very helpful in understanding the size and composition of your target universe.

There are some interesting techniques that can be used to help establish why and where you need direct marketing support. One approach is to use Intensive Planning. This a concept that encourages communication, problem definition and problem resolution.

Intensive Planning

Intensive planning sessions normally involve all of the individuals in a particular function. It should be done off site and in an informal and relaxed environment. Normally the session will take two full days. We have run sessions for all the top management in a company to identify programs to allow the company to attain its objectives. The same type of session has been effectively executed for a sales unit to identify programs to allow it to attain its objectives.

The planning session needs to be coordinated and controlled by an outside individual. Consultants, experienced in this type of planning, are excellent session moderators. The moderator and senior manager or executive should meet prior to the planning session and establish who should participate and the short and long term objectives to be planned during the session.

The planning session should be convened off site where there can be no interruptions. Meals should be available at the site to keep breaks to a minimum. The rooms used for the planning sessions should have a lot of wall space, as you'll be writing on flip charts and hanging the results on the walls. You'll also need two flip chart easels, flip chart paper, masking tape and several different colored markers.

Once everyone is present, the senior manager or executive starts the session by reviewing the objectives for the unit. These objectives should be both short term (next 12 months) and long term (next 3 years). The objectives should be written on a flip chart prior to the session. The objectives are then taped to the wall after they have been reviewed and explained by the senior manager. The senior manager will become a participant in the planning session after the objectives are presented. He/she will only have a single vote equal to any other member of the group.

Planning Session Rules

- One speaker at a time
- Everyone is equal
- All problems are to be stated in complete sentences -- no abbreviations and should state cause and effect.
- If anyone leaves the room all planning stops
- The person with the marker is in charge
- All problems must have unanimous agreement to be included.

Illustration 2-5: Intensive Planning Session Rules

The rules for the planning session are very simple:

- Each person has one vote, no matter their level or position.

- All problems will be written in complete sentences stating a cause and effect.

- In order for a problem to be included in the final planning document, it must be unanimously agreed to.

- Only one speaker at a time, no side conversations.

- The person with the writing marker is in charge.

The first day will be spent on identifying only the problems that interfere with the objectives. The second day will focus on grouping the problems and creating action programs to solve the problems.

After the objectives are reviewed, the group will define all the problems interfering with the attainment of the objectives. No problem is too small as long as the group unanimously agrees to include the problem.

One participant is appointed to act as moderator and given the marker. The moderator position will be rotated periodically. Initially, the outside participant who controls the session should moderate the session. The two flip chart stands are set up in the front of the room. One chart will be used to write all the problems agreed to. Each problem will be numbered and each chart will be numbered. The other easel is used as a scratch pad to write the problem and ensure it is in a complete sentence, clearly states the problem and is a problem that the whole group agrees to.

One speaker at a time states a problem in a complete sentence defining both the cause and effect. It is very difficult to discuss problems without trying to solve them; strong control must be exercised to focus only on problems.

If the problem is that the sales force needs qualified leads, a more complete statement should be established. For example: "The sales force needs qualified leads to sell in order to meet this years sales objectives." The cause and effect are defined. When you read this problem later in the day or at some point in the future, it will be easy to understand what was meant.

The problem is transcribed to the scratch flip chart. After clearly stating the problem, the group then discusses the problem. If there is unanimous agreement, the problem is copied to the final charts.

As a final chart fills, it is removed from the easel and taped to the walls. The charts and problems should be kept in order. By keeping the problems in clear view, the group can refer to the charts and ensure no duplication. The complete sentence, cause and effect, makes understanding the problem easy.

The problem definition phase is the longest and toughest part of the planning session. It should continue until all the problems are described and written on the charts. It is not unusual to have more than 100 problems. Frequently, the problem definition phase will go late into the evening because only one day has been allocated for this phase.

The group dynamics and communication forced during the problem definition phase can be as important as the actual problem resolution.

During the second day, all the problems should be grouped into several broad categories. Training, Communication, Compensation, Personnel, Engineering, Etc. are some groups, but you should create your own groups. There are no rules for which problem goes in which group. One problem can appear in more than one group. It is easier to use different colored markers to write the group next to the problem number.

After each problem is grouped you can begin to establish action programs to solve the problems. Every problem has to fall within a group, or have its own group. Some problems will be outside the sphere of control of the group and cannot be solved. These are environment issues and should be grouped within a special group called Environment.

Additional charts are then created for each group. Each problem number is listed. When the charts are later transposed and typed, the group resolution charts should contain the complete problem description.

Sales Problems			
Problems	**Actions**	**Who**	**When**
2,41,43	Align sales compensation programs to insure consistency.	SJ	12/1
4,6	Establish accurate forecasting system.	TM	5/1
1,21,89	Develop hiring program to add 1 salesperson per month starting 6/1	SJ	6/1

Illustration 2-6: Example of action plans from planning session

Obviously, you can't solve the problems in a two day planning session. However, you can establish action programs with target dates for completion and the individuals who are responsible. The set of charts listing the action program, target date and individual responsible becomes your activity plan for the future.

The planning session has focused on all of the problems interfering with the attainment of your objectives. The activity programs that come from this session should resolve most of the interferences to attaining your goals.

If a session like this is conducted with sales, advertising, data processing and marketing, the reasons for direct marketing will be very clear. More importantly, everyone signs up for the solution. You will get great support for all the required elements of direct marketing and everyone knows why you're doing the project.

It is critical that all the parties who will be involved understand and agree to the direct marketing program. Throughout this book we continually stress the need to communicate why and how you'll implement direct marketing. The biggest cause for failure in any direct marketing project is an unrealistic expectation level at the onset.

Direct Marketing Strategy

The primary difference between strategy and tactics is scope and the dimension of the undertaking. Tactics are the things we do to execute a strategy. Strategy defines where you would like to go over the longer term. Strategy is the war, while tactics are the equivalent of the battle we're fighting.

So far you have identified the background of the company, its organization structure, the current costs and why you need direct marketing. You are now ready to establish long term goals and objectives. For example, you may decide to reduce sales expense from 20% of revenue to 18%. More realistically, you may only want to hold sales expense at a certain rate, while costs are escalating. (Several high technology industries have been trying to deal with the dual problem of increasing selling expense and decreasing revenue per product.)

As you establish your strategy, remember that you must consider its long term implications. You may want to test and evaluate whether another channel of distribution is appropriate. Direct marketing or direct mail and/or telemarketing to sell the product directly may be reasonable, but you may have to introduce these programs in steps.

During the strategy review, keep media and direct marketing techniques to a minimum. They are the tactics and are not as critical as the ultimate direction you want to achieve. Part of your strategy may be to establish a database for ongoing direct contacts. We have worked on projects where the only objective was to establish the database for future contacts.

Actually, when you defined why you need direct marketing, the strategy was also defined. You now must establish a plan for testing and evaluating whether direct marketing can work for your company.

Measurement

How you plan to measure the program must be determined before you define all the elements to be executed. In selling to the consumer, marketers appreciate that most buying decisions are made in a relatively short period. Most of the time, the targeted consumer can make the decision. The environment for selling to businesses is quite often more complicated. A single selling cycle can span many weeks and months.

If you won't find out whether a prospect has purchased for several months, how will you measure the success of your efforts? Simply design a program that allows you to measure the project in stages and evaluate your success against interim objectives. Your business plan should contain these complete objectives for front and back-end results. Response expectations and actual results to the initial offering can indicate whether the program will succeed. Keep in mind, however, that the ultimate measurement will be purchases.

A complete financial operating plan should be created for each aspect of your direct marketing program. This operating plan includes the costs and expected results of the program. As you execute different parts of the plan, you can compare results to expectations.

We have been involved in programs that could never succeed because of impossibly high expectations. It seems as if every executive expects a 20% response in the mail. High results (20% response is extremely high) may be possible but shouldn't be required in order to conduct a successful program.

Another gratifying result of all of your planning is that you don't have to implement a program with unreasonable expectations. Just take your ultimate objective, and plan backwards. If you need an order cost of $200, you can establish a financial and operating plan that produces that kind of result.

You may not realize how low a response rate you actually need to create a successful program.

Let's look at a direct response ordering program:

Average Order	$400.00
Allowable sales expense rate	20%
Allowable sales expenses dollars	$80.00
Cost per 1000 pieces mailed	$750.00
Required Response Rate ($.75/$80)	.94%

Let's assume that we are trying to sell a $400 average order. If our planned sales expense is 20%, we can spend $80 per order. If we're spending $750 per 1000 pieces to mail to the universe, a 1% response will produce 10 orders per 1000 pieces mailed. The total selling expense will be $75 per order. To arrive at the minimum response rate that is acceptable, you establish the cost per contact ($750 ÷ 1000 = $.75) and then divide by the allowable sales expense. In our example this is 0.94%.

This was a very simple example that didn't consider returned orders, bad payment or any other fulfillment factors to complicate matters. However, it does illustrate how as little as a 1% response may be all you need to conduct a successful direct response ordering program.

Lead generation programs, or those campaigns that have multiple steps before closing the sale, are more difficult to measure but can also be planned by using the same techniques. Along with the previous measurements given, you must add the cost of sales calls and the anticipated closing rates to arrive at the complete cost per order.

A simple example of a measurement plan for lead generation:

Average Order	$5000.00
Allowable sales expense rate	20%
Allowable sales expenses dollars	$1000.00
Cost per sales call	$250.00

Closing Rate	30%
Salesperson cost per order	$833.33
Allowable cost per Direct Mktg Lead	$176.67
% Responders Qualified as Leads	40%
Allowable cost per responder	$70.80
Cost per 1,000 piece mailed	$750.00
Required Response Rate	1.06%

A number of elements will have to be measured to verify whether this plan succeeded. The first and easiest piece will be to establish the response rate to the mailing. If you get 1.06% response or better you're ahead of your planned expectations. If 40% of the responders qualify as referrals and are sent to the sales force, you again are ahead of the plan. If your initial response rate was higher but your qualification rate lower, you can still be ahead of the plan. As long as you produce a qualified lead for $176.67 or less, you are meeting the plan.

In both examples, the program was successful if we could produce about 1% response. This response rate range is reasonable and attainable for most programs. If you present a detailed plan that focuses on cost per order, you'll probably have a chance for success. Lead programs have their own set of measurement problems that will be discussed in Chapter three.

XYZ Coffee Service Business Plan

If this approach to planning seems a little far fetched or difficult to grasp, let's look at a real life example. We recently did a business plan that establishes the required response rates in a lead generation program for a sales force using only telemarketing. The company sells a coffee service to other businesses. The objective was to generate sales leads that are interested in trying the coffee service.

XYZ Coffee Service Current Sales Approach

Average Earnings per Salesperson	$25,000

Factor to Mult Avg Earnings to include
Gen & Adm Costs & Mgm't   2.00

Total Cost per Salesperson per year $50,000

Average Customer Expenditures per year $1,200

Annual New Sales Quota per Salesperson $144,000

Average New Customers per month per salesperson   10

New Customers per year per salesperson   120

Average Face to Face Sales Calls per Week   21

Sales Calls per Year   1,008
(Assume 48 Weeks allowing for Vacation and Holidays)

Sales Calls per Month   84

Closing Ratio (Orders per month/Sales Calls per month)   11.90%

Cost per Sales Call $49.60

Cost per Order $416.67

Life Time Value of the Customer
  % Loss of Customers per year   30.00%
            Value Year 1 $1,200
            Value Year 2 $840
            Value Year 3 $588
            Total for 3 Years $2,628

% Cost of Sales of 1st Year Revenue   34.70%

% Cost of Sales of Total Revenue   15.90%

Anticipated Results with Telemarketing

Planned Closing Ratio of Leads generated from
Telemarketing   30.00%

Number of Calls to Non-Ordering Prospects   1
    (Trial Service is delivered by Service Rep. Salesperson
    calls near end of trial to convert)

Number of Calls to Purchaser   2
    (Sales Rep has to make a second call to get contract
    signed)

Total Face to Face Sales Calls per Order   4.3
    (Prospect Calls/Closing Ratio less 1 Call who
    became a purchaser plus Purchaser Calls)

Total Salesperson Cost per Order $213.28
    (Total Face To Face Calls multiplied by Current Cost
    per Sales call)

Cost of Trial of Service $35.00
    (Cost delivering & picking up equipment and cost of
    coffee)

Total Cost of Trials per Order $116.67
    (Cost of Trials divided by Closing Ratio)

Total Selling Cost per Order $329.95
    (Cost of Salesperson plus Cost of Trials)

Allowable Direct Marketing Cost per Order $86.72
    (Current Cost per Order less Total Selling Cost with
    Telemarketing)

Telemarketing Cost per Hour $30.00
    (This assumes a $3.00 cost per follow up phone call)

Names consumed per hour	10
% of consumed that are completed	65.00%
Number of Completed Calls per hour	6.5
Required Orders per hour	0.35
Required Response Rate of Original List	3.50%
Required Response Rate of Completed Calls	5.38%

In creating this business plan, management was unable or unwilling to reveal the entire marketing budget so we used the average earnings of the salesman for our budgeting calculations. The cost of the salesperson was estimated at $25,000 per year. This number was doubled to arrive at the approximate true cost of the average salesperson of $50,000 per year. It was interesting to observe that even with this company's extremely low cost per sales call figure, the average cost of an order was still fairly high.

The average customer historically spent about $100 per month. This monthly sales expenditure was used to arrive at the average annual value of $1,200 per customer.

Each salesperson had an annual sales quota for new business of $144,000. This quota was used to establish the number of customers required by dividing by the $1,200 to establish the annual new customer objective for each salesperson of 120 customers. The monthly quota of 10 new customers was developed by dividing the 120 by 12.

It was then estimated that the average salesperson made 21 sales calls per week. The annual estimate was established by multiplying the 21 by 48 weeks to establish 1,008 sales calls per year. The 48 weeks allowed for vacations and holidays. It really didn't allow for sick, personal and other time off. Although somewhat overstated, it was management's numbers and the credibility of the plan meant more than fighting for a more conservative estimate. The 1,008 calls per year was divided by 12 to establish the monthly sales call volume of 84 calls per month.

Now that we knew the total number of calls and the total number of orders per month, it was fairly easy to establish the closing ratio, cost per sales call and cost per order. The Closing Ratio is established by dividing the number of orders by the number of sales calls ($10 \div 84 = 11.90\%$). The Cost per Sales Call is established by dividing the annual cost per salesperson by the number of sales calls made per year ($\$50,000 \div 1008 = \$49.60$). The cost per order can be established two different ways with the same results. (1) Divide the annual cost of the salesperson by the number of orders per year ($\$50,000 \div 120 = \$416.67$). (2) Divide the Cost of the sales call by the closing ratio ($\$49.60 \div 11.90\% = \$416.81$). There is a slight difference due to rounding.

Many businesses fail to examine the costs of acquiring a customer against the lifetime value of that customer. It is unfair to judge a program against only the first year's sales of a customer if that customer will continue to purchase product for a longer period. In this example, customer turnover or attrition rate was about 30% per year. Therefore, the average customer will last somewhat longer than 3 years. When considering turnover and lifetime values of customers, keep in mind that the turnover rate is always on the remaining balance, therefore it will never drop completely to zero.

The turnover rate of 30% was used to establish the value of the customer for the next three years. Although this was understating the lifetime value of the customer it did allow us to work with a more realistic estimate of revenue from each customer. In addition, we didn't use present value techniques to establish the real return on investment. So being a little off in the value estimate was balanced against the missing factors of cash flow and net present value of money.

In year 1 the customer contributes $1,200 in revenue. The year 2 value is 70% (100% - 30% = 70%) of the $1,200 or $840. Year 3 is 70% of the $840 or $588. As you can see the number will never go to zero. For example, year 4 would be 70% of $588 or $412; year 5 would be $288, etc. For our example we stopped the revenue, for evaluation purposes, after three years and totaled the revenue at $2,628.

The cost of selling can now be compared to both the annual revenue and the lifetime revenue of each customer. The annual revenue comparison shows that the cost of selling is almost 35% of the first year's revenue. This would make the cost of selling prohibitive in most businesses and suggests that you can't afford to sell. When the comparison is extended to include the lifetime value, it is about 16% of sales. This is a more realistic selling expense.

As you can see it takes a great deal of work to establish the costs of current approaches to selling before beginning to develop the direct marketing approach. But you really should be armed with sales costs on a current basis to objectively compare them with your direct marketing results. Most sales executives are not aware of how expensive it has become to close an order.

XYZ Coffee Telemarketing Plan

We first established that the quality of the lead we wanted to generate should be able to close at a 30% rate. After some prospect qualification on the telephone, we were planning to telemarket an offer for a one month free trial of the coffee service. Prior experience with trial service had shown these offers to close at about 30%. The trial service would be delivered by the sales representative. If a prospect didn't order, it was felt that the salesperson would only have to make a single sales call to determine that the prospect would not become a customer. Prospects that became customers required a second call to have the service contract signed.

The total number of face-to-face calls required for this program was established by adding the total prospecting calls that didn't order to the calls that did order to the calls to customers who did order. It took 1 call to determine the quality of the prospect and 30% of these would yield a customer. Therefore, $1 \div 30\% = 3.33$ Sales Calls to qualify prospects and 1 additional call to the customer who bought. The total sales calls required was 4.3.

The cost of the sales calls was established by using the current sales call cost and multiplying it by the total sales calls required per customer. Therefore, 4.3 x $49.60 = $213.28 in salesperson selling costs for each order. In addition, there was a cost to have the trial coffee service installed. The cost per trial service was $35.00. The total cost for trial service was established by dividing the single cost per service by the closing ratio. The total cost of the trials was $116.67 ($35.00 ÷ 30%).

The total sales expense per order was the sum of the salesperson costs and the cost of the trials. The total sales expense was $329.95 ($123.28 + $116.67). We then established the allowable direct marketing expenses.

The total planned selling expense was subtracted from the current selling expenses to arrive at the allowable direct marketing expense of $86.72 ($416.67 - $329.95).

Because telemarketing was going to be used to generate the trials, we had to establish its cost. (We go into more detail in a later Chapter on how to plan a telemarketing program.) For this example, we used the cost per telemarketing hour of $30.00. We expected to consume ten names per hour of activity and 65% of the consumed names completed contact. Therefore, we will have 6.5 completed contacts per hour. A completed contact is contacting the prospect and getting a decision on the offer.

We then established how many acceptances we needed to generate for each hour of activity by dividing the cost per hour by the allowable direct marketing expense. We needed to generate .35 orders per hour ($30.00 ÷ $86.72). With the completed contacts per hour and the required orders per hour in hand, we then established the required response for both the total number of records used and the actual people contacted with telemarketing. From the original list, this program required a 3.5% response rate (.35 ÷ 10) and of the total contacts, 5.4% (.35 ÷ 6.5).

This was a program designed only for telemarketing and the response rate required to make the program successful was modest. This type of planning can defuse expectation levels that may not be realistic.

Even before you get into the specifics of your program, measurement has to be considered and evaluated. First, you have to determine how you'll measure the program, and how much you can afford to spend. With a firm understanding of the tolerable selling costs, you can design and plan the direct marketing effort.

Tactics

As you define the actual direct marketing tactics you'll be using, be sure you document and chart the flow of the program. The biggest single problem we've encountered in direct marketing programs is not anticipating all the necessary and possible alternative steps. A complete flow chart will force you to consider all of the alternatives.

You're designing an operating system when you design a direct marketing program. The database, promotional material, controls and analysis, fulfillment and marketing integration must be anticipated. By developing a complete flow of the activities, you will be forced to anticipate all of the possible alternatives. As part of the flow chart, you should consider time frames and contingencies that can affect the program.

As you can see in Illustration 2-7, you should first anticipate what lists to use and where they will come from. These lists will then be merged to create a single mailing list. The duplicate names on this list should be eliminated or purged. Duplicates are expensive and can have a seriously adverse effect on your prospects, especially if you will be using telemarketing.

At the same time that the lists are merged and the duplicate records are

eliminated, the list should be source coded to allow measurement. In
our example, we planned testing three groups of customer lists and
two outside lists for the direct marketing project. Each of the five lists

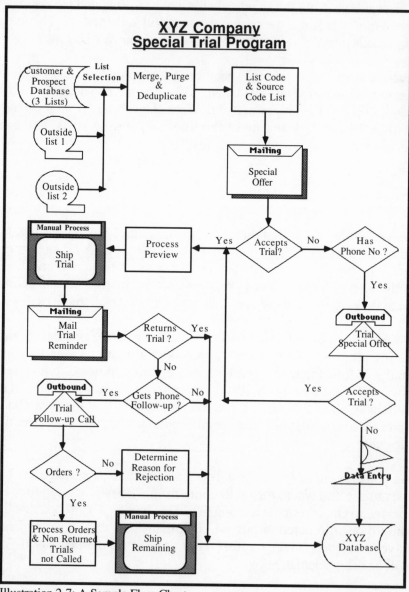

Illustration 2-7: A Sample Flow Chart

had to be coded with special sourcing information to allow measurement.

The mail was then dropped to all of the prospects. The prospect could respond by mail or through an inbound 800 number. These responders were processed and if possible eliminated from the telephone marketing list. We recognized that a prospect could have already responded and still receive a phone call. The script was designed to deal with this situation.

Acceptances were sent a trial of the product and a portion scheduled for a follow-up telephone selling call 14 days after the trial was mailed. The trials that did not receive a phone call received mail reminders. This was a method to test the impact of the second phone call. The second phone call also provided information on why the prospect was rejecting the trial and not purchasing the product. Any prospect that decided to purchase the product was shipped the remainder of the order and added to the customer file.

Prospects who did not respond to the mailing and who had a phone number, received a telemarketing call 15 days after the mail was dropped. If the prospects accepted the offer, they were processed similarly to the mail acceptances.

From the acceptances, telemarketing and follow-up telephone and other information, a complete prospect database was established for future activity. A business plan was developed from the flow chart to establish a methodology for measurement of the program.

XYZ Direct Marketing Program - February 1987

	Cust A	Cust B	Cust C	List 1	List 2	Total
Mail Activity						
Tot Rec on list	1,299	6,500	6,500	4,500	2,500	21,299
Mail Response Rate	3.00%	2.00%	2.00%	1.00%	1.00%	1.73%
Total Resp/Trials	39	130	130	45	25	369
Proj Conv Mail Trial	25.00%	20.00%	20.00%	20.00%	20.00%	20.60%
Mail Orders	10	26	26	9	5	76

Mail Cost/1000	$400					
Mail Costs	$520	$2,600	$2,600	$1,800	$1,000	$8,520
Cost per Responder	$13.33	$20.00	$20.00	$40.00	$40.00	$23.09
Cost per Order	$52.00	$100.00	$100.00	$200.00	$200.00	$112.00

Phone Activity

% of List Contactable	70.00%	70.00%	0.00%	0.00%	0.00%	70.00%
Total Contacts	909	4,550	0	0	0	5,459
% Request Trials	30.00%	25.00%	25.00%	20.00%	20.00%	25.85%
Telemktg Trials	273	1,138	0	0	0	1,411
% of Trials Converting	20.00%	20.00%	20.00%	20.00%	20.00%	20.00%
Number of Orders	55	228	0	0	0	283
Telemktg Contact/Hour	8	8	8	6	6	
No. of Init Telemktg Hrs	114	569	0	0	0	683
No. Prev F/U Telemktg Hrs	34	142	0	0	0	176
Total Telemktg Hrs	148	711	0	0	0	859
Cost/Telemktg Hr	$35.00	$35.00	$35.00	$35.00	$35.00	$35.00
Total Telemktg Costs	$5,180	$24,885	$0	$0	$0	$30,065
Cost per Trial	$18.97	$21.87	$0.00	$0.00	$0.00	$21.31
Cost per Order	$94.18	$109.14	$0.00	$0.00	$0.00	$106.24

Mail & Phone Combined

Total Previews	312	1,268	130	45	25	1,780
Total Orders	65	254	26	9	5	359

Costs

Direct Marketing	$5,700	$27,485	$2,600	$1,800	$1,000	$38,585
Cost of Goods	$4,875	$19,050	$1,950	$675	$375	$26,925
Cost of Previews	$6,240	$25,360	$2,600	$900	$500	$35,600
Commissions	$3,510	$13,716	$1,404	$486	$270	$19,386
Total Costs	$20,325	$85,611	$8,554	$3,861	$2,145	$120,496
Costs per Order	312.69	337.05	329	429	429	335.64
Revenue per Order	$900	$900	$900	$900	$900	$900
Gross Revenue	$58,500	$228,600	$23,400	$8,100	$4,500	$323,100
Contribution	$38,175	$142,989	$14,846	$4,239	$2,355	$202,604
% Rev as Contribution	65.00%	63.00%	63.00%	52.00%	52.00%	63.00%

The business plan for direct mail is done based on experience and known costs. The total number of records on each list starts the business planning process. We have to know how many of each group will be used for direct marketing. If you already have had experience with a particular list segment, those results should be used during the planning process. Certain segments of the customer list may perform better than others. In our example, the different response rates were based on our experience with that type of list. The total response rate, which is the weighted average for all of the list segments, was also calculated. This is done by dividing the total responses by the total mailed. The total response is the sum of the response for each list category.

The total responses by list segment and total for the test are easily established using the projected response rates. Again, experience with various list segments can be used to project the closing ratio of each group of responders. The weighted average closing ratio can also be established. This is done by dividing the total number of orders by the total responders. The total number of orders is the sum of the orders for each group.

The cost for the mail is used to calculate the mailing cost for each segment of the list. The total costs are the sum of the costs by list category. The cost per responder and the cost per order are now easily established.

A similar approach to planning the direct mail campaign is used for planning the telemarketing and telephone sales activity. As you'll note from the plan, only a small portion of the list had phone numbers and could be used for telemarketing. We established the responders and orders from telemarketing by using the same methodology employed for direct mail. As we discuss in Chapter 6, only a percentage of the list we start with will be able to be contacted with telemarketing. Note that only the total records used for telemarketing is included in the Totals column.

A follow-up phone call is planned to those prospects who accept our offer to try to convert the trials into orders. The number of anticipated contacts per hour is used to determine the number of calling hours required for both the initial and subsequent follow-up calling. As you'll note from the plan, $35.00 per calling hour was used as the cost for telemarketing. From that cost, we can establish the cost per responder (trial) and the cost per order.

The combined results of the program have now been established. The results are combined by list segment and then totaled for the entire program. The total orders and previews are summarized by type of media and list segment.

The costs are then established for the direct marketing effort. In addition,` the cost of goods for orders, the cost of goods for the previews and any commissions paid for orders are also established by list segment.

The plan then establishes the total costs by summarizing all the costs for the project by list segment. The cost per order is easily determined by dividing the costs per order by the total number of orders. The revenue per order is reviewed and then the gross revenue is calculated by multiplying the revenue per order by the total number of orders. The costs are subtracted from the revenue to determine the contribution by list segment. The percent contribution is determined by dividing the contribution by the revenue.

Contribution is a term that describes the amount of gross profit made by a specific activity. In many companies, this is the method of measuring the effectiveness of any marketing program. In essence, it is the gross profit of a project after allowing for cost of goods and cost of selling including commissions. It doesn't normally include general and administrative expenses or other overhead items. The concept of contribution is more fully described in the Chapter on catalogs.

By tracking the costs and results by list segment, the effectiveness of each list and facet of the marketing program can be accurately evaluated. You'll be able to determine if the overall program was a success or failure and which portions of your target audience were more profitable than others.

On-going Direct Marketing Program Planning

Once you have established the background and strategy for your direct marketing programs, each new program you execute is much easier to plan. You still want to focus on the definitions of the prospect, offer and universe you're trying to contact, but you don't have to spend much time on the historical issue. In addition, most of the anticipated results will be based on the experiences you've had in other direct marketing efforts.

We have included a sample plan of an on-going program to give you a model to use.

Acme Computer Corporation
Marketing and Sales Department
Sales Operating Guide

Section:	**Sales Programs**	
S/G:	Shared Data Program - Fall 1987	S/G #: 20-05

This guideline identifies and explains a special marketing program to generate sales leads and expand the customer base. The program uses direct marketing to make the offer to an appropriate group of prospects and then the salesperson is given a lead to follow-up.

1.0   Objective.

This program is to develop qualified sales leads for the sales people to follow-up. A special offer is used to get the prospect involved and interested in Acme Computer. Because it has been determined that selling relational database as a concept is very difficult, this promotion emphasizes the need to share information when several computers are involved. The concept of purchasing equipment has a higher perceived level of risk and is more difficult to sell. This promotion is targeted to reduce risk and make the decision to try a ACC system virtually painless. The offer is targeted to allow the prospect to feel the decision is similar to the free 30 day post installation trial they receive when they acquire software.

The prospect, after indicating an interest and concern in sharing information, is offered to install an Acme Computer AC300 system for 30 days and find out for themselves how easy and flexible sharing data is when using a Acme Computer System.

The Acme Computer system will be installed by the customer after some training and assistance by Acme Computer personnel. The system will be installed using RS-232 communication and the initial target audience will be primarily the DEC VAX user who is also using PC's.

2.0   The Universe.

  2.1 The universe of prospects for this promotion has been identified to consist of three unique groups of people.

    2.1.2   Businesses that have only an IBM host system installed and are also sharing information with a network of PC's.

    2.1.2   Businesses that have an IBM host system, DEC VAX system and a network of PC's sharing information.

    2.1.3   Businesses that have a DEC VAX host system installed and are also sharing information with a network of PC's.

  2.2   The primary target in each group of prospects will be the executive or manager responsible for the data processing installation.

  2.3   Prospect objectives in accepting the free trial offer:

Section: **Sales Programs**
S/G: Shared Data Program - Fall 1987   S/G #: 20-05

2.3.1   Determine if he can share data across multiple hosts and users.

2.3.2   Is Acme Computer a potential solution for sharing data problems.

2.3.3   Installing the AC300 is an easy way to test new technology and relational database.

2.3.4   The DP manager is pro-actively examining alternatives for both current and future problems. The trial is an opportunity to educate himself and his staff on an available approach.

2.3.6   Users will be able to see their own little applications running with the AC300.

2.3.7   Access to data will be offered to the users without having to write application programs. The prospect will be shown how to use simple query and 4GL approaches to access the information.

2.3.8   Installing hardware has been perceived as difficult and hard to learn to use. The trial program will give the prospect an opportunity to disprove this perception.

3.0   Prospect Qualification.

3.1   A qualified prospect is currently using PC's and any of the following hosts:
DEC VAX
Sun
Apollo
AT&T

Section: **Sales Programs**
S/G: Shared Data Program - Fall 1987   S/G #: 20-05

3.2   If the prospect is using an IBM VM/CMS host, he can take advantage of the special offer if he can provide a block multiplexor channel connection and additional programmer support to implement the AC system.

3.3   The prospect has to be able to identify an application that will be used for data sharing after the trial.

3.4   The prospect must have reasonable credit worthiness.

3.5   The prospect must be an end-user. VAR's and resellers are excluded.

3.6   The ACC salesperson will obtain the following additional qualification information:

   3.6.1   Types of hosts

   3.6.2   Number of hosts at the site.

   3.6.3   Number of hosts to be used during the trial installation.

   3.6.4   Application for data sharing after the trial.

   3.6.5   Schedule for the implementation of the trial and the schedule for the application.

   3.6.7   What alternatives are there for the application besides the ACC solution.

   3.6.8   How will the prospect pay for the solution after the trial. The salesperson has to establish the availability of funding.

Section: **Sales Programs**
S/G: Shared Data Program - Fall 1987   S/G #: 20-05

    3.6.9   The salesperson has to ensure that the prospect understands the costs to continue with the AC system.

    3.6.10 Establish the authority of the prospect to accept the trial.

    3.6.11 Establish the decision criteria and individuals for acquiring the AC system after the trial.

    3.6.12 Get a letter of commitment signed by the prospect. This letter will identify the ACC responsibilities for the trial and prospect responsibilities to implement the trial.

    3.6.13 Establish the criteria for evaluating the trial and what it will take to convince the prospect to continue using a AC system.

4.0   Offer.

    4.1   Free trial of AC300 for 30 days.

    4.2   System will be installed for sharing of data between PC's and supported hosts.

    4.3   ACC will provide training, system, installation support and guidance on conversion of data files to the AC300.

    4.4   Prospect provides:

        4.4.1   Files for use on the AC300

Section:　　　**Sales Programs**
S/G:　　　　　Shared Data Program - Fall 1987　　　S/G #: 20-05

4.4.2　Users (prospect will train users with ACC assistance)

4.4.3　Site and site preparation including electrical and environment if needed.

4.4.4　Communication facilities.

4.4.5　Host and PC's to work with the AC300. The PC will have a minimum configuration of at least an XT with 4 meg free.

5.0　Direct Marketing Approach

5.1　Flowchart Explanation.

5.1.1　Lists will be acquired for targeting the offer and the direct marketing program. The internal lists of prior respondents and customers will be used as the base list to start all activities. The Computer Intelligence Corporation (CIC) list of

VAX systems will also be used. A subscription list of VAX systems will be acquired for direct mail and telemarketing activity.

The DEC Professional list or Gary Slaughter Compiled list will be used.

The list will be name directed when ever possible. The target contact will be the director or manager of data processing.

Additional lists will be tested to include IBM VM/CMS sites. The same list sources will be

Section: **Sales Programs**
S/G: Shared Data Program - Fall 1987   S/G #: 20-05

Shared Data Promotion - Fall 1987

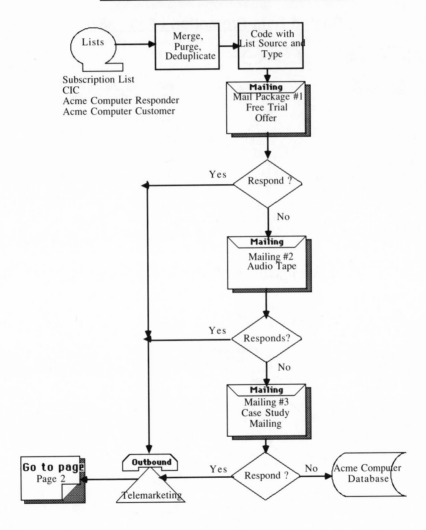

-Flowchart page 1-

Section: **Sales Programs**
S/G: Shared Data Program - Fall 1987   S/G #: 20-05

Shared Data Promotion - Fall 1987

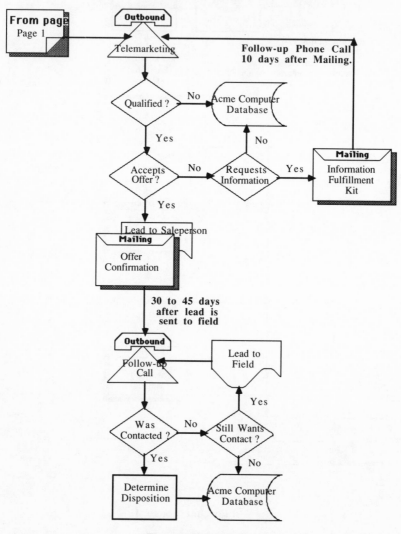

- Flowchart page 2 -

Section: **Sales Programs**
S/G: Shared Data Program - Fall 1987   S/G #: 20-05

used but will specifically be targeted for IBM. During the initial mailings only DEC users and Telco managers will be used.

If possible, sites that have both IBM and DEC hosts will be identified and coded on the list to allow testing of all types of prospects.

If telemarketing is used, the combined unduplicated list will be sent to a service bureau specializing in appending phone numbers to the record. This will be done in parallel to the mailing and normally takes about two weeks and is about 50% effective on the list supplied to the service bureau.

5.1.2   The lists will be sent to an outside service bureau and combined to eliminate duplicate names and sites. The primary list will be the Acme Computer customer, next in hierarchy will be the former respondent list. CIC will be next in the hierarchy and the subscription lists will be last.

5.1.3   The service bureau will code each record with the list source:

List Source	System	Code
Acme Computer Customer	Unknown	ACC0
Acme Computer Customer	VAX	ACC1
Acme Computer Customer	IBM	ACC2
Acme Computer Customer	AT&T	ACC3
Acme Computer Customer	Other	ACC4
Acme Computer Prospect	Unknown	ACP0
Acme Computer Prospect	VAX	ACP1
Acme Computer Prospect	IBM	ACP2
Acme Computer Prospect	AT&T	ACP3

Section: **Sales Programs**
S/G: Shared Data Program - Fall 1987   S/G #: 20-05

Acme Computer Prospect	Other	ACP4
CIC	Unknown	CIC0
CIC	VAX	CIC1
CIC	IBM	CIC2
CIC	AT&T	CIC3
CIC	Other	CIC4
Name of Publication	Unknown	SU10
Name of Publication	VAX	SU11
Name of Publication	IBM	SU12
Name of Publication	AT&T	SU13
Name of Publication	Other	SU14

Acme Computer only offers complete coverage in selected cities. The list will be extracted to only include selected sectional centers that are geographically within the covered areas. This will be explained in a memo prior to the mailing.

5.1.4   All of the un-duplicated names will be mailed package number 1.

5.1.5   Respondents to the first mailing will be sent to the local sales office for telemarketing and actual follow-up.

5.1.6   Non respondents to the mailing will be mailed a second time. This will be mailing #2.

5.1.7   Respondents to the second mailing will be sent to the local sales office for telemarketing and face-to-face sales follow-up.

5.1.8   Non respondents to the second mailing will be mailed a third mailing package.

Section: **Sales Programs**

S/G: Shared Data Program - Fall 1987 S/G #: 20-05

5.1.9 A database will be developed and only those records that are the property of Acme Computer will be included (Acme Computer Customers, Acme Computer Prospects, CIC).

5.1.10 If the prospect is qualified during the telemarketing effort, the prospect will be offered to receive a visit from an ACC salesperson visit to review the free trial program and discuss how it can be implemented. The mail solicitations will offer the prospect the opportunity to try the AC system for 30 days free. The salesperson will determine the prospect's qualification level in order to receive the free trial.

5.1.11 The prospect may refuse the offer and ask for additional information. This group will be fulfilled with an information package.

Ten days after the information package is mailed, this group will be re-contacted via telemarketing to try to convert to a sales lead.

5.1.12 Unqualified prospects and those prospects that refuse the offer will be updated on the database and held for possible future activity.

5.1.13 Accepters of the offer will receive a letter confirming their acceptance, giving the name of the salesperson or sales manager responsible for their being contacted.

A sales lead will be sent to the salesperson. Both the confirmation letter and lead will be mailed within two business days of the contact.

Section: **Sales Programs**
S/G: Shared Data Program - Fall 1987   S/G #: 20-05

5.1.14 All leads will be re-contacted via telemarketing 30 to 45 days after they were mailed to determine the disposition of the situation. If the lead wasn't contacted by a salesperson, he or she will be offered the opportunity to be re-contacted.

5.1.15 If the prospect wants to be re-contacted, the lead's name will be telephoned to the regional director and mailed the same day.

5.1.16 If the prospect was contacted, the disposition will be determined and the database updated.

6.0   Financial Projections

Anticipated Results

Number of Records for Analysis	20,000
% of Records lost via merge, purge, de-duplicate	25.00%
Number of records lost via merge,purge, de-duplicate	5,000
Records receiving pre-mailing	15,000

Group	AC Prosp	Dec Prof	CMP	Total
Mail				
Total Records - Mail #	13,000	10,000	2,000	15,000
Mail Resp Rate	1.00%	1.00%	1.00%	1.00%
Total Respondents	30	100	20	150
% Leads of Respondents	60%	60%	60%	
Leads	18	60	12	90
% Trials of Leads	60%	60%	60%	
Trials	11	36	7	54
% Orders of Trials	30%	30%	30%	
Orders	3	11	2	16
Total Records - Mail #2	2,970	9,900	1,980	14,850
Mail Resp Rate	1.00%	1.00%	1.00%	1.00%
Total Respondents	30	99	20	149

Section: **Sales Programs**

S/G: Shared Data Program - Fall 1987   S/G #: 20-05

% Leads of Respondents	60%	60%	60%	
Leads	18	59	12	89
% Trials of Leads	60%	60%	60%	
Trials	11	35	7	53
% Orders of Trials	30%	30%	30%	
Orders	3	11	2	16
Total Records - Mail #3	2,940	9,801	1,960	14,701
Mail Resp Rate	1.00%	1.00%	1.00%	1.00%
Total Respondents	29	98	20	147
% Leads of Respondents	60%	60%	60%	
Leads	17	59	12	88
% Trials of Leads	60%	60%	60%	
Trials	10	35	7	52
% Orders of Trials	30%	30%	30%	
Orders	3	11	2	16

Total Mail Results (3 Mailings)

Respondents	89	297	60	446
Leads	53	178	36	267
Trials	32	106	21	159
Orders	9	33	6	4

Total Mail Results (2 Mailings)

Respondents	60	199	40	299
Leads	36	119	24	179
Trials	22	71	14	107
Orders	6	22	4	32

Costs

Mail Costs

Cost per Direct Mail Piece for Package 1 (w/postage)	$1.89
Cost per Direct Mail Piece for Package 2 (w/postage)	$2.89
Cost per Direct Mail Piece for Package 3 (w/postage)	$1.89
Cost per Requests Literature Fulfillment Kit	$3.00
Cost per Lead Confirmation Mailing	$1.50

List Costs

Cost per Name with Processing	$0.15
Cost per Name for Phone number	$0.30
Cost per Lead Processed	$1.50

Section: **Sales Programs**
S/G: Shared Data Program - Fall 1987   S/G #: 20-05

Telemarketing Costs
Cost per Telephone Call $5.00

One Time Costs
Development $20,000

Program Costs - 3 Mail List	AC Prosp	Dec Prof	CMP	Total
Initial Name	$0.00	$4,500.00	$900.00	$5,400.00
Phone Number	$0.00	$0.00	$0.00	$0.00
Lead Processing	$79.50	$267.00	$54.00	$400.50
Total List Costs	$79.50	$4,767.00	$954.00	$5,800.50
Direct Mail				
Package #1	$5,670.00	$18,900.00	$3,780.00	$28,350.00
Package #2	$8,670.00	$28,900.00	$5,780.00	$43,350.00
Package #3	$5,670.00	$18,900.00	$3,780.00	$28,350.00
Lit Req Fulfill	$51.00	$177.00	$36.00	$264.00
Lead Confirmation	$79.50	$267.00	$54.00	$400.50
Total Mail Costs	$20,140.50	$67,144.00	$13,430.00	$100,714.50
Telemarketing Costs				
Lead F/U Call	$445.00	$1,485.00	$300.00	$2,230.00
Tot Telemktg Cost	$445.00	$1,485.00	$300.00	$2,230.00
Development Costs				$20,000.00
Total Costs	$20,665.00	$73,396.00	$14,684.00	$128,745.00
Total Leads	53	178	36	267
Total Trials	32	106	21	159
Total Orders	9	33	6	48
Cost per Lead	$389.91	$412.34	$407.89	$482.19
Cost per Trial	$645.78	$692.42	$699.24	$809.72
Cost per Order	$2,296.11	$2,224.12	$2,447.33	$2,682.19
Avg Order Size	$95,000	$95,000	$95,000	$95,000

Section: **Sales Programs**
S/G: Shared Data Program - Fall 1987   S/G #: 20-05

	AC Prosp	Dec Prof	CMP	Total
Total Revenue	$855,000	$3,135,000	$570,000	$4,560,000
% Rev/Direct Mktg	2.42%	2.34%	2.58%	2.82%
Program Costs - 2 Mail List				
Initial Name	$0.00	$3,000.00	$600.00	$3,600.00
Phone Number	$0.00	$0.00	$0.00	$0.00
Lead Processing	$54.00	$178.50	$36.00	$268.50
Total List Costs	$54.00	$3,178.50	$636.00	$3,868.50
Direct Mail				
Package #1	$5,670.00	$18,900.00	$3,780.00	$28,350.00
Package #2	$8,583.30	$28,611.00	$5,722.20	$42,916.50
Package #3	$0.00	$0.00	$0.00	$0.00
Lit Req Fulfill	$72.00	$240.00	$48.00	$360.00
Lead Confirmation	$54.00	$178.50	$36.00	$268.50
Total Mail Costs	$14,379.30	$47,929.50	$9,586.20	$71,895.00
Telemarketing Costs				
Lead F/U Call	$300.00	$995.00	$200.00	$1,495.00
Tot Telemktg Cost	$300.00	$995.00	$200.00	$1,495.00
Development Costs				$20,000.00
Total Costs	$14,733.30	$52,103.00	$10,422.20	$97,258.50
Total Leads	36	119	24	179
Total Trials	22	71	14	107
Total Orders	6	22	4	32
Cost per Lead	$409.26	$437.84	$434.26	$543.34
Cost per Trial	$669.70	$733.85	$744.44	$908.96
Cost per Order	$2,455.55	$2,368.32	$2,605.55	$3,039.33

Section: **Sales Programs**
S/G: Shared Data Program - Fall 1987   S/G #: 20-05

Revenue per Order	$95,000	$95,000	$95,000	$95,000
Total Revenue		$570,000	$2,090,000	$380,000	$3,040,000
% Rev/Direct Mktg	2.58%	2.49%	2.74%	3.20%

7.0 Direct Mail Copy Platforms

7.1 Package #1 - Initial Free Trial Offer

This package will create a high impact, perhaps in a three dimensional format. It will introduce the concept of sharing data, and call the prospect to respond to Acme Computer to have a salesperson visit, and explain how the prospect can take advantage of the free trial offer.

This mail package must paint a conceptual picture of the sharing data problem while also convincing the prospect that he/she is experiencing this problem. After reading the mail package, he/she should want to learn more about how the Acme Computer system can help solve the data sharing problem.

The proliferation of PC's should magnify the intensity of the data sharing problem and the prospect should be interested in learning how to resolve this issue.

The target group of data processing managers is heavily mailed to by a large number of vendors and the mail piece will have to break through the clutter.

The response vehicle will be a BRC or BRE which should supply a minimum of qualification information. An 800 response phone number can also be used.

Section: **Sales Programs**
S/G: Shared Data Program - Fall 1987 S/G #: 20-05

7.2 Package #2 - Audio tape free trial offer.

This package will create a high impact, perhaps in a three dimensional format. It will introduce the concept of sharing data and call the prospect to respond to Acme Computer by allowing a salesperson to visit and explain how he/she can take advantage of the free trial. Package #2 will follow mailing package #1 by about three weeks.

It may be wise to ultimately test this package by itself as a stand-alone mailing.

This mail package should also paint a conceptual picture of the sharing data problem while convincing the prospect that he too is experiencing this problem. After reading the mail package he should want to learn more about how the Acme Computer system can help solve his data sharing problem.

The proliferation of PC's should magnify the intensity of the data sharing problem and he should be interested in learning how to resolve this issue.

The target group of data processing managers is heavily mailed to by a large number of vendors and the mail piece will have to break through the clutter.

The response vehicle will be a BRC or BRE which should supply a minimum of qualification information. An 800 response phone number can also be used.

7.3 Package #3 - Offering Free Trial of AC300

This package also will create a strong impact, perhaps in a three dimensional format. It too will introduce the concept of sharing data , call the prospect to respond to Acme Computer

Section: **Sales Programs**
S/G: Shared Data Program - Fall 1987   S/G #: 20-05

by allowing a salesperson visit and explain how the prospect can take advantage of the free trial. The third package will follow mailing package #2 by about three weeks. It may be wise to ultimately test this package by itself as a stand-alone mailing.

This mail package has to paint a conceptual picture of the sharing data problem and have the prospect internalize this problem. After reading the mail package, he should want to learn more about how the Acme Computer system can help solve his data sharing problem.

The continuing proliferation of PC's should be magnifying the intensity of the data sharing problem and he should be interested in learning how to resolve this issue.

The target group of data processing managers is heavily mailed to by a large number of vendors and the mail piece will have to break through the clutter.

The response vehicle will be a BRC or BRE which should supply a minimum of qualification information. An 800 response phone number can also be used.

7.4 Lead Confirmation Mailing.

This mailing will be to confirm to the prospect that he will be contacted by a AC sales representative shortly to explain the free trial of the AC300 system.

The purpose of this mailing is to open a door of communication if the salesperson is late in getting back to the prospect. It acknowledges that we know the prospect has accepted our offer.

Section: **Sales Programs**
S/G: Shared Data Program - Fall 1987   S/G #: 20-05

7.5 Send Literature Fulfillment

> Package #1 initially will be used to fulfill literature requests. Ultimately a separate package to fulfill literature requests should be developed.

We used an outlining format for this business plan in order to make additional programs easy to test and document. You should try to establish a consistent format for developing your own follow-up programs.

Planning Summarized

By now your business plan looks like a major tome. It contains as much as you'll ever want to know about your company, why you need direct marketing and what results you expect from the direct marketing program. As we said at the start of this chapter, reading about business planning isn't very exciting. Most of the information is common sense and has probably already been developed within your company.

The development of the program you're going to implement is the only fun part of planning. It may seem easier to just start doing something, but without prior planning, your chances for failure are very high. Much of the remainder of this book describes different tactical approaches to implementing business-to-business direct marketing.

By forcing yourself to examine the basics of your business, you'll ensure that the implementation of direct marketing will have the highest chance to succeed. Your company organization may require unique implementation considerations and reporting programs. Establishing the current selling costs will allow you to effectively measure and evaluate the direct marketing effort. Finally, the overall planning phase will help clarify why you need direct marketing and what results you should expect.

Once you've developed a documented direct marketing business plan, it will be easy to communicate your program to others within your company and to outside vendors you might need. In addition, the documented plan will give you a basis from which to build new programs.

We know how hard it is to read about planning, but using some of the examples we've given, we hope you can do a little better job. Don't sell business planning short. The effort you spend up front could be the best investment you'll make to ensure that your program is successful.

Chapter Three - Lead Generation Programs

Real World

The most frustrating possible direct marketing objective to launch must be generating sales leads for a field sales force. As the direct marketing manager, usually you have no control over the ultimate success of the project and it's almost impossible to measure the results. Let's see how we can do better.

Virtually every business-to-business direct marketing professional can tell war stories of attempted lead generation projects that were never continued because the program's results couldn't be measured. The reason for difficulty in measurement of a lead program really starts in not understanding the environment. We, the communications and direct marketing departments, perceive our mission to be to help the sales force by generating sales leads. Yet, the field organization frequently has a different perception of our role. They feel it's "the staff at headquarters, in their ivory towers" versus "the field force, where the rubber meets the road". If you examine their side of the story, their perception is frequently partially accurate.

Most lead generation program failures occur due to one or a combination of two fatal flaws. First, in many instances, the direct marketing program is designed with little or no input from the field sales force. The results are feelings of suspicion, distrust and downright hostility because we only encumber the salesperson with additional reporting requirements and a lot of paper work and supposed leads whose value has not been explained.

Second, we often find lead generation programs have been designed for the outstanding performers of the sales force. We ask this group to qualify and sell the lead and then report back on the success of the lead program. This poor targeting has probably done more damage to lead programs than any other factor.

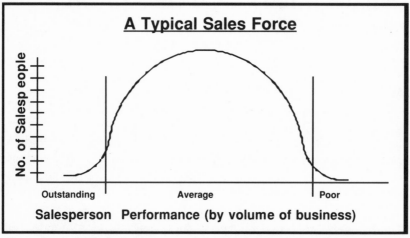

Illustration 3-1: The bell shape curve as it relates to a typical sales force.

Why? A sales organization will normally fall into a bell shaped curve, similar to Illustration 3-1. The left end of the curve, the outstanding salesperson, needs little or no help. However, if sent leads, this group is most likely to follow-up and even generate orders. They are not at all threatened by outside help and support.

Them right end of the curve, the poor salesperson, wants help but has trouble accepting it. He is threatened and constantly looks for excuses. His excuse for failure will be directed at the poor leads we are sending to him.

The group in the middle, the average salesperson, is where our program should be targeted. If we can move this group to the left, even a small amount, we can have a dramatic impact on the success of the company.

Our goals in this chapter are how to make a lead generation program work; how to build measurement programs on the quality and results of the lead program that we can control; and how we can solicit and get the support of the sales force in our program.

The Use of Sales Time

The statement,"the only real resource we have in business is time", could not be more appropriately applied than in sales. The effective use of time is the key to the salesperson's success. The more time the salesperson has in front of a prospect or customer, the better the odds of making a sale.

Sales managers have to be very selective when they require the sales force to perform functions that take them away from contact with prospects or customers.

IBM measures their entire field force at least annually to determine how time is being used. The results are used to determine resources needed for products and services and how the organization might be improved. In 1979, it was discovered that only 33% of work time was being spent face-to-face with customers. It was alarming to find that 2/3 of the sales force's time was being spent in non-customer related activities.

This situation really sounds extreme. Yet, you may be surprised to learn that within your own company your sales force may actually spend only half their time in front of customers. Vacations, holidays and personal time off, probably take more than one month out of every year away from available time to sell. Consider the sales contests and travel awards you run and you probably loose another week or two. Education and product training will again reduce the available selling time from the sales force. Look at the weekly sales meetings, reports and special projects required and it is easy to see as much as 50% of available selling time lost.

The Laboratory for Advertising Performance, a division of McGraw-Hill, New York, conducts a bi-annual survey to determine the effectiveness and costs of average sales forces. Part of this ongoing research establishes the average cost of a sales call in many industries

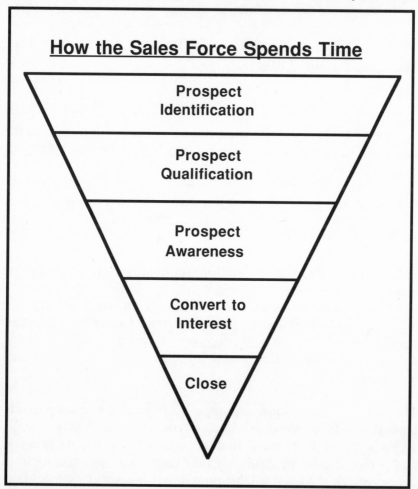

Illustration 3-2: Where sales time is typically spent.

and the average cost to close an order with a sales force. The survey conducted for 1985 activity determined that the average cost of a single sales call across all industries was in excess of $250.

When you couple this high cost with how little time salespeople actually spend in front of customers and prospects, illustration 3-2 becomes even more meaningful. This diagram illustrates that most selling time is spent finding qualified prospects and making them aware of your offerings.

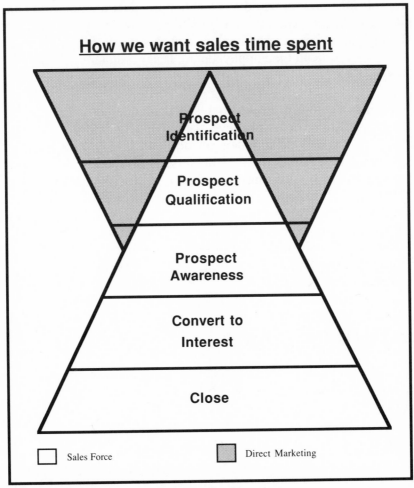

Illustration 3-3: Where we would like sales time spent.

Your objective is to invert the way sales time is spent to correspond with Illustration 3-3. Direct marketing should be used to move the prospect through the identification, qualification, awareness and interest stages. Of course the salesperson will not be completely eliminated during these stages, but his or her involvement should be reduced substantially.

If this is such a simple concept, why then isn't it happening naturally? Any salesperson will readily agree that prospect identification and qualification isn't something he or she likes to do. The sales force would prefer to have these functions done for them. Why then do we have such a difficult time implementing lead generation program with the sales force?

No one has a complete answer to this difficult question. We speculate that the sales force doesn't believe that anyone can perform this function as well as they do and their performance is ultimately based on new leads. They don't trust anyone else to do their job, especially staff generals who don't have regular contact with the field. Also, often their prior experience with leads hasn't been good. Finally, the sales force typically currently creates the time to do the identification and qualification phases. If the sales force had an adequate and ongoing supply of highly qualified referrals, their opinions and work habits might change. This is not a short term problem with short term answers.

Lead Generation Questions

As you begin to plan your lead generation program, a number of critical questions will need to be resolved. Illustration 3-4 identifies the six major issues.

Lead Program Questions to Resolve

1) What is a good lead?

2) How many leads is enough?

3) Which is worse--no leads or too many?

4) How do you track leads?

5) What about turnover?

6) How do you get feedback?

Illustration 3-4: The six major issues involved in a lead generation program.

1) What is a good lead?

Some of the experiences we had in designing a lead program at IBM will probably sound familiar to you.

The lead program was a test to support 90 salespeople in five branch offices. The salespeople were responsible for selling new account, first time users of computer systems. During the design phases of the project we brought 16 of the salespeople together to get their opinions on several issues.

The 16 salespeople were asked to define what they felt to be a good lead. We wrote the definitions on charts as the salespeople gave their requirements. When we were finished there were 21 different definitions of a good lead.

It is intriguing that while the success of any lead program will ultimately be judged by the quantity and quality of the leads generated, we have yet to get a group of salespeople to agree on what is the definition of good lead. On only one point they do agree: "A good lead is one that closes." As direct marketers, salespeople feel we should be able fore tell that a specific lead will purchase a product or service.

Later, we will discuss some issues to address in establishing the quality of a sales lead. During the IBM planning session, we ultimately agreed that a good lead had affirmatively answered the following questions that met the sales group's predetermined qualifications:

• Were they evaluating a computer, bookkeeping machine or word processing equipment within the next 12 months?
• When they were planning to acquire the system?
• How many clerical people they had?
• Had they added any clerical personnel in the last 12 months?
• Did they anticipate adding clerical people in next 12 months?
• Did they have an Accounts Receivable problem?
• Did they have an Inventory Control problem?

Any prospect who was evaluating a product in the next 12 months was considered a lead and sent to the sales force. The salespeople had determined that they wanted an opportunity to sell any prospect who was in the process of product evaluation. This was a serious flaw in the structure of this program and will be discussed later.

2) How many leads is enough?

This question is also very difficult to get a consensus opinion from the sales force. They all agree that we should just send them the sales leads and they could handle them.

The same group of IBM salespeople originally answered that

they wanted as many as 20 leads per day. We had discussed with them our plan to use direct mail and telemarketing to generate the leads. Our plan was to give them their required number of leads every day. This was a new concept to the sales force, they had never experienced a sustained and ongoing flow of leads.

The sales force we were dealing with was selling computer products at a starting price of $14,000 or more. It took at least three sales calls to sell the product. When you consider 20 leads per day, that is 20 follow-up calls each salesperson would have to make to qualify the lead and schedule for an appointment. If the phone call took only 15 minutes, the sales force had just signed up for five hours of telemarketing every day. We were able to convince the sales force to take only three sales leads per day.

This ultimately proved to be about three times as many leads as the salespeople could handle. A lot of the problems associated with the leads really tied back to our definition of what was a good lead. In a 90 day period we generated over 12,000 leads.

The correct number of leads is directly related to the quality of follow-up required and the number of orders you want to generate as a result of the lead program. As discussed in the business planning chapter, the key to the success of any program is the expectation level. You'll never be able to completely replace the identification and qualification functions of the sales force. In the beginning, you should anticipate only a small portion of the salesperson's business coming from the lead program. As the program gains credibility, you can expect a higher contribution from the leads.

3) **Which is worse --**
   No Leads?
   Too many Leads to follow up?

We have constantly asked this question of direct marketing executives and sales executives alike. The answers seem to follow a pattern.

The sales executive, sales manager and salesperson always answer no leads to follow up as being the worse alternative. The sales force only wants an opportunity to sel; they never think about the issue of being unable to follow up on any lead. A lead to a salesperson means a potential order, and that is all they think of.

On the other hand, the direct marketer knows it's almost impossible to measure the results of his lead program. Generating excess leads only complicates the problem.

In addition, when you send too many leads to follow up to the sales force, all the leads become poor quality. The sales force can't handle the volume, therefore the leads can't be that good. An excessive quantity of leads is normally a turn off to the sales organization. They now perceive all the leads to be of lower quality and tend not to follow up, or screen the leads and follow up selectively. This type of program tends to be non recoverable; you can't expect the sales force to ever accept the leads positively in the future.

A final point about too many leads. A prospect who has been promised that a salesperson will call, expects to be contacted. When you fail to follow up, how do you think this person feels about your company and products? Quite probably he will be upset and may never do business with you. We call the concept of sending too many leads to follow up "poisoning your universe."

Obviously, the right number of leads to be followed up is best. No leads, although probably better from a direct marketing point of view, will yield no business. Too many leads can destroy the opportunity for the direct marketing program to succeed.

4) How do you track leads?

Within this issue are a number of points that need special attention for a successful generation program.

• There must be specific objectives.

Lead programs frequently fail because of unrealistic expectations. For example, only a portion of the leads will actually be followed up and only a portion of the leads followed up will actually buy.

Our experience indicates you can expect only about 30% of the leads that are generated to be followed up. This sounds somewhat absurd, but nevertheless it's true. Salespeople will attempt to reach a prospect and if they are unable to contact the individual after several attempts, they will move on to someone else.

In the best of programs we are surprised to receive a 60% follow up. We have seen follow up levels as low as 10%.

Only a certain amount of leads actually followed up will buy. Perhaps you're expecting 25% of the leads to close. With excellent cooperation from the sales force you get 60% follow up. That means you will actually achieve 15% of the leads closing. Not a bad program, but if you expected 25% to close, the program will be perceived as a failure.

You really have to get everyone involved in the program to agree on very specific objectives .

• There must be commitment

Once you've established reasonable expectations for the lead program, everyone involved needs to commit to the project. Frequently, the direct marketer is behind a project but sales and sales management haven't truly signed up. Only when everyone involved in the project agrees to meet specific expectations and responsibilities does the effort stand a chance to succeed.

Commitment to the lead program must start from the salesperson, all the way up to the VP of Sales. The best situation is to have the sales organization involved in the design of the program. The more the program belongs to them, the higher the odds for success.

The lead program cannot succeed without feedback on the quality of the leads and how they can be improved. If management and the sales force aren't committed to giving feedback and helping to track the leads, the program will fail.

- **The system must be heuristic**

Heuristic means to teach yourself and to learn from experience. With specific agreement to realistic objectives, commitment to follow up the leads and provide feedback, the program can become heuristic. As we learn about the quality and quantity of the leads program, we can use the feedback to improve and make the program better. Similar to the computer in the movie "War Games", the lead system can continue to learn from itself.

These issues truly affect our ability to track and understand the results of the lead generation program. Before you start the project, the issue of tracking the results needs to be resolved. As we look back on the IBM program, it was because we didn't originally anticipate these issues that ultimately led us to making substantial changes. However, we constantly had to return and resell management on why the project should be continued and expanded.

5) What about turnover?

The real question is: What happens to your leads when the salesperson leaves? In most programs we've reviewed, the leads leave with the salesperson. It is not common to have kept a copy of the lead or have entered the lead information into a computerized database.

Leads are expensive. After the lead has been followed up only once, it has become downright valuable. You probably have invested $300 to $500 in each lead. Part of designing your lead program must address the inevitable turnover within the field force and what will happen to the leads.

6) How do you get feedback?

As we mentioned earlier, feedback is one of the most critical elements in the ultimate success or failure of the lead program. The design of the lead document can radically affect the feedback of the program.

In the IBM project we did not effectively anticipate how the lead information would be returned. Most salespeople operate out of their briefcases or cars and normally do not have the ready capability to copy or reproduce the lead information. In addition, the information returned by the sales force needs to be in a format appropriate for analysis. You may want to establish a coding plan to allow the salespeople to identify the quality of the lead.

Again at IBM, we established several questions with coded answers that allowed us to evaluate the lead and any additional activity required to help convert the lead to an order. Illustration 2-5, was the reporting system we designed. Unfortunately we had to change the salesperson's lead form three times to include this system. It is always difficult to change a program after it has started. By anticipating how

Lead Qualification Reporting

Disposition Codes

1) Actively working - prospect has agreed to further contacts.
2) Prospect not handled by this location.
3) Prospect referred to another location.
4) Prospect ordered.
5) Already a customer.
6) Prospect rejected us:
   a) They are too small
   b) We are too expensive
   c) We are not competitive
   d) Performance
   e) Deferred decision
   f) Satisfied with current
   g) Other
7) Prospect wants to be deleted from our files.
8) Prospect bought competition within the last one year.
9) Unable to contact the prospect within the last 30 days.
10) Other - _____
    _____

Lead Quality Analysis

Likelihood to buy

1) Definitely will buy
2) Probably will buy
3) Uncertain
4) Probably won't buy
5) Definitely won't buy

Likelihood to buy from you

1) Definitely will buy
2) Probably will buy
3) Uncertain
4) Probably won't buy
5) Definitely won't buy

Timing to buy

1) Immediate
2) Less then 3 months
3) Less then 6 months
4) Less then 1 year
5) One year or more
6) Probably won't

 Disposition Code

 Liklihood to buy

 Liklihood to buy from you

 Timing to buy

Illustration 3-5: A typical lead quality reporting mechanism.

you'll receive feedback about the lead you can avoid problems in the future.

The lead form we used was made up of four part carbonless paper. The salesperson only had to fill in the appropriate codes and return the copies to the lead generation center. All the lead information was included on the form but the salesperson was also asked to update with any changes. We anticipated giving the salesperson and the sales manager a copy of the lead, which was the reason for the additional copies. As we all know that computers aren't sold on the first sales call. We provided an extra copy to report the initial call disposition and the final disposition of the lead. We even provided a binder with tabs to make territory organization easier.

The feedback on lead quality is as important as the lead generation itself. Most times this is an area that is overlooked. You can't measure and control a program without information on the lead and the effectiveness of the program.

Lead Quality

Every salesperson has a different definition of a good lead. They rarely agree on criteria and have a difficult time expressing what qualities they would like in a lead to be considered 'qualified'.

Over the years we have found four categories to establish lead qualification guidelines. These categories are especially helpful if you're going to use telemarketing to qualify the lead prior to making a sales call.

As an aside, one of the problems in using telemarketing is the ease in which you can get additional information. Often we confuse lead generation and market research when performing the lead qualification process. Always ask yourself whether the information you're requesting is really necessary to establish if a prospect is qualified as a sales lead.

The major categories to use in lead qualification are :

Money
Authority
Need
Desire

As you may notice, the first letter of each word spells MAN with a D. This is a convenient way to remember the four qualification areas. It also spells DAMN!

Hopefully, if the prospect is interested in your product or service, he/she can afford to purchase from you. In reality, there are three areas to look for financial justification in almost any business decision:

1) Displaceable Expenses - dollars already being expended for similar or like services. You may find displaceable expense in related areas of the business as well as the primary area you're trying to address.

2) Avoidable Expenses - dollars that the company can avoid having to spend in the future if they were to buy your solution.

3) Increased Revenue and Business Growth - dollars that the company might generate due to better procedures or approaches to their business. We have often had this area addressed as intangible. Many business decisions are made on emotion based on the intangible value to be derived. We cannot overlook this as a primary justification.

As you try to establish the ability of a company to buy your solution, remember not to get bogged down with unnecessary details. Sometimes it's nice to have additional facts, but they don't really improve the quality of the lead. We often forget that the salesperson will generate his or her own level of information. We may be getting too much detail just to qualify the sales lead.

Authority often is difficult to establish. To determine if the person you're trying to sell to has the authority to buy from you is tough. Ego being what it is, some business people cannot admit to people outside their own company that they have limited power. Lead quality normally suffers the most in this area. Many techniques try to subtly establish buying authority. However, the best method is to ask the prospect directly if he can make the decision to buy your product or service.

Establishing need is the area we all tend to over complicate. We think you should try to limit your questions and probes to one or two major criteria. Keep in mind that you're trying to qualify a sales lead to be followed up by a salesperson. The salesperson will sell the product or service. Many companies perform an excess of market research under the guise of trying to determine prospect need.

Finally, a lead isn't qualified until the prospect has accepted the offer and agreed to see a salesperson. During the IBM program, we initially sent a prospect's name to the sales force when the prospect indicated plans to acquire a machine in the next 12 months. The prospect did not indicate any desire to talk to the salesperson. Obviously, when the salesperson called, the prospect wasn't certain of the purpose of the call. The quality of the lead was immediately questionable in the mind of the salesperson.

The whole process of establishing lead quality should be started on a blackboard with the salespeople. Write the four major categories on the board and ask the sales force what one single question in each area, if answered, would help to confirm the quality of the lead. You'll ultimately get more than one question. To eliminate the other questions, try to determine if the information is absolutely necessary to establish the qualification of the lead.

You can sometimes resolve the Money, Authority and Desire issues with one question that introduces the price of your product and an offer. Prospects may respond that they can't afford it or that they have to talk to someone else. Remember, a prospect isn't qualified unless he/she agree to become a referral.

The Sales Attitude

The Sales Attitude
or what traits make a good salesperson

- **Greed motivated**

- **Large ego**

- **Hates paperwork**

- **Protective of his/her territory**

- **Won't do anything in which he doesn't see a personal gain.**

- **Over-achiever**

Illustration 3-6: The sales attitude

In Illustration 3-6, the traits that make up a good salesperson are reviewed. As sales managers, these are the characteristics we look for when hiring a salesperson. These traits are common in the successful salesperson.

Every sales manager has his or her own opinion regarding the characteristics desirable in the perfect salesperson. The list in Illustration 3-6 seems to agree with most the characteristics mentioned by sales managers we talked to. The real issue is how different the definition of direct marketing as discussed in Chapter one (presented again as

The Definition of Direct Marketing

- **An organized and planned system of contacts**

- **Using a variety of media -- seeking to produce a lead or an order**

- **Developing and maintaining a database**

- **Measurable in cost and results**

- **Works in all methods of selling**

- **Expandable with confidence**

Illustration 3-7: The definition of Direct Marketing.

illustration 3-7) is with the the salesperson's attitude.

Generalizations are always dangerous, but bear in mind the target is the center of the bell curve, the average salesperson. The sales attitude is built around a very large, yet fragile ego. It is hard for salespeople to accept that you can find a prospect in their territory that they didn't already know about. Our requirement to track the lead and determine its quality goes directly against the key elements of the sales attitude. An individual who hates paperwork, is protective of his territory and doesn't do anything that doesn't produce a personal gain is not likely to help us measure and control the lead program.

Direct marketing people and salespeople even have very different views on what our objectives are. As you may recall from Chapter one, the grid in Illustration 3-8 shows how direct marketing views its mission. Then review Illustration 3-9 and look at how the salesperson views the same objective.

The salesperson is not that far from wrong. Our objective is to reduce the cost of selling. We want him or her to spend more time in better

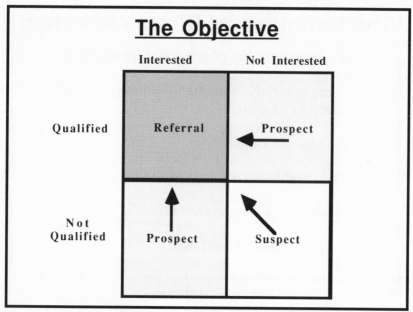

Illustration 3-8: The real objective of Direct Marketing.

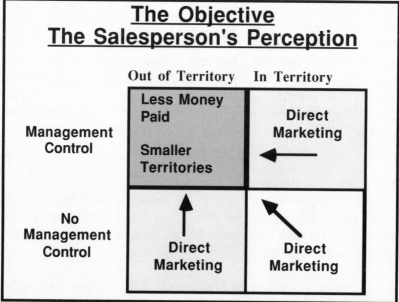

Illustration 3-9: The salesperson's perception of Direct Marketing.

selling opportunities. Clearly, part of the direct marketing program has to sell the sales staff on what we're trying to do.

The sales attitude can seriously affect the success of the direct marketing program. Without statistics, we will never be able to measure the success of the project. When you design the lead generation program, you should consider how the salesperson will perceive your efforts.

Lead Management

You must design your system to get information for measurement and tracking of the leads. Over the years, many systems have been created and refined to generate information about lead disposition. It seems that every company initially goes through the same process. Illustration 3-10 shows the typical lead tracking approach.

The key element is the chastisement of the sales organization when the lead information isn't returned. This is especially difficult if we generated more leads than the sales organization could follow-up. The more pressure that is put on the organization to return the lead information, the more likely the data will be inaccurate.

Here's a typical scenario: The pressure is applied to the sales force to return the lead information. The sales force reacts to the pressure by taking all the leads and coding them as bad leads.

Lead management is frustrating and difficult. Many companies give up and send leads without any attempt to measure the results. In fact, the Direct Marketing Association's Business-to-Business Council conducted a survey in 1979, 1980 and 1981 to determine direct marketing effectiveness. The full survey is available in the DMA Fact Book and can be purchased from the Direct Marketing Association. Two of the questions indicate the measurement and follow-up being done.

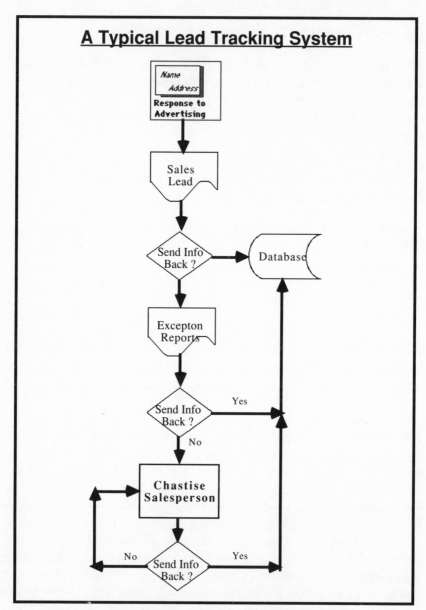

Illustration 3-10: A typical lead tracking system.

Business/Industrial Council
Research - 1986 Fact Book

	1979 Office Equip Manufacturers	1980 Printing Industry	1981 Wholesale Durable Goods
How frequently do you set objectives when mailing to prospects?			
Rarely	16.6%	27.8%	30.7%
Never	30.2%	27.7%	30.6%
o you measure conversion of leads into actual sales?			
Yes	-	43.3%	27.3%
No	-	55.8%	72.7%

Most of the time, when direct mailing to prospects, objectives are not set. And measurement is even less likely. The typical tracking system is only used in less than 50% of the leads generated. Remember that this survey represents a group of people who have tried to measure, and who have learned the harsh realities of trying to interface sales leads to a reluctant sales force.

We encourage people to continue to work with the sales force on measuring lead quality. However, why not consider also asking the prospect what finally happened? Illustration 3-11 indicates an approach that could give you the lead quality information you require.

It is somewhat hard to believe, but when this approach has been used we have found less than 50% of the leads generated were ever followed up by the sales force. This really isn't a condemnation of the sales force but a reflection on the reality of the environment. If we generated more sales leads than can be followed up, obviously we only confirmed that situation. Additionally, the salesperson probably tried to reach the prospect on more than one occasion. After several

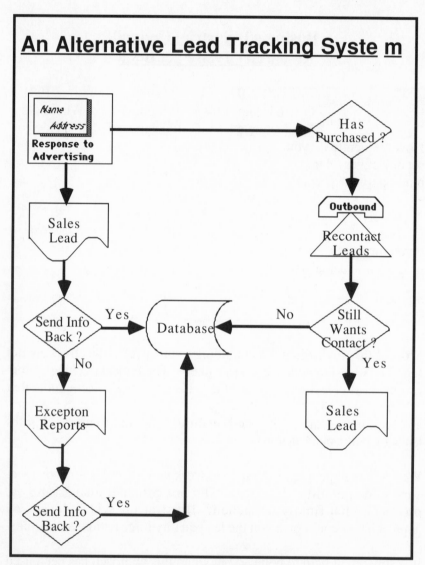

Illustration 3-11: An alternative lead tracking system.

attempts, the salesperson is off doing something else. In the crush of
business, the lead may get lost. Our follow-up allows us to determine
the final outcome. If the lead wasn't contacted, there is still a sales
opportunity.

Lead measurement and tracking need to be considered in the initial program design. You should establish a lead tracking system which is based on sales force interaction and by direct contact with the prospect. You get invaluable information on the quality and quantity of sales follow-up. You also will gain great insight into what and why prospects are buying, including competition.

Scoring

With the IBM program, lead quality became a major issue. The sales force had asked for many more leads than they could possibly follow up. Ultimately we returned to the drawing table to try to define a good lead.

During the telemarketing effort we had the communicator input prospect responses directly into a computer. The computer was used to determine the quality of the prospect and only offer a referral to the salesperson.

The communicators were part time employees who were not knowledgeable in the IBM product line. They had been trained in good telephone techniques and the telephone call was completely scripted. The script itself was manual using a flip card approach, but the scheduling and data capture were interactive with the computer. The following Script was used during the telemarketing call.

If Name Directed: Good (morning/afternoon) (FIRST AND LAST NAME OF DECISION MAKER) please? IF NO LONGER AT FIRM, ASK FOR HIS/HER REPLACEMENT, (Record on screen).

If Not Name Directed: Good (morning/afternoon) Please connect me to your office manager -- but before you do, I need to know his full name and title.

If Asks who is calling: This is (YOUR FULL NAME) calling on behalf of IBM. Is Mr(s) _____ in?

If not available: Will (He/She) be in later today -- or will (He/She) be in tomorrow at this time?

Introduction to Switchboard-Establish Decision Maker   **1**

Mr(s) _____? I'm (YOUR FULL NAME) and I'm calling on behalf of IBM. You are the (TITLE) for (COMPANY), right?

   If No: Please tell me, what is your correct title?

Then you're the person I should be talking to, because IBM has recently introduced a new line of computers that can now give companies the benefits of data processing at a cost far below what you may have associated with us in the past. I am not asking for any confidential information. The purpose of my call is to see if you're thinking about getting a small computer, a bookkeeping machine or perhaps word processing equipment? (PAUSE)

   If Yes or Unsure: Go to Define Decision Status - Card 3

   If No: Go to Gather Data - Card 4

Introduction to Decision Maker-Verify Title and Establish Interest   **2**

Tell Me, about when will you be making a decision?

Immediately   3 Months

Qualified

9 Months   12 Months

Must be Qualified on other data from card 4.

Define Decision Status   3

I hear that often ... Let me ask you ...
   1.How many total employees do you have at your location now?
   2.How many are performing clerical or accounting functions?
   3.Have you had to add clerical personnel in the past 12 months?
   4.And, do you anticipate needing additional resources for cleri-
     cal functions in the next 12 months?

Mr(s)____, accounts receivable and inventory control are business related areas that lend themselves to data processing.

   5.Mr(s)___, many businesses are experiencing more over due
     accounts receivable. Have your accounts receivable grown by
     more than 20% in the last 12 months?
   6.And, does your business have inventory? Has it increased by
     more than 20% in the last 12 months?

Gather Data - Screening   4

A. And do you use a computer now?

  If Yes: Is it your own?   **If Yes**: Do you rent it?
  Or did you purchase it?
B. Do you use a Service Bureau, Mr(s)____?
  If No to both: Go to appropriate close based on qualifying instruction.
  If Yes to either A or B: Continue

  What Kind is that?
  And how long have you used it/them?
  About how much do you spend a month?
  And, are you satisfied that you are getting all your data processing needs covered by your current procedures?
Go to correct close based on qualifying instructions.

Gather Data - Data Processing Experience   **5**

Thanks so much for talking with me today. Could I have one of our representatives call you to talk about your needs further?

  If Yes: Fine. You'll be hearing from us soon.
  • And, what would you like a computer to do to help your business, Mr(s)____?
  • What products or services does your company specialize in?
  • Could you give me a general idea of your companies annual sales volume?

  If refuses rep call: Go to appropriate objection.

Making Decision: Offer IBM Rep Contact   **6**

Mr(s) _____? Your business sounds like it is growing significantly and perhaps you're not aware that the cost of data processing has gone below what you might spend for a single clerk, or bookkeeping machine. Now may be the time to evaluate if data processing can help you.

IBM offers many services to help you determine your needs and implement the right solution for ;your business. Can I have one of our representatives call to discuss this with you further?

If Yes: Fine. You'll be hearing from us soon.
* And, what would you like a computer to do to help your business, Mr(s)____?
* What products or services does your company specialize in?
* Could you give me a general idea of your companies annual sales volume?

If No: Go to Gather Data - Card 4

Not Making a Decision but qualified: Offer IBM Rep   7

Thanks so much for your courtesy. By the way, what products or services does your company specialize in?

We'd like to keep in contact with you, Mr(s) _____, so you'll be hearing from IBM from time to time -- and please give us a call when you feel you have to add equipment or personnel.

Thanks again -- have a very nice day. Good-bye.

Close: If not qualified or refuses all offers   8

The script had other branches available for answering questions and handling objections.

This script was developed with the sales staff and focused on screening prospects before being sent to a salesperson for follow-up. Initially, any prospect that was in the process of evaluating a system within three months was sent out as a lead regardless of the prospect's desire to see a salesperson. We used binary decision making; that is the prospect answered a question a certain way (yes or no) and qualified themselves. If the prospect was making a decision within six months, they were automatically qualified to be offered to be contacted by a salesperson. If the decision was to be made within three months, the prospect was sent to the salesperson, regardless of whether he/she agreed to see a salesperson or not.

If a purchase was planned for the future, the other qualification criteria was examined to determine if the prospect should be offered a salesperson. Again, all the questions were really binary. The prospect answered yes or no to meet the criteria. If the prospect gave answers to certain questions, he/she would qualify to be offered a salesperson.

When the IBM script was developed, we didn't understand or relate to the MAND concept that was discussed earlier. The sales force asked for three sales leads per day. If the prospect had answered certain questions, they wanted to have that prospect as a lead. We quickly had severe lead quality problems. Many prospects were evaluating 'personal computers' that cost approximately $2,000. The smallest IBM systems were then priced at about $15,000. The salespeople were unhappy with the leads.

With the manual scripting techniques we've demonstrated, you really don't have many options on lead qualification. You can link different binary decisions, but the qualification process becomes more and more difficult to implement.

The IBM salespeople asked for less leads but of higher quality. We tried to establish what is considered higher quality, but again had the same problem of definition of a good lead. Which was better: A prospect making a decision in 90 days or less with only one clerical person; or a similar prospect not making a decision for more than six months but with eight clerical people?

Computer Decision		Clerical Employees		Total Employees	
Immediate	35	6 or more	15	100+	15
Less then 3 mos	25	3 to 6	10	50 to 99	10
3 to 6 mos	15	2	5	25 to 49	5
6 to 12 mos	10	1	0	less than 25	0
Unsure	5	0	(10)		
Not Evaluating	0				
Added Clerical in last year		Will add clerical		Account Rec'vble	
Yes	10	Yes	15	Yes	10
No	0	No	0	No	0
Inventory Growth		Using Data Proc		Annual Sales	
Yes	10	Purch Sys>1 yr	5	25 million+	10
No	0	Purch Sys<1 yr	(10)	1 to 25 million	5
				500k to 1 mill	0
		Serv Bureau	15	less than 500k	(5)
		Not Satisfied	15		

Illustration 3-11: A lead scoring system.

We began to evaluate the relationship of the answers to the qualific-tion questions. This relative lead qualification procedure was a tremendous breakthrough, and finally would allow us to differentiate between prospects and referrals.

We established point values for each answer and were able to score the lead. The scoring system in Illustration 3-11 is an example of the algorithms we used.

This system is almost impossible to implement with a manual script and a communicator trying to score manually while on the phone.

The ideal situation would allow the prospect to be scored during the phone call and enable the score to be used to determine the appropriate offer.

We worked with the sales force to establish the values of each answer. Bear in mind that the best scoring system would change and modify itself as you learn from leads you've already generated. We went back and scored all the leads we generated prior to the scoring system introduction, and found the average lead to be worth about 20 points. It was interesting that the sales force did not like almost 65% of all leads generated. They were not happy with the quality of the leads.

We automated the scheduling process of the telemarketing calls and placed terminals in front of each communicator. We used a relative approach to determine lead quality and the appropriate offer to make to the prospect. The computer was programmed to evaluate the answers. If the prospect crossed a certain threshold, the offer was made. For the first time we could actually differentiate between prospects and referrals.

A prospect was established as having a score between 20 to 39 points. Referrals were established to have a score above 40 points. A key decision was made that a single question could not qualify a referral. The average referral or lead had a score of 47 points after the introduction of the scoring qualification system. More importantly the salespeople now liked 65% of the leads and were unhappy with only 35%. Order information is not released by IBM.

We have used scoring algorithms in many other programs with the same kinds of results. When we work with clients on defining the values for scoring, no one question will qualify a prospect to be a referral. The MAND concept makes evaluating the right questions to ask easier. It is very difficult to implement a scoring system to determine the offer without being interactive with a computer during the telephone call. However, scoring after the fact can be very valuable to determine lead quality, the results of your offers and list usage.

Scoring solves many problems but creates a whole new set of opportunities. In the past, every prospect meeting a certain criteria was sent to the sales force for action. With scoring you identify the best referrals to send to the salespeople. You also identify a group qualified as prospects but not qualified enough to be referrals. What do you do with this group to ultimately turn them into referrals and customers? We discuss one alternative in the following section using conditioning and regeneration.

You can accomplish similar scoring results by using two step mailing techniques. Initial responses are mailed a second piece which has qualification information that can be returned. After the second response, the prospect can be considered a referral. Obviously, this technique will substantially reduce the number of referrals sent to the salespeople.

Conditioning and Regeneration

Most companies have a limited universe within the business-to-business arena. A prospect is very valuable and, even if one does not buy from you now, he may buy from you in the future. When you talk to the sales organization, you learn that a prospect takes time to nurture and sell. Our selling activity really is the same. Once a prospect is identified, we should continue to market this prospect even if he or she became a lead or referral and were sent to the sales force.

During the IBM lead program we learned there is a difference between prospects and referrals. When operating a lead generation program, the referrals are to be sent to the sales force and prospects should be nurtured and conditioned into referrals. We also know that not all the leads will be followed up with the same quality.

We designed a direct mail program that involved multiple contacts spread over a three to four month period. After the prospects or referrals were identified, they were mailed a conditioning series of mail pieces to move them along through the sales cycle. The series was not product oriented. It focused on the buying decision. Need and desire were the themes used throughout the series. Cost justification, application needs and identification, and how to use a computer in your business were three of the pieces in the series. All the pieces asked the prospect to get involved with the material. They all contained involvement gimmicks.

Prospects and referrals were tested to determine the effectiveness of this approach. Lead quality improved dramatically and the sales force wanted to add their own prospects to the existing database to have them receive the mail series.

Conditioning and regeneration are key elements to continuing to work the prospect and referral universe. If you're unable to close the business today, this technique allows you to get the business in the future. Good salespeople perform this function independently. When a salesperson identifies a qualified prospect, he/she begin to work to sell that prospect over time. The salesperson will send literature, letters and make many phone calls until the prospect succumbs to their efforts. Tenacity is a trait we all look for in an aggressive salesperson.

We should learn from our sales force. This repetitive activity works in direct marketing as well as in direct selling. The sales force should be consulted to determine those techniques that are successful. You should try to implement a uniform system to condition prospects to become referrals and to regenerate referrals into customers over time.

Lead Programs Summarized

This chapter covered a lot of ground. We've talked about the inconsistencies in lead follow up, the difficulty in lead definition and how to implement leads with the sales force. Whenever you implement a lead program, you try to reduce the cost of selling by improving the effectiveness of the sales force. The lead program has to work as a tool for the sales force. It should not be perceived by the salespeople as an alternative to their efforts. Nothing will destroy the effectiveness of the project faster then if the salespeople feel that we are trying to replace them with direct marketing. Work with your sales organization to create the lead program as complementary to their efforts as opposed to an alternative.

When the decision is made to implement the lead program, do not reduce commissions or territories. For the lead program to be successful, you need the support of the salespeople. Anything that affects their perception of the direct marketing effort in a negative way, should be avoided at all costs. Sell the direct marketing program to the sales force. If mail is being used, send a copy of the piece to the homes of the salespeople. Put them on your list.

In order to measure the effectiveness of the lead program, you must have feedback. Salespeople perform a variety of activities. Unfortunately, their highest priority will not be to give you information on the quality of the leads. You should design a lead tracking and management system to control the distribution and reporting of the leads. Ask sales management to get involved and help with reporting. However, do not chastise the salespeople for not returning sales leads. Consider positive actions such as contests for the most leads followed up. Make sure you publicize sales successes from the sales leads. Nothing will motivate a salesperson to follow up the leads more than sales success.

Design a way to ask the prospect directly what has happened. Special offers that give a premium for buying as a result of the lead are interesting methods for measuring conversion of leads to orders. Giving a coupon or special discount to the lead also will help measure some of the conversions.

A questionnaire or telephone call some period after the lead is generated is an ideal way to determine lead quality and lead conversion. Go directly to the referral and ask about the quality of the lead follow up. You can find out what the prospect bought, if anything; why the prospect bought or didn't buy; and you can determine if that prospect is still a sales opportunity for you.

Remember, most salespeople are operating from their briefcases of car trunks. They normally don't have a copier or filing cabinet. When you design the lead report format, help the salesperson organize and manage their territories. Use multiple copy formats if you want information returned, so the salesperson only has to fill in the blanks and return it. Make forms easy to use and understand. Give the salesperson an easy way to file and manage the information you're sending to them. All leads should be sent to the field in the same format. We prefer a three-ring binder, with pre-punched lead information. Cards and other formats are just as effective, as long as you think of the salesperson first.

One final point. Any information you have on the prospect or referral should be sent to the salesperson. Don't hide any data. Most salespeople are entrepreneurs and believe they are running their own businesses.

Chapter Four - Database

As we mentioned in Chapter one, "database" may be the most mis-used term in direct marketing. Database has become the new buzz word and concept for direct marketing. Everyone uses and embraces the term, but few people understand what it means. The concept is so new that most dictionaries do not even include a definition. One dictionary definition (The World Book Dictionary) defines database "as a large collection of records stored on a computer system from which specialized data may be extracted or organized as desired".

Historical Development

Let's review database within the context of a quick history of data processing. In the evolution of data processing, information was originally captured on punched cards. Each card had a physical limitation of only being able to hold 80 characters of information. The machines that processed this information were initially limited to a series of registers that could perform arithmetic functions. Additional information created during the processing were printed or punched into another card.

The first computer system, ENIAC, developed in the late 1940's, weighed several tons and filled a large room. Today that same computing power is available on a micro chip. It is mind boggling how far and fast data processing technology has come. Our ability to store, retrieve and process data has grown exponentially over the last 40 years.

In the 1960's the storage of information progressed from storing information on punched cards to storing the data on magnetic tape. This medium had many advantages over punched cards. However, tape processing was limited in its ability to store and retrieve data.

Information in punched cards is limited to 80 characters of data per card. Files could contain more than one card per record. However, multiple cards per record made the processing slower and more difficult. In order to read and process information, you had to read the cards sequentially. If multiple cards were used, they had to be sorted and merged prior to processing. If new information was created as a result of processing, a new card or series of cards had to be created.

You are probably familiar with the use of magnetic tape for storing and playing music. If you want to play a song on the center of the tape you have to play through or fast forward to the appropriate part of the tape. This type of information storage, reading one item at a time, is called *sequential processing*. Having to move through all the preceding songs is one of the primary limitations of sequential pro-

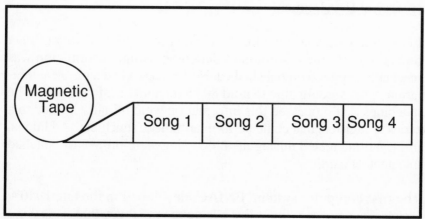

Illustration 4-1: Sequential Tape Processing

cessing. To play song 4 in Illustration 4-1, you first have to play songs 1, 2 and 3.

Besides the difficulties in reading a song in the middle of the tape, imagine the difficulty in combining songs from multiple tapes.

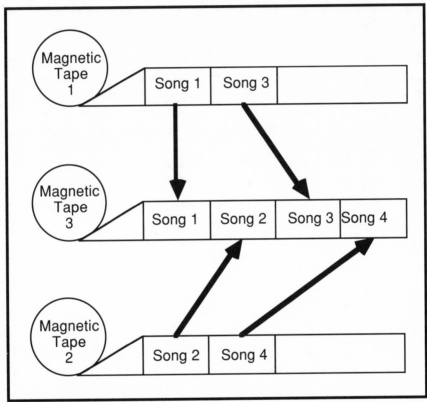

Illustration 4-2: Sequential tape processing.

Illustration 4-2 shows that in order to write or record in the center of a tape, you must first erase any existing information on the tape. Creating a new tape of information or music then requires reading information from one device and writing information on a different device. So while tape processing allows for storage of more than 80 characters of information in each record, it has limitations in reading, writing and processing.

Tape processing permits almost unlimited strings of data. Therefore, you can store all pertinent information in one record without the physical limitations of the punched card. Still, processing and creating new information required creating a new tape on a different device. If only one record was processed, the whole tape had to be read and a new tape created.

During the 1970's, the data storage medium changed significantly to allow for the direct access of information. Using the music example, if we were listening to a record and wanted to play the fourth song on that record, you could lift the arm directly to that song. This technique is similar to *disk processing* in data processing. In Illustration 4-3, data is stored in tracks on a rotating magnetic surface. A movable arm is directed to a specific track location. As the rotating surface passes under the access arm, the required data is read.

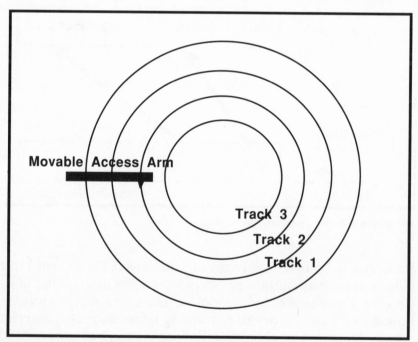

Illustration 4-3: Disk Processing

Disk processing allows the computer to randomly address information. It enables information to be retrieved randomly. In addition, disk processing also permits the writing and updating functions to be accomplished simultaneously. We no longer have to read sequentially and then write the processed information onto a new tape. We can now read, write and update simultaneously.

Disk processing permits the random processing of information. The introduction of *random direct access processing* has allowed for the development of dynamic databases.

With tape processing, lists could be compiled that contained more than 80 characters of information per record. The larger size of the record permitted the addition of demographic and psychographic information to these lists, further enabling better segmentation and targeting techniques. Tapes also facilitate the interchanging and exchanging of list information with other companies.

The technological advancements in data storage and retrieval have significantly improved our ability to conduct sophisticated direct marketing. Unfortunately, many companies today are still using tape and punched card processing. This is not because the equipment required to upgrade to newer techniques is too expensive, but rather because it is perceived that the change to the newer technologies would be too difficult and risky.

Computer programs are traditionally written to deal with files whose records have specific characteristics. If the record format is changed, the computer programs that deal with that record will all have to be modified. It is not unusual, as a system evolves, to have hundreds of computer programs involved in the processing of information. Introducing a new piece of information, such as the average earnings per household, could require a major programming effort. This big "change" is not to create the new information, but to modify the existing programs to handle this new piece of data.

Traditional computer programs deal with fixed length and formatted files. Your data processing department is probably using programs and files. In addition, if your company is a long time user of data processing, you probably have a number of program applications based on tape processing. This doesn't mean that your data processing system is antiquated, but just reflects the natural business perspective of if it isn't broken, why fix it. Your data processing department is never starved for things to do. Updating an application that is working always will be assigned a lower priority than needed new applications or fixing existing programs that are not functioning properly.

As data processing equipment technology has improved, so have the programming and processing techniques. In the 1980's, the state-of-the-art has evolved to computer programs that can deal with data independently of the programs. This means that the computer programs don't care about the format of the information. A series of utility programs have evolved to manage data independently of the computer programs. These database management systems (DBMS) allow the data processing departments to write programs that will not have to be modified when information is added or changed within the system.

These database managers operate independently of the application programs. Most database management systems will allow an unsophisticated user to perform his/her own inquiries into the computer without the aid of the data processing department. This new technology has great promise in being able to reduce the backlog of new applications to be developed by the data processing department. More importantly, it will put the power of the computer into the hands of the end users without having to make them computer programmers.

A computer database program to manage information is a relatively new concept. Most companies are not yet using this new technique; more than likely they are still using application programs and files to manage their information. It is ironic that while the cost and effort to convert existing applications to a database management system may be prohibitive, the cost of the actual DBMS program is fairly modest.

Technological enhancements over the last few years have produced a whole new set of applications. Because the data is now randomly available and the computer is powerful enough to process one transaction at a time, *on-line transaction processing applications* have evolved. This new application series has placed added demands on data processing to provide instant availability of data.

When many computer programs originally were written, the available data and necessary reports were perceived to be relatively fixed. If the programmer who initially designed the system didn't anticipate a requirement for information in the future, that information became very difficult to obtain. Data availability was controlled by the computer and data processing department, not the user of the information. This accounts for the usage explosion of personal computers within business. End users were frustrated with the "long" delivery time from data processing. They want to control their own information and not be limited in what information they can receive.

Database management systems offer a way to solve both the user's and data processing department's problems. Still, business decision makers are faced with some very difficult questions:

1) Which database management system is right?

2) Does the economic benefits of transferring information to the user outweigh the additional computer power needed for rapid information delivery?

3) How difficult will it be to convert to a database management system?

We have provided this background to demonstrate the different meanings for database. As you probably have noticed, data processing people use the term database to mean a management system to control data. The direct marketing definition of database is totally different.

Because most data processing centers are still using programs and files to process information, greater care in planning for the data requirements of your direct marketing program will be needed. As we discussed in Chapter one, you must have five specific elements (Illustration 4-4) for a successful direct marketing program.

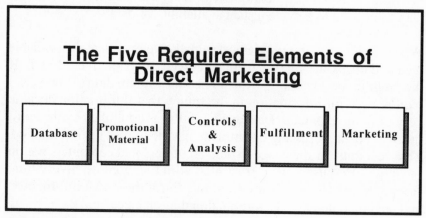

Illustration 4-4: The elements of Direct Marketing

Two of these elements are directly related to our discussion:

• **Database**

• **Controls & Analysis**

As we reviewed earlier, and again in Illustration 4-5, the definition of direct marketing includes a definition of database. Let's again examine the various parts of the direct marketing database:

• **Database provides names of customers or prospects.**

The original name and address list is an important part of the database, but all of the activity relating to each of the names on that list is also essential.

The Definition of Direct Marketing with Database Defined

- An organized and planned system of contacts

- Using a variety of media -- seeking to produce a lead or an order

- Developing and maintaining a database

  - **Providing Names of Customers, Prospects**

  - **Vehicle for Storing, Measuring Responses**

  - **Vehicle for Storing, Measuring Purchases**

  - **Vehicle for Continuing Direct Communication**

- Measurable in cost and results

- Works in all methods of selling

- Expandable with confidence

Illustration 4-5: The definition of database.

- **Database is a vehicle for storing and measuring responses.**

  Once you reach the targets you identified and they respond to your offer, the database should provide the ability to track each contact and each response.

- **Database is a vehicle for storing and measuring purchases.**

  Now that you know if a prospect has responded to your direct marketing program, you want to track whether these respondents actually become buyers.

The back end conversion of respondents to orders is the key measurement in evaluating the success of the direct marketing program. By tracking the actual respondents who purchase, you can establish the cost per order and the average order size.

• **Database is a vehicle for continuing direct communication to the prospects, respondents and customers.**

The database should allow you to have a sustained and complete ability to contact the initial list of prospects, the group that responded and the group that became customers.

As you can see, the measurement and controls of the direct marketing program are directly tied to the database. It is very challenging to anticipate the information you'll have to capture to measure and evaluate the program, prior to starting the project. Because most data processing departments are using programs and files as opposed to database management systems, adding or changing data is more difficult.

Lists

As we have mentioned earlier, some direct marketers consider their lists to be the complete database. In reality, the list is just the initial building block of the database.

There are basically four kinds of lists:

- House or Customer Lists
- Compiled Lists
- Respondent Lists
- Subscription or Membership Lists

Each list has different characteristics that may make it worthwhile for your business to use. The lists you select for your direct marketing effort will be the single most important decision determining the success or failure of the project.

In real estate, there are three things that are important in a piece of property:

1) Location
2) Location
3) Location

Direct marketing has a similar series of important elements:

1) List
2) List
3) List

To underscore the importance of the list, carefully consider this direct marketing axiom: an outstanding offer made in an outstanding package to a poor list will produce poor results. On the other hand, a mediocre offer, in a mediocre package made to a good list will probably produce good results.

Let's look at the different kinds of lists and their characteristics:

House or Customer Lists: These are people that have previously responded to you or have already become customers. This is the most valuable list source you have and will produce the highest results when used in a direct marketing project.

Develop as much geographic, demographic and psychographic information as possible on your house lists. The more information you have on people who have already bought from you, the easier it is to select prospects who may buy from you. There are some scientific computer methods, called regression analysis, available to review customers and determine their areas of similarity.

The existing sales force, if you have one, can be very helpful in establishing a profile of likely prospects to purchase your products or services. Again, people who have already purchased your products are the best indicator of others who should be your customers.

House lists, particularly if you're billing the customer, are fairly current and up to date. These lists will normally contain phone numbers and name and title information. Depending on the product you're selling the contact name and title may or may not be appropriate for your needs. Depending on your company's credit policies, your house lists may not contain industry and sizing information. Your customer list may contain 'ship to' and 'bill to' information and may not contain the contact you're looking for.

Evaluate your house lists for application to your needs. House lists are excellent for cross selling, upgrading and generating repeat business. You have established a working relationship and can capitalize on that relationship in your direct marketing programs.

Compiled Lists: There are many companies that compile and develop lists as their primary business. You're probably familiar with the largest, Dun and Bradstreet (D&B), a well known business information provider. Some list compilers have specialized in specific market niches. They may use direct mail and telephone interviewing to build and verify the information. You can even contract with a list compiler to build a unique list to meet your special needs.

Compiled lists are typically used by marketers to fulfill a unique requirement so compiled list owners normally append some additional information to the basic name and address. Most use SIC codes as a primary segmentation tool. Frequently, compiled lists will have more than one contact per business. Some of the major list compilers have built total lists of all available businesses with some sizing and other demographic information.

Compiled lists are normally updated on a periodic basis, usually annually or bi-annually. Some lists are compiled from the yellow pages, therefore they are only updated once per year. With the frequent changes of title and position in American industry, compiled lists tend to 20% to 40% outdated. The basic sizing and segmentation data doesn't change significantly.

Compiled lists are excellent resources when you are looking for additional information to help you target a promotion. If you want to reach a segment of the market that can only be identified by very specific criteria, compiled lists are probably the best source.

Respondent Lists: People who have previously purchased or responded to direct marketing are more likely to respond to direct marketing again. The more people respond, the more likely they will respond again. Direct marketers commonly weigh the value of a respondent in terms of how *recently* he/she has responded, how *frequently* he/she has responded and the *monetary* value of the purchase. This concept is called *RFM* (Recency, Frequency and Monetary). Catalog marketers are very familiar with this concept and frequently score their lists using RFM techniques.

Other direct marketers will frequently rent their respondent lists to others. Renting lists can provide excellent opportunities for you to sell your products or services. You will have to evaluate the type of products responded to and the affinity towards your products or company. Business list brokers can provide valuable insight to list usage by other marketers and list selection recommendations based on years of experience in the list rental business.

In most cases, respondent lists do not contain very much additional information concerning the prospect or company beyond RFM. It is unusual for the respondent list to contain a phone number.

Respondent lists can be fairly current, depending on the group that you decide to rent. The more recent the purchase, the more accurate the list. If the list is aged, you run the risk of renting a high rate of not reachable names commonly called a *Nixie*.

Subscription and Membership Lists: This group of lists has demonstrated an affinity with a common set of interests. In the business community, a group that subscribes to a trade journal probably has an interest in that activity. By advertising, mailing or phoning to this group we are targeting the identified interest. This type of affinity is called a *psychographic* characteristic -- how people feel about things. Membership and subscription lists include people who have made an overt decision to participate. They raised their hands and said I want to belong.

Membership lists may contain industry, sizing and other pertinent information. Most frequently these lists only contain name and address data, though telephone number may be available. These lists can be out of date. Frequently, membership lists are not purged and kept current with name and address information.

Subscription lists usually only contain the name, title and address information. The publication is being sent to the name on a periodic basis and therefore the name and address information is accurate. Most subscription lists do not include telephone number, title or industry information.

There are two types of subscriptions:

Paid Subscription: The subscriber has paid to receive the publication. Although there is very little additional information available about the subscriber, he paid to belong to this group. Paid subscriptions might also be classified as respondent lists because they are direct response purchasers.

Controlled Subscription: This is a free subscription. The reader fills out an application to qualify to receive the publication. Controlled subscription publications have additional information and can be segmented and targeted better than paid subscription. Because it is free, the reader may not have as strong an affinity as the paid subscriber.

Selecting the appropriate list types will depend on the direct marketing promotion. Each list type has its own advantages. As you design your direct marketing program, we suggest you test different lists and list types to determine your most effective list source.

Combining Lists

In the business-to-business environment there are over 40,000 lists available. It is impossible to know about every list. As part of your direct marketing business plan, you will identify the most likely prospect for your products. After you define your marketing program, you may want to consider using a list broker to help select and evaluate the best lists.

Once you select the various lists you plan to use, your database effort will really begin. Using various computer routines, you'll want to combine the lists and to the best of your ability eliminate duplicate records. As you may recall from Chapter one, de-duplication in the business-to-business environment is more difficult than when marketing to consumers.

Even the use of telephone number, which you may or may not have, will not guarantee the elimination of duplicate records. Many businesses provide direct phone numbers for individuals and a different number for company. On the other hand, some businesses only have a central phone number. It is impossible to use the phone number to eliminate duplicates with any degree of accuracy.

Based on our experience, the best de-duplication routines will be only about 60% effective in the business-to-business environment. Consider using an outside service to eliminate duplicates and combine the lists. Each record should be updated to reflect the list that it came from. This will allow you to perform an analysis of each list source.

If you're planning to use telemarketing, you may want to send the combined, de-duplicated list to a service bureau to have the phone numbers appended to the record. These same service bureaus can also add industry, sizing and other demographic information to your list.

What started as a simple mailing list, is now growing into a database containing other valuable pieces of information. At this point, you can fulfill the first requirement of the direct marketing database - - you can reach a group of prospects or customers. Frequently, this is where the database effort ends. We often find internal databases with no measurement information about respondents or purchasers. It is also fairly common to find that the respondents from a mail campaign were never recorded and sent to the field force for handling.

Measuring Response

Your data processing department may not be able to handle additional information because of the modifications required to their existing programs. If an application system is being designed to support your needs, you should evaluate all of the additional information required for your database.

The database should be capable of measuring that group of people who responded to the direct marketing promotion. This sounds simple, but it can prove to be very difficult depending on the type of your direct marketing program. As you define your database requirements to the data processing department, make sure they understand that you'll need to identify respondents and, ultimately, buyers.

Lead generation and traffic building programs (those campaigns that ask prospects to respond by going to a specific location) are difficult to measure. You may have to design a special method to capture respondent information. Special coupon or premium offers that are only available as a result of the direct marketing program can be useful in establishing measurement information.

As you design your database requirements, you may want to include:

> Type of contact
> Date of contact
> Response date
> Response request (what did the prospect ask for)
> Source of response (mail, phone)

This information can be helpful in evaluating the success of your program, and determining your next logical step. By building a transaction file detailing the activity and results, you'll be able to follow the sales cycle from start to finish.

If you are only making one contact per prospect, this information is not difficult to record. The situation gets more complex and difficult if multiple contacts and types of contacts are used to the same list. For example, you may decide to mail to several different titles in the same business. Tracking response from this program can become difficult.

Lead generation programs get more complicated because you involve a variable that you can't control -- the salesperson. As we discussed in Chapter three, lead programs need very special attention in both measurement and control.

Being able to measure respondents is easier in the consumer environment because the list is simpler. The consumer will frequently purchase as the response, therefore you don't have to deal with a response and purchase separately. Business-to-business is more complicated because there is no easy way to manage the name; the decision cycle is longer, more complicated and may have more than one player. All of these factors require a more sophisticated database in business marketing than in the consumer world.

Measuring Purchases

As we mentioned earlier, the real measurement of the success of any direct marketing program is the ultimate cost per order and the profitability of the program. But if the measuring of a respondent can get difficult, the measuring of a purchase can become impossible.

Frequently, a prospect will respond to a direct marketing program with a different company name than the name used during the purchase. A prospect may respond to the offer as an individual yet the purchase is then actually made by the company.

Your database must first measure respondents and then those respondents that ultimately convert to orders. If you're selling a product directly and not using a sales force, the problem is a little less difficult. You will ultimately know that a sale took place. In a lead generation program, as we discussed earlier, you may never find out that there was a sale.

Several methods can help you measure the actual purchases made because of the direct marketing program.

- As we mentioned earlier, make a special offer only available through the direct marketing program. If this offer is fulfilled, you'll know that the order came as a direct result.

- Ask the customer after the fact, how they heard of your company and the primary reason he/she purchased.

- Pay special incentives to the distribution channel for ordering through the direct marketing program.

- Use a computer matching routine to identify orders from direct marketing.

- If you are using a sales force, ask the salespeople what has happened.

Don't limit your measurement program to the these ideas. As part of the creative process in designing your direct marketing program, make measurement a part of the process.

In a lead generation program, the problem of measuring sales is frustratingly complicated. The salespeople do not like to admit that you helped them. They are reluctant to give credit to the direct marketing program for the sale. In addition, as we mentioned in Chapter three, many leads are not even followed up by the salespeople. The same techniques described above for measuring orders can also be used to measure the effectiveness of your salespeople. Frequently, direct marketers elect to ask the sales force to evaluate the quality of the leads. This seems to be the least effective technique for evaluating the success of the direct marketing program.

Some information you may want to add to your database to help evaluate purchases:

Date of purchase
Product purchased
$ Amount purchased
Method of purchase (retail, salesperson, direct)

Continuing Communication

Any respondent to your direct marketing programs -- whether for information or actual purchases -- will become your best opportunity for additional response in future programs. The respondent list could become one of your most valuable assets.

As you use direct marketing programs to contact your "house" list, be sure you provide a way to keep the list up-to-date. If names, addresses, phone numbers or contact information change, your database should reflect the most current information.

Your least expensive respondent, lead or order will be generated from our "house" list of prior respondents and customers. That means this list will represent your most profitable universe for selling products or services. Very often we'll see respondents to direct marketing programs stacked in boxes with nothing being done to further the sales effort. Other than existing customers, those "bad" leads represent your best selling opportunity.

Building a Relational Database

Relational database technology now allows you to separate your data into unique elements and only store one version of information for multiple uses. For example, you can create a single company name and address that can be used for contacting multiple people within that company. If the address changes, you only have to make the address change once for all contacts within the company.

Information in a relational database is stored in *tables.* The database table contains *columns*, that are similar to the fields in a normal data processing file. The members of the table are called *rows.* These are similar to the records in standard data processing files.

In the past, if you needed to capture multiple options for a specific question that allowed more than a single response, you probably created a separate 'bucket' for each possible response. In database design, you would create a separate table for these responses and relate them through a common key.

For example, you have allowed your prospects to respond to a mailing by indicating their desire to receive additional information; attend a seminar; have a salesperson contact them; or have their name added to a mailing list. Prospects will often select more than one option. To capture this information with traditional file processing, a separate bucket for each option would be necessary. Additionally, if you offered an additional option on a subsequent program, you would have to change all of the files and programs involved.

Using a relational database, a table for prospect requests is created and linked via a common relation to the *Names* table. Normally, the common relation is a name number. Each separate request is entered into the prospect request table. New or additional requests are added independent of prior activities.

Location addresses are stored in a separate table and individuals are related to the location table by a common location identifier. If the address changes, only the location table need be changed. Each individual's contact address is automatically updated by the change.

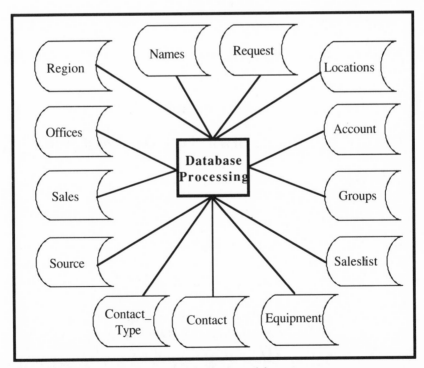

Illustration 4-6: A direct marketing database model.

A Database Model

Illustration 4-6 is a database model that establishes commonly used information for direct marketing purposes. Your needs may vary significantly, but this model gives a basis for creating a database.

The *Names* table is used to store the marketing contact name, title and telephone number information for marketing purposes.

The Names table will be related to the *Locations* table for establishing the address information to contact the individuals in the *Names* table.

The Names table will be related to the *Source* table for establishing how a name was added to the Names table.

1.0 Table Layout

Column Name		Description	Format
1.1	Names_Id	Unique Identification #	N6
1.2	Loc_Id	Location Identification # - this identifier will link the names table to the *Location* table. It is the key to the *Location* table.	N4
1.3	Lname	Last name	A15
1.4	Fname	First name	A14
1.5	MI	Middle initial	A1
1.6	Salt	Salutation - (Mr, Mrs, Ms)	A3
1.7	Title	The functional business title used by the individual like DP/Manager or VP/MIS.	A15

1.8 Phone   The phone number of the name. The   A17
             phone number also contains up to a 4
             position extension.

             Any field includes special editing
             characters - ie. (800)555-1234-1234

1.9 Dec_status   Decision status. This represents the   A1
                  individuals involvement in the decision to
                  add or change alternatives.
                  1=Makes the decision
                  2=Investigates and recommends
                  3=Not involved in the decision

1.10 Source_Id   This is a code that identifies the source   N4
                  that added this particular name to the
                  names table. The Source_Id is the link
                  to the *Source* table. It is the key to the
                  Source Table.

1.11 Update   The last date this row of the table was   A8
               updated or changed.

The *Request* table is used to store the detailed information about each name in the name file and the requested disposition that name has given to you. Names can request multiple types of dispositions.

The *Request* table is related to the *Names* table.

1.0 Table Layout

Column Name	Description	Format
1.1 Names_Id	Unique Identification # for a particular Account.	N4
1.2 Request	This is the description of the particular	A25

request made of the prospect to Britton
Lee

Send Additional Information
Attend a Seminar
Have Sales Rep Call

The *Locations* table is used to store the name of the company,
address and other master information about a particular company or
location.

The *Locations* table will be related to the *Sales* table for establishing
the information about the salesperson assigned to a particular location.

1.0 Table Layout

	Column Name	Description	Format
1.1	Loc_Id	Unique Identification # for a particular location.	N4
1.2	Sales_Id	Salesperson Identification # - this identifier will link the *Locations* table to the*Sales* table. It is the key to the *Saless* table.	N4
1.3	Company	Company name	A35
1.4	Address1	First line of street/mailing address	A25
1.5	Address2	Second line of street/mailing address	A25
1.6	City	Address city A16	
1.7	State	The standard two position state code	A2

1.8	Zip	The Zip Code which can be 5 or 9 positions.	A10
1.9	Phone	The phone number of the company.	A12
1.10	Parent	If the company is a subsidiary or division of another company, this is the Location_Id of the parent company.	N4
1.11	SIC	This is the Standard Industrial Classification (SIC).	A5
1.12	Update	The last date this row of the table was updated or changed.	A8

The *Account* table is used to store the details about accounts within different locations. A location can have several Account records for different applications or opportunities. The *Account* table should be created to contain your own specific qualification information. It is where you store the unique data about a specific account. Remember, if you are storing multiple types of similar data, you should create a separate table. In this example, we will have multiple types of equipment so we should create a separate *Equipment* table.

The *Account* table will be related to the *Names* table for establishing the primary sales contact with the prospect business.

The *Account* table will be related to the *Location* table for establishing the company address and master information.

The *Account* table will be related to the *Equipment* table for establishing the quantity and type of equipment installed at each account.

1.0 Table Layout

Column Name		Description	Format
1.1	Account_Id	Unique Identification # for a particular Account.	N4

1.2   Names_Id   This is the primary sales contact.   N6
                     The Names_Id will be used to identify
                     the Name Identification # - this identifier
                     will link the *Names* table. It is the key
                     to the *Names* table.

1.4   Unique   The rest of this table will contain the unique
                     data you're capturing for a specific account.

The *Groups* table is used to store the details about each name in the name file and relate names to particular accounts in the *Account* table.

The *Groups* Table is related to the *Names* table. This table will enable establishing all of the individual names involved in a specific account.

1.0 Table Layout

Column Name		Description	Format
1.1	Account_Id	Unique Identification # for a particular Account.	N4
1.2	Names_Id	Names_Id is the unique identification number that links the Names table. Names_Id is a unique identifier of a person on the names file and is the key to the *Names* table.	N4

The *Saleshist* table is used to store the details about a salesperson's activity or history with a specific account. If you are using a sales force, this is the table that is used to store activity with the prospect.

The *Saleshist* table will be related to the *Account* table for establishing the salesperson's historical selling activity with a specific account.

1.0 Table Layout

	Column Name	Description	Format
1.1	Account_Id	Unique Identification # for a particular account.	N4
1.2	Date	Date of activity	A8
1.3	Activity	The type of activity I=Init Call Q=Stage 1, Qualification P=Stage 2, Proof S=Stage 3, Proposal/Sale O=Stage 4, Order	A1
1.4	Disposition	The disposition of the Account as result of the contact activity. 1=Actively Working 2=Account Rejection 3=Sales Rep Rejection	A1
1.5	Odds	Odds that this account will order	N2
1.6	Nxt_Date	The anticipated date to move to the next sales stage.	A8
1.7	Order	This code indicates if the account has ordered and is now a Customer. Y=Customer	A1

The *Equipment* table is used to store the details about equipment or other unique products or services used in each account.

The *Equipment* table will be related to the *Account* table for establishing the account the equipment is installed in.

1.0 Table Layout

	Column Name	Description	Format
1.1	Account_Id	Unique Identification # for a particular Account.	N4
1.2	Vendor	This is the manufacturer of the equipment.	A15
1.3	Model	This is the model of the equipment	A10
1.4	Description	Description of the equipment installed.	A50
1.5	Quantity	The quantity installed	N5

The *Contact* table is used to store the details about each sales contact. It contains a description of the contact, costing information and the program that is related to this contact.

1.0 Table Layout

	Column Name	Description	Format
1.1	Contact_Id	Unique Identification # for a particular Contact.	N4
1.2	Names_Id	This is the name of the target we contacted.The Names_Id will be used to identify the Name Identification # - this identifier will link the *Names* table. It is the key to the *Names* table.	N6
1.3	Type_Id	This is the contact_Id # that is used to identify the type of contact that was made to this name. The Contact_Id is the identifier that will link the	N4

Contact_Id table. It is the key to the
Contact_Id table.

1.4	Date	This is the contact date	A8

1.5	Disposition	The result of the contact	N2

01=Responded
02=Rejected-Not Qualified
03=Rejected-Prospect not interested
04=Lead Generated
05=Ordered
06=Requested Literature
07=Requested Seminar
08=Complaint

The *Contact_type* table is used to store the details about each sales contact. It contains a description of the contact, costing information and the program that is related to the contact.

1.0 Table Layout

Column Name		Description	Format
1.1	Type_Id	Unique Identification # for a particular contact.	N4
1.2	Project	This is the name of the program that is being supported with this type of contact.	N6
1.3	Program	The program that this project and contact are a part of.	N6
1.3	Description	A complete description of the contact.	A50
1.4	Costs	The estimated or actual costs of the contact.	A8

The *Source* table is used to store the details about lists and other sources of names. This table will be used to determine the effectiveness of various list sources and to determine the best sources for new names.

1.0 Table Layout

	Column Name	Description	Format
1.1	Source_Id	Unique Identification # for a particular source.	N4
1.2	Name	The name of the source.	A15
1.3	Description	Description of the source.	A50
1.4	Date	The date that the source was acquired.	A8
1.5	Count	The number of records this source contained.	N8

The *Sales* table is used to store the information about each of the salespeople. The table will contain information on salespeople and sales managers. This table will contain home addresses and phone numbers to allow them to be added to direct marketing programs. The start date and last date will allow you to evaluate the sales performance over time.

The *Sales* table will be related to the *Offices* table for establishing the address information to contact the individuals in the *Sales* table. Consolidation of information by sales office will also be possible with the *Offices* table.

The *Sales* table will be related to the *Region* table for establishing the reporting structure of each individual.

1.0 Table Layout

	Column Name	Description	Format
1.1	Sales_Id	Unique Identification # for each sales person.	N6
1.2	Office_Id	Office Identification # - this identifier will link the *Sales* table to the *Office* table. It is the key to the *Office* table	N4
1.3	Lname	Last Name	A15
1.4	Fname	First Name	A14
1.5	MI	Middle Initial	A1
1.6	Salt	Salutation - (Mr, Mrs, Ms)	A3
1.7	Title	The functional business title used by the individual like Senior Sales Rep or Account Executive.	A15
1.8	Phone	The phone number of the name. The phone number also contains up to a 4 position extension.	A17
1.9	Addr1	Home Address	A25
1.10	City	Home City	A16
1.11	State	The standard two position state code	A2
1.12	Zip	The Zip Code which can be 5 or 9 positions.	A10
1.13	Phone	The home phone number.	A12

1.11 Start	The start date of employee.	A8
1.12 Finish	The last day of employment	A8
1.13 Region	The Region_Id. This establishes the affiliation of the individual with his/her immediate manager.	N4

The *Office* table is used to store the information about each of the offices to allow for contacting the personnel in each office.

1.0 Table Layout

Column Name	Description	Format
1.1 Office_Id	Unique Identification # for each field office.	N6
1.2 Street	Address A25	
1.3 City	City A16	
1.4 State	The standard two position state code	A2
1.5 Zip	The Zip Code which can be 5 or 9 positions.	A10
1.6 Phone	The phone number.	A12

The *Region* table is used to store the information about each branch office or sales region. It establishes the reporting structure of the individual salespeople.

The *Region* table is related to the *Sales* table to capture the name and address information of the Regional Manager.

1.0 Table Layout

Column Name	Description	Format
1.1 Region_Id	Unique Identification # for each field office.	N6
1.2 Name	The name of the Region	A25
1.3 Manager	Sales_Id of the regional manager. The Sales_Id will link the *Region* table to the *Sales* table. Sales_Id is the key to the *Sales* table.	A16

This database model may not fit your business. However, it demonstrates how involved the database becomes. You must keep repetitive data in separate tables to permit maximum flexibility. This database model will give your data processing department an idea of your requirements and allow you to perform the database functions inherent in the direct marketing definition.

A number of relational database management systems (DBMS) are available that make implementing this approach easier. In the PC market, Paradox and Dbase II are two alternatives. Oracle and Ingres are DBMS alternatives on some mini-computers and main frames. An independent system that allows you to share databases between systems is offered by Britton Lee.

Database Marketing

This the newest marketing concept and the current buzz word that everyone is using to describe their marketing efforts. As you have already seen, a database means different things to different people. This marketing concept presumes that each marketing contact is stored on the computer database. The prior contact history will be used to establish the next logical contact and marketing activity. This almost sound like "Star Wars". Because most business are still using programs and data files, they are probably unable to implement database marketing today.

To properly implement database marketing, you must be able to change your data requirements as your needs change. It is possible to require a change based on each contact you make to the database. This could mean dedicating a computer programming staff to the direct marketing project. The use of a dynamic database probably requires a database management system. Again, it is very difficult to operate and control database marketing with the older technology of computer programs and fixed files.

Your need to capture information about each contact and results will require a significant amount of computer storage and the flexibility to change the files each time you introduce a new marketing program. If you have this capability, you will be able to automatically generate contacts to your customers and prospects based on the results of the last contact.

The real question becomes: does database marketing offer you an opportunity to generate a less expensive order and increased profits? Based on our experience, database marketing substantially improves results.

Cellular Company Database Case Study

Let's examine a lead generation program that ultimately evolved into a significant database marketing program.

Cellular Company is a major supplier of cellular telephone equipment and was interested in generating sales leads for their independent distributors in several market areas. Broadcast, radio, television, space ads in both newspapers and magazines, and direct mail were used to generate responses. As you'll note in Illustration 4-7, the responses were handled by an independent telemarketing service bureau. The independent firm was fully automated and handled both mail and phone responses. If the response was via telephone, the inbound communicators were scripted and fully interactive with a computer.

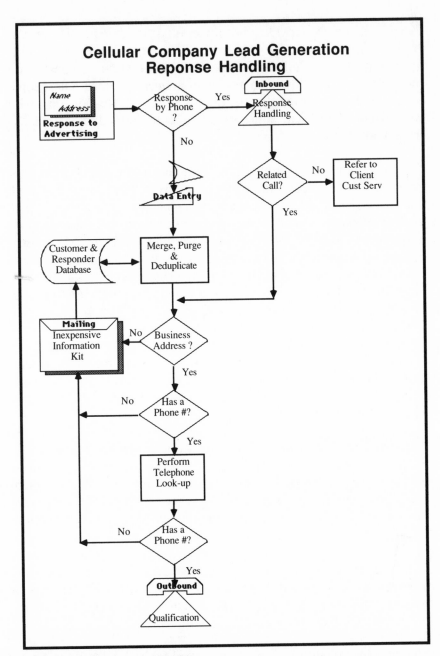

Illustration 4-7: Response Handling

The prospect was considered of lower quality if he/she did not provide a company name. These prospects were sent a less expensive fulfillment package. Cellular Company did not feel that a salesperson could effectively follow-up a responder at his/her home. Salespeople have a tendency to prejudge the quality of leads. Respondents who only provide their home address are frequently judged to be tire kickers and not buyers.

All respondents were added to a database and each contact was tracked. As new respondents were received, they were checked against the database to ensure that they hadn't already been handled in the last 90 days. Quite often, a prospect who hasn't had a timely response will respond a second time. Cellular Company was selling through outside distributors and there were several distributors in each market. An attempt was made to ensure that the same prospect wasn't sent to two different distributors. An attempt was made to eliminate prior responders. As discussed earlier, de-duplication routines in business-to-business are not very effective.

All respondents were qualified via telephone. If a mail respondent did not provide a telephone number, and the number wasn't available through directory assistance, the record was considered not qualified and sent the less expensive information package.

At the onset of the project, Cellular Company recognized that their product was unique and there would be a lot of interest from people who were not qualified. In addition, Cellular Company had a limited geographic area in which they offered services. In order to deal with the not qualified prospect, either through geography or qualification criteria, a less expensive generic fact kit was developed.

The qualified prospects, those with business addresses and phone numbers, were contacted via outbound telemarketing. Each prospect was screened for qualification and offered a salesperson. The telephone screening approach is detailed in Illustration 4-8.

The same lead qualification script was used for both inbound and out-

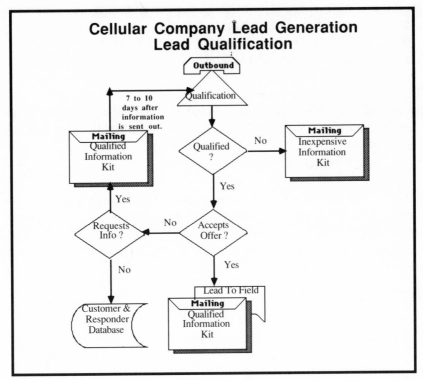

Illustration 4-8: Lead Qualification

bound telemarketing. If the prospect wasn't qualified . . . they didn't meet the criteria for Money, Authority, Need and Desire . . . they were sent the inexpensive mail kit. Qualified prospects were offered the opportunity to be contacted by a salesperson.

We knew that many prospects request literature before they agree to be contacted by a salesperson. We also knew that a substantial percentage of prospects requesting information could be converted to a lead if they were contacted after the material was received.

In telemarketing, prospects will frequently request additional information. One group of people who respond to a telephone offer with a request for information use it as an easy way to terminate the call. However, there is another group who are interested in the offer but want more information prior to making a commitment. All prospects who request additional information should be dealt with as legitimate prospects. In our experienced, about 25% of these literature requestors can be converted into leads.

Keeping track of who requested literature; when the literature was fulfilled; and when the prospect should be re-contacted will require some form of database. Small volumes allow you to handle the database manually. However, as the volumes become larger the database will require a computerized approach.

Initially, Cellular Company management wasn't concerned about the return of information from the sales force. Management was convinced that the sales force would follow-up on every lead and provide feedback about lead quality. Cellular Company didn't feel that a lead management and control system was necessary.

After several months of lead generation and several thousand leads, only 5% of the leads had been returned with any information. Cellular Company couldn't evaluate the success of the lead program. Senior management received verbal feedback that lead quality was not very good. They were considering shutting down the project.

To evaluate the success of the lead program, a mail questionnaire was sent to all leads to determine their disposition. The respondent database made re-contacting the leads very easy.

The results were startling. Only 40% of the leads had been contacted by the sales force. In our experience, this is a good follow-up rate. We have seen follow-up as low as 8% of leads generated in other campaigns. In this instance the leads proved to be of very high quality. Of the leads contacted by a salesperson, over 60% had purchased a product.

Management was alarmed about the business opportunity that had been lost due to no sales force follow-up. Several action programs were implemented to ensure that Cellular Company could capitalize on the opportunity within their current and future respondent

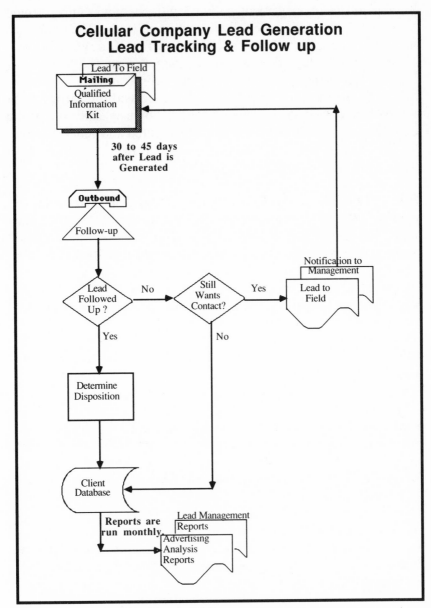

Cellular Company Lead Generation
Lead Tracking & Follow up

Illustration 4-9: Lead Tracking and Follow up

database.

A complete lead management and tracking system was implemented to ensure that the sales force followed up on all leads. The leads were only given to a distributor salesperson for 30 days. Cellular Company used telemarketing to re-contact prospects 30 days after the leads were generated to determine their disposition. The follow-up call determined if the prospect had received the information requested and if he/she had been contacted by a salesperson. If the lead was not contacted, it would be regenerated and sent to another distributor salesperson. Illustration 4-9 reflects the flow of activity in the lead tracking and follow up system.

The results of the project were very rewarding. Follow-up improved to almost 80% of leads generated. More importantly, the closing rate of all leads generated climbed to over 30%. The cost per lead and cost per order were substantially less than originally anticipated.

The database allowed continuing contact with the respondent. It also allowed an accurate measurement system to be developed to evaluate the success of the lead generation program.

Additional direct mail followed by outbound telemarketing programs were developed and the database was naturally used as a list source. Prospects on the database were contacted three additional times in the first year to generated more leads. Only those prospects who had already purchased were not included in the continuing direct marketing program. Not surprisingly, the least expensive leads and orders were derived from the database because these database names performed at a higher level of response than other lists.

Each time a contact was made, it was added to the database to track and evaluate the effectiveness of each step of the direct marketing effort. The database also contained all of the information captured during the telemarketing contacts and this data became valuable market research.

The results of each contact established the next activity for the prospect. The storage, retrieval and updating of the information as a result of each contact developed a dynamic marketing database. The results of each contact had to be evaluated to determine the next step.

The use of this information to condition the next selling activity is the essence of database marketing.

These results and benefits justify the investment to implement a dynamic database. You can experiment with database marketing by handling your literature requestors similarly to the methods we discussed earlier. Send the information to the respondent and then follow-up with a telephone call to attempt to convert the prospect to a lead or an order. We think you'll find the results very encouraging.

Database Summarized

As we indicated earlier, database maybe the most misused and misunderstood term in our marketing language. It means different things to different people.

Data processing people think about a database in terms of how the computer information is going to be managed and controlled. To them, database means DBMS or database management systems.

The conversion of existing files and programs to a DBMS is a large effort and has substantial impact on data processing. Computer programs are written to deal with data formatted in a specific way. Changing the format of the data normally means having to change any computer program that will deal with that data. Even adding a small piece of information to existing systems can mean a massive change to computer programs.

Database management systems separate the data from the computer programs and make changing and adding information relatively easy. DBMS systems allow adding or changing of information independent of computer programs. They also move the control of information from the data processing department to the end-user.

The list industry definition of database is different than data processing and direct marketing. The list industry considers the term to mean an expanded list. Several list companies now offer databases that are the result of combining several lists and then adding demographic, geographic and physchographic data. These combined lists are referred to as databases. They are a significant improvement over prior list sources because you can be more effective in selecting and segmenting your target audience.

Other departments within your business can probably give you additional definitions of database. All of the definitions may be correct for their particular application. For the purposes of business-to-business direct marketing, the definition we've been using throughout our discussion is most appropriate.

Direct marketing will develop and maintain a database which:

- Provides names of customers or prospects

- Is a vehicle for storing and measuring responses

- Is a vehicle for storing and measuring purchases

- Is a vehicle for on-going communication with customers and prospects.

Throughout this book, we've continually reviewed each element of the direct marketing database definition. In this chapter, we have explained the four different list types:

- House or Customer Lists
- Compiled Lists
- Respondent Lists
- Subscription or Membership Lists

We discussed the characteristics of each list type and how to combine them to create a target universe for your direct marketing promotion. Once you begin direct marketing, your database needs to be able to measure responses and then measure purchases. We tried to discuss the minimum elements needed for both of these functions.

A complete database model was provided to allow you to evaluate the amount of information you may need for direct marketing. The model could be used to work with your data processing department to design your own direct marketing database.

Database marketing offers great promise in reducing costs and increasing results. A complete program was reviewed to demonstrate the elements of database marketing. We discussed how to use the database to condition additional contacts to the prospects and customers.

We tried to provide an explanation of database that will allow you to effectively communicate with data processing and direct marketing. Database is one of the required elements of direct marketing. If you don't have control of the database, your efforts will probably fail. If you can't automate the database with your data processing department, consider using another alternative that will give you control.

Chapter Five - Promotion

__Promotion Defined__

Promotion can be defined as the further development and encouragement of prospects to purchase one's products or services.

Promotion may be viewed as having two aspects:

- Technical
- Creative

The effort and importance of these two aspects may be evenly divided, but it is more likely that the distribution is 60% to 70% technical and 30% to 40% creative.

Technical elements are those elements that are a must if you are going to execute successful direct marketing: product information, reply device, pricing and acceptable format for the media being used are some of the areas to be considered. In addition, the approach must conform to legal and trade practices as well as internal product and credit requirements.

Creative aspects are the big ideas that clothe your information to make it more appealing to its market. Big ideas can be serious, funny, direct or oblique in describing product positioning.

Technical Promotion

Let's now focus on how to make you a better technician. Our goal is not to make you a creative director, but to give you the tools to develop the thought processes needed to become a better manager of the direct marketing process.

Promotion has four parts:

1) List
2) Offer
3) Format
4) Copy

Lists are discussed in Chapter four, Database. Lists represent those people, from whatever source you select, you have chosen to target. The action you want the prospect to take is your offer. The method you select for delivering the offer to the prospect is the format and the copy is how you say it. Understanding these parts of promotion will provide a basis for evaluating and implementing the direct marketing concept.

If you were to weight the four elements of the direct marketing effort, based on the relative value each has to the ultimate success of the project, they would appear the following way:

List   50%
Offer   25%
Format   15%
Copy   10%

These percentages are not in concert with what most of us do most of the time. Most of us spend 80% of our effort on copy, 15% on format, 5% on list (generally a last minute detail) and 0% on offer.

Why is there such a wide variance between what we do and what should be done to bring about or effect good direct marketing? Simple. We all love our "**It**."

> **It** *(noun) the product or service a company or individual makes available for someone to buy.*

Picture your **It** in front of you. Isn't it the most beautiful **It** in the whole world? Isn't it the most easily understood, most needed, problem solving, cost effective, efficient and user-friendly **It** ever discovered?

Isn't it difficult to understand why people aren't lined up to purchase your **It** ? How simple their lives would be if only those people out there would buy and use your **It** .

Before getting too worked up, let's determine how much we know about competitive **Its** . A little? Some? We don't have time to learn about their **Its** because we're to busy trying to get them to understand our **It.** We're also trying to fulfill our day-to-day administrative tasks while having some free time for fun. There just isn't enough time to understand and appreciate their **It**.

So the best thing to do is to describe our **It** in eloquent prose. We can never tell people too much, because our **It** is so great. Since everyone needs our **It**, they will take the time to read about our **It**. Then they will surely take action. So, let's spend hours and hours on every verb, noun and adjective. Better still, let's get a committee together to help write the copy -- "The words."

After spending ten weeks getting "the words" just right, we are five weeks behind schedule so let's just blast the copy out into the market. Let's run it up the flagpole and see who salutes. Let's throw it against the wall to see what sticks. What sticks?

Nothing -- Or, very little.

Those stupid people don't know what they're missing. We told them about our **It** and they still don't care. They don't know what's good for them.

But it's not their fault, it's ours. We have spent 80% of our allotted time on just 20% of the of the areas needed in a direct marketing program.

Look through some promotion pieces you've received. How much of each do you read? 10%? 30%? 50%? 100%? And the parts you did read are headline, graphics, captions, call-outs and subheads -- and maybe 10% to 15% of everything else.

How do you get people to pay attention to your message? Talk with trained successful salespeople and learn what they do to succeed. After conducting a number of interviews, develop a model and approach similar to the one used by a successful salesperson.

Initially the salesperson develops an understanding of the best market to sell to by trying the pitch on anybody who will listen. After a few thousand "nos" the salesperson learns who not to pitch. While screen doors are a little used item in the manufacture of submarines, listen to your instincts, but don't be afraid to test a new market from time to time. They may be great inside a submarine.

Like the salesperson, spend time seeking out the right market. Define the correct individual to market to within the market. You may have to market to both a decision maker and an influencer. This is one of the most important aspects of the technical preparation of the direct marketing program. The list work makes the difference between success and failure. If you don't spend the effort on understanding and evaluating the list, you'll experience thousands of "nos" in terms of non-response.

You may still believe the best use of your time is in forming the most eloquent description of your **It**. If you do decide that the description of your **It** is most important, go to your sales force to learn how they are selling. Their approach to describing the features and benefits of your **It** will be strong indicators of how your copy should be written.

Let's again review the four elements of promotion:

List -   The customers or prospects to whom you plan to target your marketing effort.

Offer -   The proposition you are making to your customers or prospects in order to get them to respond. It is the action you want the prospect to take.

Format - The vehicle for delivering the offer to your market: mail, phone, print, broadcast.

Copy -   The words you use to communicate your offer to the market.

For promotion to be effective, follow the same steps the sales force does in developing a sale. Use your promotion as a surrogate salesperson.

An easy formula to help remember the elements of direct response promotion is *AIDA* -- **A**ttention, **I**nterest, **D**esire, **A**ction. While general advertising has attention and interest as its goal, direct marketing goes further to include desire and action. These last two elements separate general advertising from direct marketing.

Just as an experienced salesperson does not bother trying to gain the attention of the wrong people, you should not use the wrong list. Once the salesperson has identified a valid prospect, he/she will try to generate a sale.

The salesperson's presentation will include a complete needs assessment of the prospect. A good salesperson will find out the prospect's problems. As a surrogate salesperson, your direct marketing promotional material must exhibit knowledge and empathy to gain the prospect's interest.

Once the salesperson can identify and understand the problems of the prospect, he/she can begin to relate the features of his/her **It** to the specific needs of the prospects. He/she does so by demonstrating how his/her **It** will solve the prospect's problems thereby creating a level of desire to make a change. Chapter one discusses this concept in detail in its review the Buying Decision.

In your direct marketing program, you should perform the same function by proposing to solve problems you already know exist. Format and copy should focus the prospect on his/her need and how your **It** will solve his/her problem. This is the first part of your offer.

Like a good salesperson, you should ask for the order. This is the second part of the offer. Move the prospect to action. Desire and action are easily affected when offer is compressed by limitations of time, quantities or pricing for a period of time.

This process can be applied when selling an **It** or when asking for an appointment for selling an **It**. Just like the salesperson, the direct marketing surrogate salesperson can make several contacts with a prospect before asking for an order.

A salesperson may make several contacts within an organization before finding out with whom to speak. Keep this in mind when contacting a company; it is a little presumptuous to believe a single promotional effort can reach the right person in any given company. Based on the price of the product being offered, it may even be presumptuous to believe the second effort will get the order.

An initial contact may merely be a probe to discover the name or title of the best person to establish a relationship within a company. This can be accomplished by contacting, much like our salesperson does, a receptionist or switchboard attendant and asking who is the most appropriate person to contact. This kind of information can be obtained by mail or phone.

This could be a waste of time and money if your **It** is easily understood, inexpensive and generates a strong contribution to overhead and profit. In this case, broad based promotion can be most cost effective.

If your product is expensive and requires more than one individual to make a buying decision, direct marketing can be an effective enhancement to the selling effort. It may be worthwhile to spend the time and money to make sure you are speaking with the person that will act as a "champion" for your **It** during the review and buy-in cycles.

You can also use direct marketing to sell many individuals within the company on the advantages and benefits of your product. While a salesperson can't talk to more than one person at a time, direct marketing will allow your message to reach as many individuals as needed on the same day.

Whatever approach you select, direct marketing can be used effectively as a lead generator for your sales force after you've established awareness, interest and desire. The action can be the opportunity to be visited by a salesperson.

Before discussing offers, let's explore the major difference between corporate life and entrepreneurial life. A great deal of the offers received in the business environment have to do with saving time and/or money. This can be expanded into the trite combination: efficiency and effectiveness. In truth, people who work for a corporations don't care much about time and money. They say and act as they do because that is the company line. Time and money are not personal needs.

To make an effective offer to employees, appeal to them as people. In general, corporate employees are interested in following:

1. Getting promoted
2. Reducing hassles
3. Covering their rears

Let's review these interests in terms of life as an employee in a medium to large corporation. Getting promoted means more status, more money, more power and all the reasons people hang around a corporation. If offered an opportunity to be promoted as a result of making a buying decision, an employee would find a way to make that decision.

Reducing hassle is a game frequently played by the corporate employee. If a promotion is not attainable, then most will try to reduce the chaos experienced on the job. If this can be done via making a buying decision, most will take advantage of hassle reduction so they can spend more time on getting promoted.

Covering the rear is the avoidance process most people in corporate environment practice. This is the process of getting others to share the risk of decisions so that no one can pin the tail on them. It is also the process of making decisions that can be revised in the event things don't work out as planned. Also, making decisions to go with the industry choice will probably allow them to stay clear of ridicule. As a rear cover, most employees will respond to suggestions from others within the company -- especially from persons ranked above them in the organization. Other reasons to make a decision could be guarantees with a right of return or offers that are supported by industry belief.

If an employee's rear is exposed, he/she won't have time to reduce hassle and get promoted. If your offer is aimed at the personal motivation of the company employee you're trying to reach, your odds of success are increased.

The owner of the business will be interested in the benefits of time and money as a result of purchasing your **It**. Business owners are saving their own money rather than the money of a corporation. The business owner seems to have better skills at using time. While the corporate employee is willing to delay decisions, the business owner makes decisions fast, especially when there is a way to save time or money. He/she doesn't need committee support to make a decision.

Lists

The lists you select are clearly the most important part of your direct marketing efforts. Unfortunately, the list is often the area you spend the least amount of time evaluating.

Earlier, during the planning phase, you should identify the characteristics of your customers and prospects. The identification phase should include a detailed description of the specific individual and types of individuals you are trying to reach.

In the consumer universe, you can select prospects by demographic and geographic characteristics. Several firms specialize in creating complete lists of households with selected similar demographic characteristics. Some of these firms attempt to overlay lifestyle characteristics with demographic and geographic information. In essence, you can select households meeting almost any criteria.

Business list selection does not enjoy the same luxury of finite selection information. Business demographics do not exist, even though this concept is frequently discussed. The demographics are those characteristics that are available based on the business itself. The concept of lifestyle would be applicable if we could analyze the corporate culture of all businesses.

Here are some characteristics of businesses that can improve your ability to select lists:

- Annual sales or revenue

- Number of employees

- Standard Industrial Classification (SIC)

- Geography - state, ZIP, SCF (Sectional Center Facility - first three digits of the ZIP code)

- Assets

- Credit Rating

- Types of equipment being used

- Expenditures above a certain value in any specific area

- Area of business activity: regional, national, international

- Multiple locations

- Titles

- Functions

As you can see the business list selection variables are quite different from those in the consumer world. The above list may not be complete for you needs. Only by evaluating your customers and prospects and the products you are trying to sell can you arrive at the criteria you should use for list selection. All the characteristics you feel are necessary may not be available on every list you evaluate. This problem is compounded by the limited size of business lists; you might use an entire list just testing it.

A lack of standards in company names and abbreviations, and numerous telephone numbers per company prevent elimination. No matter how hard you try, you will never be able to eliminate all of your own customers from a prospect mailing. In addition, you will probably have duplicate mailings and contacts to a single individual, even when using a single list source.

Subscription and membership lists may be a poor selection when you are planning to market in a tight geographic area. The publication or organization may not have enough people in the selected area. Tight geographic marketing may necessitate the use of compiled lists.

On the other hand, compiled lists may not have complete contact names so you may be forced to solicit a title or function. This may not be so bad since testing has indicated that there is not that marked a difference between title addressing and name addressing. Obviously, it is better to use the name if you have it. However, the wrong name may never get delivered.

The rate of change in contact name and address in the consumer world runs about 15% to 20% per year. In the business environment, change can run as high as 40%. Compiled lists tend to be about one year old and can have a substantial error rate in the contact name. Responder and subscriber lists may be updated more frequently and the contact name could be more accurate, but remember, you don't have the same number of selection criteria for these lists.

Even your own customer list has to be evaluated as a direct marketing list. Is the contact on your list the person you want to solicit for additional business? If not, you should implement a program to add the proper person to your file. In order to update you can address solicitations to your own customers by title or function without damaging the relationship.

It is often possible to trade customer lists with associates in similar businesses who are not selling competing products. For example, if you sell office supplies and an associate sells cleaning supplies, you can exchange or rent the other list and even use the associate's name in your solicitation. Customer lists always respond better than general prospect sources.

If you're selling a business publication, soliciting another business publication list is far better than a compiled list. Evaluate your product and target market to identify the best list opportunities. Test all types of lists to determine which ones meet your cost per order criteria. You will always be making compromises in selection criteria, contact name and other characteristics that are important to you.

Business lists are normally much smaller than consumer lists. When you begin testing, be careful not to test too many lists lest your results per list may be so small you cannot adequately evaluate any list.

Some final thoughts on lists: Even after you have done a relatively good job of identifying the characteristics of the universe you want to solicit, the actual list selection is still going to be a gamble. There are many list brokers, direct marketing agencies and list compilers who can help you select and test list alternatives.

A good list broker can be an important addition to any direct marketing resource team. Most brokers are paid a standard industry commission of 10% to 15% by the list owners, therefore you incur no fee. List brokers have experience with many lists and can recommend specific lists to meet your needs. The Direct Marketing Association can provide the names of list brokers in your area.

Offers

The offer is the proposition you make to your prospects to motivate them to respond to your promotion. Whether you are selling a notebook or a lifetime of financial counseling, you must get your prospect to take the first step that will achieve your objectives. You need to get the prospects to feel good about your offer so they can overcome fear, uncertainty and doubt (FUD) about your company and its product.

Your offer will include your product, price, payment terms and any incentive you are willing to include, along with special conditions you may attach to the offer. In his book, Profitable Direct Marketing, Jim Kobs listed the following 99 direct response offers. This list comprehensively covers consumer and business offers.

BASIC OFFERS

1) **Right Price** - The starting point for any product or service being sold by mail. Consider your market and what's being charged for competitive products. And make sure you have sufficient margin for your offer to be profitable. Most products sold by mail require at least a three-time mark-up.

2) **Free Trial** - If mail order advertisers suddenly had to standardize all their efforts on one offer, this would no doubt be the choice; it's widely used for book and merchandise promotions. Looking at it like a consumer, the free trial relieves the fear that you might get stuck buying by mail because the advertiser is willing to let you try *his* product before he gets *your* money. Most free trial periods are 10 or 15 days, but the length of the trial period should fit the type of product or service being offered.

3) **Money-Back Guarantee** - If for some good reason you can't use a free trial offer, this is the next best thing. The main difference is you ask the customer to pay part or all of the purchase price *before* you let him try your product. This puts inertia on your side. The customer is unlikely to take the time and effort to send a product back unless he's really unhappy with it.

4) **Cash with Order** - This is the basic payment option used with a money-back guarantee. It's also offered with a choice of other payment options. Incentives (such as paying the postage and handling charge) are often used to encourage the customer to send his/her check or money order when he/she orders.

5) **Bill Me Later** - This is the basic payment option used with free trial offers. The bill is usually enclosed with the merchandise or follows a few days later. And it calls for a single payment. Because no front-end payment is required by the customer, the response can be as much as double that of a cash offer.

6) **Installment Terms** - This payment option works like the one above, except that it usually involves a bigger sale price...with installment terms set up to keep the payments around $10 to $20 per month. Usually a necessity to sell big ticket items by mail to the consumer.

7) **Charge Card Privileges -** Offers the same advantages of "bill me later" and installment plans, but the seller doesn't have to carry the paper. Can be used with bank charge cards, travel and entertainment cards, and specialized cards (like those issued by the oil companies).

8) **C.O.D. -** This is the Postal Service acronym for Cash-On-Delivery. The mailman collects when he/she delivers the package. Not widely used today because of the added cost and effort required to handle C.O.D. orders.

FREE GIFT OFFERS

9) **Free Gift for an Inquiry -** Provides an incentive to request more information about a product or service. Usually increases inquiries, though they become somewhat less qualified.

10) **Free Gift for a Trial Order -** Commonly called a "keeper" gift - because the customer gets to keep the gift just for agreeing to try the product.

11) **Free Gift for Buying -** Similar to the above, except the customer only gets to keep the gift if he/she buys the product or service. The gift can be given free with any order, tied to a minimum purchase, or used as a self-liquidator.

12) **Multiple Free Gifts with a Single Order -** If one gifts pays out for you, considering offering two or more. You may even be able to offer two inexpensive gifts and spend the same as on one more expensive item. Biggest user of multiple gifts is Fingerhut Corporation. At last count, they were up to four free gifts for a single order!

13) **Your Choice of Free Gifts -** Can be a quick way to test the relative appeal of different gift items. But will seldom

work as well as the best gift offered on its own. The choice probably leads to indecision on the consumer's part.

14) **Free Gifts Based on Size of Order** - Often used with catalogs or merchandise that lends itself to a quantity purchase. You can offer an inexpensive gift for orders under $10.00; a better gift for orders running between $10.00 and $25.00; and a deluxe gift for orders over $25.00.

15) **Two-Step Gift Offer** - Offers an inexpensive gift if customer takes the first step...a better gift for taking the second step. Such as a free record album for *trying* a new stereo set, and a deluxe headset if you elect to *buy* it.

16) **Continuing Incentive Gifts** - Used to get customers to keep coming back. Book clubs often give Bonus Coupons to save up for additional books. Also suitable is silverware, where you give one place setting per order.

17) **Mystery Gift Offer** - Sometimes works better than offering a specific gift. It helps if you can give some indication of the item's retail value.

OTHER FREE OFFERS

18) **Free Information** - Certainly an inexpensive offer - and a very flexible one. The type of information you provide can range from a simple product catalog sheet to a full-blown series of mailings. If the information is not going to be delivered by a salesman, this should be played up.

19) **Free Catalog** - Can be an attractive offer for both the consumer and the business market. In the business field, catalogs are often used as buying guides and saved for future reference. In the consumer field, you can often attach a nominal charge for postage and handling...or offer a full year's catalog subscription.

20) **Free Booklet** - Helps establish your company's expertise and know-how about the specific problems of your industry. Especially if the booklet contains helpful editorial material - not just a commercial for your product or service. The booklet should have an appealing title, like "How to Save Money on Heating Costs" or "29 Ways to Improve the Quality Control System".

21) **Free Fact Kit** - Sometimes called an Idea Kit. It's usually put together in an attractive file folder or presentation cover. You can include a variety of enclosures... from booklets to trade paper articles to ad reprints.

22) **Send Me a Salesman** - This one is included here because the offer is actually a free sales call...with wording like "have your representative phone me for an appointment." Normally produces more qualified inquiries than a free booklet or fact kit. Those who respond are probably ready to order or seriously considering it.

23) **Free Demonstration** - Important for things like business equipment that has to be demonstrated to be fully appreciated. If the equipment is small enough, it can be brought into the prospect's plant or office. If not, he/she might be invited to a private showing or group demonstration at the manufacturer's facilities.

24) **Free "Survey of Your Needs"** - Ideal for some industrial products or services. Like a company that sells chemicals for various water treatment problems. Offering a free survey by a sales representative or technical expert is appealing, and gives you the opportunity to qualify a prospect and see if your product or service really fits his/her needs.

26) **Free Dinner** - Like the rest of the offers that follow to this section, this one is particularly suited to certain types of direct marketing companies. It's widely used by real

estate and land companies... who offer a free dinner at a nearby restaurant. Those who attend also get a sales presentation on the property.

27) **Free Film Offer** - Many mail order film processing companies have been built with some variation of this offer. Either the customer gets a new roll of film when he/she sends one in for processing. Or the first roll is offered free, in hopes that it will be sent back to the same company later for processing.

28) **Free House Organ Subscription** - Many industrial companies put out elaborate house organs for customers and prospects...which contain a good deal of helpful editorial material. You can offer a free sample issue. Or better yet, a year's subscription.

29) **Free Talent Test** - Popular with home study schools. Especially those that offer a skilled course, such as writing or painting. Legal restrictions require that any such test be used to measure real talent or ability, not just as a door-opener for the salesman.

30) **Gift Shipment Service** - This is one of the basic appeals of offers used by virtually all mail order cheese and gift food firms. You send them your gift list, and they ship direct to the recipients at no extra cost.

DISCOUNT OFFERS

31) **Cash Discount** - This is the basic type of discount. It's often dramatized by including a discount certificate in the ad or mailing. However, a discount offer will *not* do as well as an attractive free gift with the same value.

32) **Short-Term Introductory Offer** - A popular type of discount used to let somebody try the product for a short period at a reduced price. Examples include "Try 10

weeks of the *Wall Street Journal* for only $5.97" and "30 days of accident insurance for only 25¢." It's important to be able to convert respondents to long-term subscribers or policyholders.

33) **Refund Certificate -** Technically speaking, it's a delayed discount. You might ask somebody to send $1.00 for your catalog and include a $1.00 refund certificate good on his/her first order. The certificate is like an un-cashed check - it's difficult to resist the urge to cash it.

34) **Introductory Order Discount -** A special discount used to bring in new customers. Can sometimes cause complaints from old customers if they're not offered the same discount.

35) **Trade Discount -** Usually extended to certain clubs, institutions, or types of businesses.

36) **Early Bird Discount -** Designed to get customers to stock up before the normal buying season. A great many Christmas cards and gifts have been sold by mail with this offer.

37) **Quantity Discount -** This discount is tied to certain quantity or order volume. The long-term subscriptions offered by magazines are really a quantity discount. The cost-per-copy is usually lower on a two-year subscription because it represents a quantity purchase - 24 issues instead of 12.

38) **Sliding Scale Discount -** In this case, the amount of the discount depends on the date somebody orders or the size of the order. Such as a 2% discount for orders up to $50, and a 10% discount for orders over $100.

39) **Selected Discounts -** These are often sprinkled throughout a catalog to emphasize certain items the advertiser wants to push or give the appearance that everything is on sale.

SALE OFFERS

40) **Seasonal Sales -** Such as Pre-Christmas Sale or Summer Vacation Sale. If successful, they are often repeated every year at the same time.

41) **Reason-Why Sales -** This category includes Inventory Reduction, Clearance Sales, and similar titles. These explanatory terms help make it more believable to the prospect.

42) **Price Increase Notice -** A special type of offer that's like a limited time sale. Gives customers a chance to order at the old prices before increases become effective.

43) **Auction-By-Mail -** An unusual type of sale. Has been used to sell such items as lithographs and electronic calculators, when their quantities were limited. Customers send in a "sealed bid" with merchandise usually going to the highest bidder.

SAMPLE OFFERS

44) **Free Samples -** If your product lends itself to sampling, this is a strong offer. Sometimes you can offer a sample made with or by your product. Such as a steel company who uses take-apart puzzles made from their steel wire. Or a printer who offers samples of helpful printed material it has produced for other customers.

45) **Nominal Charge Samples -** In many cases making a nominal charge for a sample--like 10¢, 25¢, or $1.00--will pull better than a free sample offer. The charges helps establish the value of the item and screens out some of the curiosity seekers.

46) **Sample Offer with Tentative Commitment-** This is also

known as the "complimentary copy" offer used by many magazines. In requesting the sample, the prospect is also making a tentative commitment for a subscription. But if he/she doesn't like the first issue, he/she just writes "cancel" on the bill and sends it back. But legal precautions are advised, your legal counsel should review this offer before you actually make it.

47) **Quantity Sample Offer-** A specialized offer that's worked well for business services and newsletters. Like a sales training bulletin, where the sales manager is told to "just tell us how many salesmen you have, and we'll send a free sample bulletin for each one."

48) **Free Sample Lesson-** This has been widely used by home study schools, who offer a sample lesson to demonstrate the scope and content of their course.

TIME LIMIT OFFERS

49) **Limited Time Offers-** Any limited time offer tends to force a quick decision and avoid procrastination. It's usually best to mention a specific date--such as "this special offer expires November 20th" rather than "this offer expires in 10 days."

50) **Enrollment Periods-** Have been widely used by mail order insurance companies, who include a specific cutoff date for the enrollment period. It implies there are savings involved by processing an entire group of enrollments at one time.

51) **Pre-Publication Offer-** Long a favorite with publishers, who offer a special discount or savings before the official publication date of a new book. The rationale is that it helps them plan their printing quantity more accurately.

52) **Charter Membership (or Subscription) Offer** - Ideal for introducing new clubs, publications, and other subscription services. Usually includes a special price, gift or other incentive for charter members or subscribers. And it appeals to those who like to be among the first to try new things.

53) **Limited Edition Offer** - A relatively new direct response offer. But a proven way to go for selling coins, art prints and other collectable items.

GUARANTEE OFFERS

54) **Extended Guarantee** - Such as letting the customer return a book up to a year later. Or with a magazine, offering to refund the unexpired portion of a subscription any time before it runs out.

55) **Double-Your-Money-Back Guarantee** - Really dramatizes your confidence in the product...but it better live up to your advertising claims if you make an offer like this.

56) **Guaranteed Buy-Back Agreement** - While it's similar to the extended guarantee, this specialized version is often used with limited edition offers on coins and art objects. To convince the prospect of their value, the advertiser offers to buy them back at the full price during a specified period that may last as long as 5 years.

57) **Guaranteed Acceptance Offer** - This specialized offer is used by insurance firms with certain types of policies that require no health questions or underwriting. It's especially appealing to those with health problems who might not otherwise qualify.

BUILD-UP-THE-SALE OFFERS

58) **Multi-Product Offers** - Two or more products or services

are featured in the same ad or mailing. Maybe you've
never thought about it this way, but the best-known type
of multi-product offer is a catalog - which can feature a
hundred or more items.

59) **Piggyback Offers -** Similar to a multi-product offer,
except that one product is strongly featured. The other
items just kind of ride along or "piggyback" in the hope of
picking up additional sales.

60) **The Deluxe Offer -** A publisher might offer a book in
standard binding at $9.95. The order form gives the cus-
tomer the option of ordering a deluxe edition for only
$2.00 more. And it's not unusual for 10% or more of
those ordering to select the deluxe alternative.

61) **Good-Better-Best Offer -** This one goes a step further by
offering 3 choices. The mail order mints, for example,
sometimes offer their medals in a choice of bronze, ster-
ling silver, or 24K gold.

62) **Add-On Offer -** A low-cost item that's related to the featured product can be great for impulse orders. Such as
offering a wallet for $7.95 ... with a matching key case
offered for only $1.00 extra.

63) **Write-Your-Own-Ticket Offer -** Some magazines have
used this with good success to build up the sale. Instead
of offering 17 weeks for $4.93 - which is 29¢ per issue -
they give the subscriber the 29¢ an issue price and let him
fill in the number of weeks he/she wants his/her subscription to run.

64) **Bounce-Back Offer -** This approach tries to build onto
the original sale by enclosing an additional offer with the
product shipment or invoice.

65) **Increase and Extension Offer -** These are also follow-

ups to the original sale. Mail order insurance firms often give policyholders a chance to get increased coverage with a higher-priced version of the same policy. Magazines often use an advance renewal offer to get subscribers to extend their present subscription.

SWEEPSTAKES OFFERS

66) **Drawing Type Sweepstakes** - The majority of sweepstakes contests are set up this way. The prospect gets one or more chances to win. But all winners are selected by a random drawing.

67) **Lucky Number Sweepstakes** - With this type of contest, winning numbers are pre-selected before making the mailing or running the ad. Copy strategy emphasizes "you may have already won." And for those winning numbers that are actually entered or returned, a drawing is held for the unclaimed prizes.

68) **"Everybody Wins" Sweepstakes** - No longer widely used, but a real bonanza when this offer was first introduced. The prize structure is set up so the bottom or low-end prize is a very inexpensive or nominal one. And it's awarded to everyone who enters and doesn't win one of the bigger prizes.

69) **Involvement Sweepstakes** - This type requires the prospect to open a mystery envelope, play a game, or match his/her number against an eligible number list. In doing so, he/she determines the value of the grand prize he/she wins *if* his/her entry is drawn as the winner. Some of these involvement devices have been highly effective in boosting results.

70) **Talent Contests** - Not really a sweepstakes, but effective for some types of direct marketing situations. Such as the

mail order puzzle clubs and the "draw me" ad which offers a free scholarship from a home study art school.

Note - chance promotions are Locally and Agency regulated. Always be sure your offer is within guidelines. Legal review is advised.

CLUB & CONTINUITY OFFERS

71) **Positive Option -** You join a club and are notified monthly of new selections. To order, you must take some positive action - - such as sending back an order card.

72) **Negative Option -** You are still notified in advance of new selections. But under the terms you agreed to when joining, the new selection is shipped *unless* you return a rejection card by a specific date.

73) **Automatic Shipments -** This variation eliminates the advance notice of new selections. When you sign up, you give the publisher permission to ship each selection automatically until you tell him to stop. It's commonly called a "Till Forbid" offer.

74) **Continuity Load-Up Offer -** Usually used for continuity book series, like a 20-volume encyclopedia. The first book is offered free. But after you receive and pay for the next couple of monthly volumes - the balance of the series is sent in one load-up shipment. However, you can continue to pay at the rate of one volume per month.

75) **Front-End Load-Ups -** This is where a record club gives you 4 records for $1.00 - if you agree to sign up and accept at least 4 more selections during the next year. The attractive front-end offer gets you to make a minimum purchase commitment. And the commitment usually has a fixed time period for buying your remaining selections.

76) **Open-Ended Commitment** - Like the front-end load-up, except that there is no time limit for purchasing your 4 additional selections.

77) **"No Strings Attached" Commitment**- Like the above two offers, except it's more generous because you are not committed to any future purchases. The publisher gambles that you will find future selections interesting enough to make a certain number of purchases.

78) **Lifetime Membership Fee** - You pay a one-time fee to join - usually $5.00 or $10.00 - and get a monthly announcement of new selections. But there's no minimum commitment, and all ordering is done on a positive option basis.

79) **Annual Membership Fee** - Here you pay an annual fee for club membership. It's often used for travel clubs ... where you get a whole range of benefits, including travel insurance. Also used for fund raising, where a choice of membership levels is often effective.

80) **The Philanthropic Privilege** - This is the basis of all fund-raising offers. The donor's contribution usually brings nothing tangible in return - but helps make the world a better place in which to live. Sometimes enhanced by giving gummed stamps, a membership card, or other tokens of appreciation.

81) **Blank Check Offer** - First used in the McGovern fund-raising campaign. Supporters could fill out blank, post-dated checks ... which were cashed one-a-month to provide installment contributions. Later adapted for extending credit to bank charge card customers.

82) **Executive Preview Charge** - A successful offer for such things as sales training films. Executive agrees to pay $25 to screen or preview the film. But if he/she decides to buy

or rent it, the preview price is credited against the full price.

83) **Yes/No Offers** - Asks prospect to let you know his/her decision either way. In most cases the negative responses have little or no value. But by forcing a decision, you often end up with more "yes" responses.

84) **Self-Qualification Offer** - Uses a choice of options to get the prospect to indicate his/her degree of interest in your product or service. Such as offering a free booklet or a free demonstration. Those who request the latter qualify themselves as serious prospects and should get more immediate attention.

85) **Exclusive Rights for Your Trading Area** - Ideal for selling some business services to firms who are in a competitive business. Such as a syndicated newsletter that a bank buys and sends to its customers. You give the first bank that responds an exclusive for his/her trading area. The percentages that order are such that you seldom have to turn anybody down.

86) **The Super Dramatic Offer** - Sometimes very effective. Such as the offer to "smoke my new kind of pipe for 30 days. If you don't like it, smash it up with a hammer and send me back the pieces."

87) **Trade-In Offer** - An offer like "we'll give you $10 for your old slide rule when you buy a new electronic calculator" can be very appealing.

88) **Third Party Referral Offer** - Instead of renting somebody's list, you get the list owner to make a mailing for you - over his/her name - and recommend your product or service. Usually works better than your own promotion because of the rapport a company has with its own customers.

89) **Member-Get-A-Member Offer** - Often used to get customers to send in the names of friends who might be interested. Widely used by book and record clubs, who give their member a free gift if he/she gets a new member to sign up.

90) **Name-Getter Offers** - Usually designed for building a prospect list. A firm can offer a low-cost premium at an attractive self-liquidating price.

91) **Purchase-With-Purchase** - Widely used by cosmetic firms and department stores. An attractive gift set is offered at a special price with a regular purchase.

92) **Delayed Billing Offer** - The appeal is "Order now and we won't bill you until next month." Especially effective before the holidays, when people have lots of other expenses.

93) **Reduced Down Payment** - Frequently used as a follow-up in an extended mailing series. If customer does not respond to the regular offer in previous mailings, you reduce the down payment to make it easier for him to get started.

94) **Stripped-Down Products** - Also used in an extended mailing series. A home study school, for example, who doesn't get the prospect to order the full course will come back with a starter course at a lower price.

95) **Secret Bonus Gift** - Usually used with TV support. The commercial offers an extra bonus gift not mentioned in the ad or mailing being supported. Such as offering a bonus record if you write the album number in the "secret gold box" on the order form.

96) **Rush Shipping Service -** An appealing offer for things like seasonal gifts and film processing. Sometimes the customer is asked to pay an extra charge for this rush service.

97) **The Competitive Offer -** Can be a strong way to dramatize your selling story. Like Diner's Club offering to pay prospects $5.00 to turn in their American Express card.

98) **The Nominal Reimbursement Offer -** Used for research mailings. A token payment is offered to get somebody to fill out and return a questionnaire.

99) **Establish-the-Value Offer -** If you have an attractive free gift, you can build up its value and establish credibility by offering an extra one for a friend at the regular price.

Excerpted from *Profitable Direct Marketing* by Jim Kobs, published by Crain Books, 740 Rush Street, Chicago, Illinois 60611.

Here's a 100th item to this list: **the perpetual offer**. In business, this is the offer that provides personal benefit to a buyer when spending company money. One example of the perpetual offer is the airlines frequent flyer programs. Similar programs have been implemented by car rental, hotel and even catalog companies.

The growth of frequent traveler and frequent user programs has proven that prospects can become involved with a supplier on an ongoing basis. All the supplier need do is remind prospects of their current "use" status and show them when they will receive an award. The only draw back to this type of offer program is in curtailing or eliminating it. The plus of this type of program is the loyal and happy customer database it creates.

Frequent user customers on the database are less expensive to promote because they are known entities. The bonus awards cost less than promoting the market to stimulate an incremental sale. The success and continued growth of these types of programs are proof-positive of how effective marketing to this group of customers has become. In fact, the frequent traveler programs have created substantial joint ventures between airlines, hotels and car rental companies.

The offer must be in line with program objectives and with the company's operational ability to follow-up on responses. If the objective is lead generation, make an offer that will generate only as many leads as you can effectively handle. Too many leads can be even more destructive to the direct marketing program than not enough leads. Quantity will not be as important as quality.

Whether the offer is for leads or actual orders, make the offer only as enticing as you can afford. It makes no sense to give away profits to generate a response. There are exceptions when you might be willing to not make a profit on an initial order if the potential from future orders can make the customer profitable. This is fairly common in the catalog industry. You will always have to evaluate whether your offer was so lucrative that the quality of the responder is not as good as you had hoped.

When examining the economics of offers being developed, remember that the offers are a variable cost; only respondents are taking advantage of the offer. If a 10,000 piece mailing yields 500 respondents, the cost of the offer is only for the 500 respondents.

If a less attractive offer yielded 400 respondents, as opposed to the 500 mentioned earlier, evaluation is a little more difficult. Include the costs for the offer and then review the total direct marketing costs per responder and per order. Don't throw out the baby with the bath water because of the difference in response rates (400 vs. 500).

Lead programs are even more difficult to measure. You have to evaluate not just the response but the actual orders. Remember, ultimately you're in the sales business. Track your respondents to sales before you decide which offer is best.

Formats

Format represents the method selected to deliver the offer to the market. Many people refer to format as media. This definition is too restrictive since several of the formats do not fall within a media definition. Telemarketing, for example, is not traditionally defined as media. For the purpose of this discussion, we will use formats to encompass all of the ways to deliver a message to a market.

Once you have researched and determined your market segments, and have developed your offers per market segment, you are ready to select the format to deliver your message to your market. This process is often based on previous experience or on recommendations. While it's impossible to provide a fixed formula for selection of formats, it is possible to provide a structure for approaching the format decision.

There are two major selection criteria to consider when selecting formats:

1) The level of personal contact necessary to gain a sale or to generate a lead that can become a sale.

2) The dollars you are willing to spend to gain a sale or to generate a lead that can become a sale.

If we set up a hierarchy of formats (Illustration 5-1) from personal to impersonal contacts, we would see that a sales contact is on the top and as the most personal and network advertising on the bottom as the most impersonal. We will discuss each of these later in more detail. Now if we examine the associated cost per contact of each of these formats, we see that the higher the level of the personal contact, the greater the cost (Illustration 5-2).

Juxtaposing the triangles (Illustration 5-3) provides a quick reference in helping you make general format selections.

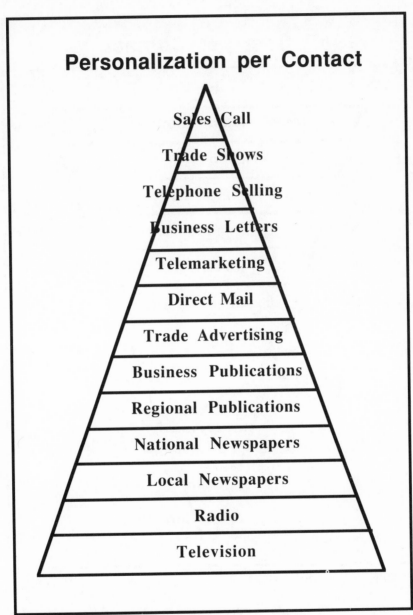

Personalization per Contact

Sales Call
Trade Shows
Telephone Selling
Business Letters
Telemarketing
Direct Mail
Trade Advertising
Business Publications
Regional Publications
National Newspapers
Local Newspapers
Radio
Television

Illustration 5-1: Personalization of the contact

Your experience, knowledge of your selling process and the financial

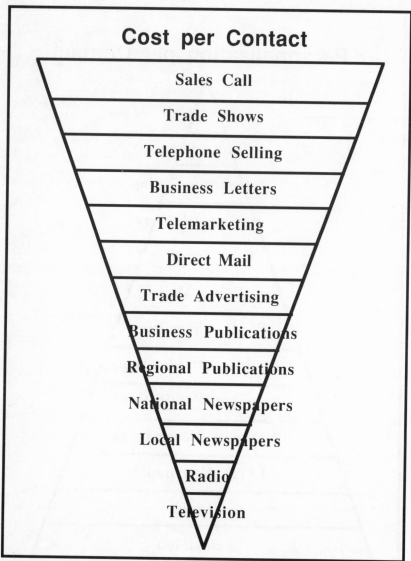

Cost per Contact

Sales Call

Trade Shows

Telephone Selling

Business Letters

Telemarketing

Direct Mail

Trade Advertising

Business Publications

Regional Publications

National Newspapers

Local Newspapers

Radio

Television

Illustration 5-2: Cost per contact

pro forma are the guides you should use when selecting formats. Most business-to-business applications use more than one format to deliver their messages to the their market. The workhorses of business-to-business direct marketing are telephone, mail and trade publi-

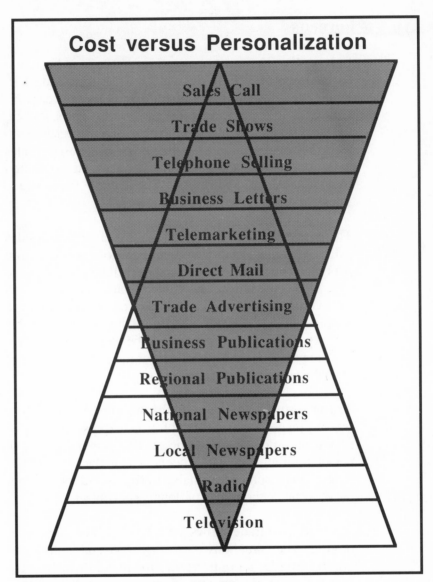

Cost versus Personalization

Sales Call

Trade Shows

Telephone Selling

Business Letters

Telemarketing

Direct Mail

Trade Advertising

Business Publications

Regional Publications

National Newspapers

Local Newspapers

Radio

Television

Illustration 5-3: Cost versus Personalization

cation space advertising. These three major formats provide the majority of business-to-business leads and orders.

Types of Formats

- **Sales calls**. The most common format used in business-to-business selling to deliver an offer to the market. While the sales call is not direct marketing, it is controllable and measurable in its cost and results. The sales call, the most personal contact, is the most expensive sales contact you can make. You can derive you own cost per sales call, as we discussed in Chapter two, or use published industry costs as a guideline. The average face-to-face sales call costs more than $250.

  This is not that high if you can make a sale on each sales call. Depending on the number of sales calls you require per order, you may find that personal selling can cost more than $1,000 per order. The same research that established the average cost per sales call also determined that the average industrial order costs more than $1,100 in sales call expenses. These costs should be part of your market plan so you can decide what part of the existing expenses should be displaced by direct marketing.

- **Trade shows**. An alternate format to personal selling where prospects are gathered for the express purpose of reviewing products and services. This is an extension of personal selling with a cost per contact in the $90. to $125 range. This assumes reasonable traffic for the show; if not the cost can be thousands of dollars per contact.

  A variation of trade shows are seminars. This technique of group sales situations is growing more and more popular. It provides an opportunity to spread the sales cost across a group of prospects. Seminars normally require a fair amount of front-end work to drive traffic but can be extremely effective in controlling the cost and quality of the sales contact.

- **Telephone selling**. Since this format represents a major opportunity for the business-to-business marketer we have devoted an entire chapter to this subject. For the purposes of evaluating the cost of this format, we will divide telephone into two major segments: telephone selling and telemarketing.

Telephone selling is when you put a qualified salesperson on the telephone to make sales calls as opposed to having the salesperson meet the prospects face-to-face. The use of telephone selling is fairly expensive per contact. Salespeople will be able to make more calls per day because travel time is eliminated. You probably will not see a rapid increase in sales when you introduce telephone selling because your sales force is already using telephone as a format. Telephone selling costs $50 to $125 per contact.

Telephone selling is difficult to measure in terms of both costs and results. In many businesses, telephone selling is considered a tool and a necessary part of the business. It is often segmented and measured. In many situations, the executive responsible for telephone selling does not even have control of or responsibility for the telephone bill. There is usually not a clear understanding of all the expenses involved in telephone selling.

- **Business Letter**. These are personal letters written, signed and mailed one at a time. They are used as a transmittal format for proposals, propositions, offers, contracts and general communication between a salesperson and his/her accounts. This format costs between $7.50 and $25 per contact.

- **Telemarketing**. This form of telephone is not dependent on the skill of the communicator but relies on a script, offer and marketing database to make a contact to the prospect. This format costs between $35 and $65 per hour of activity. Because it is a production activity, it is possible to make a business contact for $7 to $15. The cost per sale will depend on the offer, what is being sold and the leverage used in the script to increase response (premiums, incentives to the buyer, etc).

• **Direct Mail**. This is the workhorse of business-to-business direct marketing. We have provided a complete chapter on this important format. Direct mail can be used as part of an unsolicited promotion or as a form of fulfillment when a prospect requests more information about a company and its products. The cost of direct mail can range from a few cents per contact, in the case of card decks, to several dollars per contact for fulfillment or elaborate mail packages. As a general guideline, mail costs per contact range from 50 cents to $2.

• **Trade Advertising**. This is the most comfortable format used by business-to-business marketers. Trade publications are those publications that have circulation to a specific group. In most cases, subscribers do not pay for the publication: they receive the publication based on their industry, area of responsibility and/or position. To receive the publication, the subscriber completes a qualification card that provides information to the publication.

Advertisers in this type of publication can review subscriber information before placing print ads in the publication. Depending on circulation and area of concentration, cost per contact can vary. We estimate cost per contact to range between 6 cents and 15 cents. Contacts are based on circulation and are referred to as impressions, assuming that one person will see your ad one time. In addition, trade publications tend to have a high degree of pass-along to other readers. A manager will probably pass a publication to all of his/her subordinates.

Many trade publications offer reader service cards or "bingo" cards -- so called because the reader circles numbers on the card based on the numbers the magazine assigns to each ad in the book. The bingo cards are sent back to the magazine or a service bureau where they are processed. The leads are then passed along to the advertisers. Leads generated from this type of service should be carefully screened prior to being given to the sales force.

- **Business Publications**. These are general interest publications distributed as a result of paid subscriptions. Typically, little is known about their readers except what can be gained from address overlays or subscriber studies. These publications cross industries and are general in nature. If a product crosses many industries and levels of management, these books can work well for it. Like trade publications, business publications normally offer reader service cards to their subscribers. The cost per impression ranges from three cents to ten cents.

- **Regional Business Publications.** When servicing a regional market, regional business publications can be the best print investment. Regional publications are focused on business readers in a circulation area that approximates a given trade area. Regional buys in national publications may provide greater coverage than regional publications within a trade area, resulting in wasted circulation. While more expensive than national publications, regional publications may be a good alternative. The cost per impression ranges from nine cents to 20 cents.

- **National Daily/Weekly Newspapers**. There are several newsprint publications written for the business market or that have a business or money section. These newspapers have large circulations intended to cross all types and sizes of businesses. Advertising in these publications can provide large numbers of readers for a relatively low cost. Space ads run in these publications can generate a significant number of responders. Leads generated from this type of service should be carefully screened prior to sending them to the sales force. The cost per impression can be in the three cents to ten cent range.

Regional newspapers, like national dailies, can reach large numbers of readers in their business sections. Responders should be carefully screened for qualification. The cost per impression can be the same as in a national daily, however, the circulation contains some people who may not be in the business arena.

- **Local Newspapers**. This is an alternative for the business marketer who is servicing a local area. A national marketer will be concerned about costs, variations of sizes and submission requirements for ads between all of the local newspapers. Most local papers do not have a business section that will seek out target readers. An ad can be lost in the ROP (Run of Press); the publisher can place the ad anywhere in the publication. Costs range from ten cents to 25 cents per impression.

- **Radio**. This has not proven to be a successful stand-alone format for business-to-business direct marketing. Radio can support a regional or local marketing effort if the listener is going to receive printed material or additional information at a retail location. Costs per impression vary widely due to time of day, frequency of airing and the length of the ad. When planning to use radio, evaluate the type of listener the radio station represents and compare to the characteristics of your target.

- **Regional or Network Television.** Television has been used from time to time as a response format by companies that have large budgets and strong mark-ups on their products. More often, television is used as an image and awareness-builder. Direct response ads using 800 numbers can generate large quantities of unqualified responders.

Direct response television has been used successfully in the consumer world where targeting and segmentation are not as critical as in business-to-business. Because there are many people viewing the ad who are not qualified, the cost per *qualified* contact is very high. The cost per contact is very low compared to other formats, but with no way to target the message to a defined group of prospects the quality of any responder has to be carefully examined. Leads generated from this type of format should be carefully screened prior to sending them to the sales force. Most responders will not be qualified. Cost per impression can be from one to nine tenths of a cent. Although the cost per impression is attractive, there is a high amount of waste in contacting the wrong people.

Copy

This area seems to receive the most attention in the development of the direct marketing promotion. It is clearly an important element within direct marketing, however it will have the least impact on the success of your promotion. It is at the copy level that we spend the more time on the **It** than on the them -- the prospects in your market.

Richard S. Hodgson, in his book, *Direct Mail and Mail Order Handbook* (published by Dartnell, Chicago, Illinois 60640) does an excellent job of providing directions on how to prepare and review direct marketing and direct mail copy. Some of his thoughts and recommendations are given below:

Seek an Expert

The best advice on copy which can be given to any direct mail advertiser is to seek an experienced *direct mail* copy expert. Then work with him or have him work with your copywriters to develop the best techniques to meet the specific communications problems involved.

With such guidance, the odds are that you or your copywriting personnel will learn many of the techniques that lead to success, and eventually others will be turning to you for direct mail copy help.

In the absence of in-person help from an expert, turn to some of the helpful books on direct mail copywriting that are available.

Because there are so many detailed and helpful volumes available on the subject of direct mail copy, it is our primary purpose to provide some basic guidelines for successful copywriting. This material is presented to assist you in evaluating copy, rather than to try to teach writing techniques.

One technical approach to creating copy is to use the AIDA formula (Attention, Interest, Desire, Action). also used in training a sales representative an approach to selling situations.

Attention - The direct marketing contact should get the recipient to look at it and focus on its message. This is only accomplished by offering the recipients something of interest to them. Announcing a new product in the opening message does not get anyone's attention unless you relate what the new product is going to do for them.

Interest - Once you have the recipient's attention, you can deliver the benefits and offer of your promotion.

Desire - With the recipients interest aroused, you can begin to move to close. Restate points of interest in customized terms that are personalized to the recipient's needs. Do not confuse the product's features with the benefits they provide. The classic example is that you are not selling *dril! bits* you are selling *holes*.

It's easy to spend a great deal of time writing about the features of *drill bits*: hardened steel, ground edges, length, weight, etc. What the recipient wants to have is perfect little *holes*. Explain how the *drill bits* will create those perfect little *holes* to satisfy the recipient's needs. If you never make the transition from features to benefits, you will never arouse desire.

Action - This is what it is all about. Many direct marketers never call the prospect to action. You should begin all promotion efforts, including copy, by developing the action you want the recipient to take. Start with the action and weave it through the entire promotion rather than trying to tie it in as an afterthought. Don't be afraid to call the recipient to action frequently throughout the promotion. For example, each time a benefit is mentioned, explain that the recipient can have it now by going to the action step. This is no different than *trail closing* in face-to-face selling.

Illustration 5-4 gives a methodology for developing direct response copy. AIDA is only one formula you can use to organize the development of direct marketing copy. Hodgson supplies several other for-

---

Direct Marketing Copy Checklist

Before you start to write

1) Develop the action you want the recipient to take.
2) List all your product's features and associated benefits.
   This is done by listing a feature, followed by the words "What this means to you is..." Answering the statement which provides the benefit.
3) Rank benefits in order of importance to the recipient.
4) Identify someone you know who personifies the recipient you are trying to reach, so that you are writing to a person rather than a concept.

Writing Copy

1) Write your action step(s).
2) Using the AIDA formula, create several attention-getting headlines and select the best one.
3) As your message unfolds, keep your copy moving. Frequently remind the reader of the benefits your product will deliver and continually call to action.
4) As for the order. Ask for the order. Ask for the order.
5) If your message is to be printed, make sure it is appealing to the eye. Dense copy and long paragraphs produce little white space where the reader can rest.

Illustration 5-4: A direct marketing Copy Checklist.

mulas that you might find helpful. No matter what approach to copy-writing you use, Illustration 5-5, the checklist by Maxwell Ross can be helpful.

Checklist for Better Direct Mail Copy
Prepared by Maxwell C. Ross
Copy Technique

1) Does the lead sentence get in step with your reader at once?
2) Is your lead sentence more than two lines long?
3) Do your opening paragraphs promise a benefit to the reader?
4) Have you fired your biggest gun first?
5) Is there a big idea behind your letter?
6) Are your thoughts arranged in logical order?
7) Is what you say believable?
8) Is it clear how the reader is to order - and did you ask for the order?
9) Does the copy tie in with the order form - and have you directed attention to the order form in the letter?

Copy Editing

10) Does the letter have"you" attitude all the way through?
11) Does the letter have a conversational tone?
12) Have you formed a "bucket brigade" through your copy?
13) Does the letter score between 70 and 80 words of one-syllable for every 100 words of copy?
14) Are there any sentences which begin with an article - a, an, or the - where you might have avoided it?
15) Are there any places where you have strung together too many prepositional phrases?
16) Have you kept out "wandering" verbs?
17) Have you used action verbs instead of noun construction?
18) Are there any "thats" you do not need?
19) How does the copy rate on such letter craftsmanship points as (a) using active voice instead of passive, (b) periodic sentences instead of loose, (c) too many participles, (d)splitting infinitives, (e) repeating your company name too many times?
20) Does your letter look the way you want it to? (a) placement of page, (b) no paragraphs over six lines, (c) indentation and num-bered paragraphs, (d) underscoring and capitalization used spar-ingly, (e) punctuation for reading ease.

Illustration 5-5: Checklist for better direct mail copy.

Business Personalities

Successful business-to-business direct marketers try to align the personalities of their promotion with the personalities of the people who are going to receive the promotion. This means marketing to the individual -- not to his/her position within the company. However, sometimes, as we will explore later, personality type and position can be related. When a company's purchasing procedures involve multiple buyers who use a single purchasing agent, this process becomes more difficult. So we must look to the promotion itself -- through its design, copy and graphics -- to project its personality clearly, one that will match that of the business executive we are targeting.

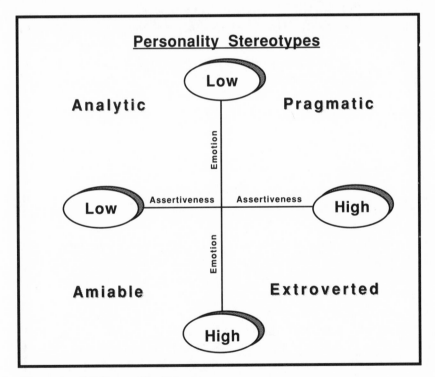

Illustration 5-6: Personality Stereotypes
The four stereotype personalities are charted by the point at which assertiveness intersects with emotion. A highly emotional but unassertive individual, therefore, can be classified as "amiable."

While all people may be created equal, all people do not make buying decisions for the same set of reasons. People are all driven by an almost unexplainable group of forces. Psychology has developed stereotypes to help categorize the many types of people.

Business purchasers can be defined using four of the major personality types: pragmatic, extroverted, amiable and analytic. These four stereotypes are determined by the intersection of a person's assertiveness and emotion, from low to high on a set of axes. (See Illustration 5-6)

Now, let's take a look at each of the personality types:

   • **Pragmatic** - These people are businesslike; they don't like to waste time or take vacations, and they make quick decisions based on facts. Pragmatic individuals buy condensed books and use a highlighter to emphasize major points. They judge a seminar on its value, not on its presentation; they would prefer to receive an executive summary of its main points. They don't like spectator sports; they would rather participate (except golf, which wastes

Pragmatic	
Do's	**Don'ts**
• Be clear, specific, brief.	• Don't ramble with long prose.
• Stick to business.	
• Provide facts and figures about effectiveness of options.	• Don't try to build a personal relationship.
	• Don't speculate or offer assurances.
• Call to action by referring to objectives and results.	
• Provide factual alternatives.	• Don't try to convince by personal means
	• Don't dictate or direct.
• Make ordering easy.	• Don't use complicated merchandising gimmicks or involvement.

Illustration 5-7: Dealing with the Pragmatic Personality.

too much time). Efficiency is important to them. They are top managers, or striving to reach that position.

- **Extroverted** - Aggressive, impulsive and very friendly, these people make fast decisions based on excitement or enthusiasm. They go to a seminar and are inspired by the presenters; they don't like charts and graphs, and their desks are usually sloppy. Motivation is a driving force. This is the type of individual most often found in sales and marketing environments.

- **Amiable** - These individuals like to develop relationships with people and things, and are probably in management positions only in larger companies where the system provides barriers against pressure. They drive older cars because they dislike car salespeople. People who fit this stereotype make decisions slowly, based on what will make everybody happy. Their reason for attending a seminar is simply to be around similar people, and while they are there, they worry about whether or not everyone is having a good time. General traits are openness and

---

Extroverted

Do's
- Offer the dream and intentions.
- Talk about people and their goals.
- Give ideas for implementing action.
- Provide testimonials from people seen as important.
- Offer special immediate extra incentives for willingness to place orders.

Don'ts
- Don't legislate.
- Don't drive facts and figures.
- Don't "dream" too much or they will put down the promotion.
- Don't be dogmatic.
- Don't be impersonal or judgmental.

Illustration 5-8: Dealing with the Extroverted Personality.

friendliness. This type of person is found in personnel, or perhaps as an administrative assistant or staff manager who has protection from dealing with front-line confrontation.

- **Analytic** - A breed apart, these individuals are comfortable with slide rules and calculators, and like to be surrounded by gadgets. Because they can't seem to get enough information, they generally make slow decisions. They can attend a 10-day seminar about coaxial cable, for instance, and feel it was a shallow presentation. Analytical people are often engineers or accountants.

It is important to note that these are broad generalizations. Everyone exhibits pieces and parts of each personality style from time to time. If, however, you have identified yourself with two of these personality types, they are most likely adjacent on the graph, and not diagonal to each other. While you can move up and down the emotional scale and back and forth on the assertiveness scale, you will seldom change styles in adjacent quadrants. This is important to remember as you define your promotion's personality.

Amiable

Do's

- Use personal comments to lead offers
- Present your case softly, non-threateningly.
- Involve the reader by explaining "how."
- Be casual and informal.
- Provide personal guarantees to minimize risks and give assurances of benefits.

Don'ts

- Don't stick coldly to business.
- Don't be domineering, demanding or threatening about position or power.
- Don't debate facts and figures.
- Don't patronize or demean.
- Don't offer guarantees or assurances you can't fulfill.

Illustration 5-9: Dealing with the Amiable Personality.

If you want to shift your promotions personality or evaluate whom you are selecting as business customers, take a look at some of the do's and don'ts for each personality type. (See Illustration 5-7 thru 5-10). Then review your (or your competitor's) promotions with these do's and don'ts in mind. To whom are you actually directing your promotion?

The common complaint of business-to-business direct marketers is, "We don't know who is doing the buying." A purchasing agent, for example, may place orders for several people or departments. But, if you allow yourself to express some opinions in your promotion, to stereotype a few titles or functions and relate them to your promotion, you can guess fairly accurately who is doing the buying.

First, we'll stereotype a few promotion personalities. As you will see, the personality of the promotion selects the personality of the reader. Then, we'll see how the promotion/person match is developed. We'll examine the personalities of catalogs as a way to contrast the different approaches.

Analytic

Do's

- Be direct; stick to business.
- Support your credibility by listing pros and cons.
- Be accurate and allow for ways to verify reliability.
- Provide solid, tangible, practical evidence.

Don'ts

- Don't be circuitous, casual or informal.
- Don't be too brief.
- Don't use testimonials.
- Don't use gimmicks or clever, quick manipulations.

Illustration 5-10: Dealing with the Analytic Personality

Quill Corporation's catalog is an example of an assertive catalog. It has pages of items and prices, best buys, guarantees and fast delivery. Star bursts and bright colors characterize this non-personalized catalog which definitely targets the pragmatic or extrovert type. There is enough information for these assertive people to make a decision on office supplies without any long explanations. If a purchasing agent or office administrator is the decision-maker, this highly assertive book may be a turn off. People on the low scale in assertiveness may not feel comfortable with the Quill Catalog, unless price alone keeps them interested.

MISCO, Moore and Sorbus catalogs on the other hand, all have low-assertive personalities. There is an occasional price highlight or vignette, but generally, they reach out to office and support personnel with a comfortable approach that features pages of consumables, as well as items to make life easier.

Inmac does an excellent job of traveling several lanes of personality selection. Benefit headlines attract the pragmatics, well written copy that leads from benefits to features attracts the analytics and the amiables. Clever use of vignettes and detailed photos provide something for just about everyone. Since research reveals that business catalog buyers purchase through a primary and secondary catalog only, Inmac is probably one of the top two in most businesses.

Wear-Guard - "America's leading supplier of work clothing and uniforms" - has taken a dramatic strategic shift in personality. Formerly Eastern Uniform, Wear-Guard has lightened up over the years, from slashed prices in red (assertive) to re-pricing in black (less assertive). Overall, though, the book was still reaching out to low-emotion buyers. Squared photos were backed by short benefit and longer feature copy, with price, sizes and colors as the copy thrust, and product personalization as an option.

Maybe the adage "Too soon old, too late smart" does not apply to Wear-Guard. A new catalog re-positioned some of the same personalized products as identity apparel or image-makers. This re-drafted catalog shows much larger, two-page spreads, of happy people displaying corporate wear. Photography, layout and design are more dramatic - and much more emotional. This re-positioning definitely reaches out for the amiables (to belong) and the extroverts (to show off) with an appeal not seen in Wear-Guard's previous catalogs.

Probably the least assertive business catalogs are those that feature industrial products, like C&H, which present page after page of merchandise displayed without emotion. This approach seems to reach for an analytic buyer. 20th Century Plastics is a good example of a nonassertive, low-emotion catalog. One of its editions throws us a ringer: a free travel alarm clock with a customer's order -- definitely an emotional (personal) appeal. (Who needs an alarm clock at work anyway?)

NEBS is a classic example of a high-assertive, low-emotion catalog. The business forms for small business cataloger presents just that - - no-nonsense pages of useful items offering forms to solve the problems of small businesses, an approach directed to the pragmatic personality. For a small business owner, this is a no-wow, no-flash book of solutions in a world of chaos.

Two of the least emotional, least assertive catalogs are the house catalogs of Hewlett Packard and Digital Equipment. Customers receive pages of items accompanied by long explanatory copy, which, because of its lack of flow, suggest that, perhaps, the catalogs were created by committee with no concept of catalog/recipient personality in mind. In both cases, the catalogs feature excellent photography and superior print production. There are attempts to include people to provide a human touch, but the results, in our opinion, are bland. Hewlett-Packard and Digital Equipment might want to re-examine their catalogs, then ask the question: If I weren't a customer, would I order from this catalog?

The use of catalogs to reach business buyers is growing. When considering catalog marketing, look carefully at whom you want to sell and define the stereotype buyer. Then develop the catalog personality to attract this buyer.

<u>Creativity</u>

Creativity is probably the one area or endeavor feared the most and understood the least. There seems to be some mystique that there are a few creative people and then there are the rest of us. The rest of us sit in awe of those few creative types that can turn a phrase, have the big new idea or draw a pretty picture. In truth, no one has any reason to take a back seat to anyone else.

By merely agreeing with the premise that only a few people are creative, you put yourself in a box that keeps you from being creative. Once you have decided that you can't be creative, you are guaranteed not to be.

The people who get the creative labels are the people who are willing to take a chance and let their ideas be revealed to the rest of the world. You may have an idea from time to time but are unwilling to make it public for fear of being ridiculed or laughed at. Your worst fear may be that you'll get the cosmic raspberry from the omnipotent grand phobia.

Ideas are like water in a brook. Sometimes the brook runs fast. Sometimes there are large pools where the brook doesn't seem to run at all. Sometimes there are falls where the water cascades into space with great force and out of control, free falling to once again join the flow as the water races to the next larger body of water.

You can and should let your ideas flow freely. Like the brook, you should get into the flow of things. Without sharing your ideas, no matter what brook you are part of, you will become stagnant, uninteresting and boring.

When you were young, no matter where you were or how many toys you had, the strangest things could provide hours of enjoyment. You would receive a new bicycle and end up playing with the box instead of the bike. Your mind would fill with so many ideas on what the box could become that there were not enough hours in the day to live out all the fantasies. Who needs reality? Nobody told you it was only a box. You might even have put the box away at night and left the bike out in the rain. Eventually the box would shred, and the bike would become a motorcycle, a chariot, or a rocket.

As we grow older, we become less free with our ideas. Peers tell us we're weird if we don't act like everyone else. Peer pressure stifles creativity. Playing in a box at eight years old is okay. At 13 it is not. It is amusing to realize that what others think of our actions can alter our creative abilities. All we're doing is suppressing the creative juices to allow us to fit into our social environment.

As we've grown older we have moved from one box that was an expression of our creative freedom, to an invisible box which curtails our creative expression. We worry about others making fun of our ideas, so we keep them to ourselves. We learn to keep our mouths shut so no one will think we're one of those weird creative people. We would rather be viewed as good managers, in control at all times and supportive of the company line. We let the creative types have all of the fun and take all of the risk. They get to play in the box without fear of reprisal. They are *supposed* to do all of the weird stuff. They are supposed to dress funny and they even get to laugh and shout. We want to be real careful not to be confused as being part of this group. Let's be sure we don't do any of the weird things because people may start thinking we're creative.

As consultants we consistently tell clients that they already have all of the good ideas. Our job is to organize their ideas into marketing programs that will help them achieve their objectives. As soon as this concept is explained, the client begins to look at us strangely. We were detailed to bring the creative dust and sprinkle it over the business plan to make magic.

Let's look at the steps you should go through to establish the creative process:

    1) State the objectives in a quantifiable form. Even creative

people need a destination. If you don't have a destination and you don't know where you're going, any road will get you there. Objectives provide the common denominator for all further discussion.

2) Gather all, or as many people in the company, that are involved in the project into a group. Review with them the objectives and the information available about the product or service to be discussed.

3) Set upon the task of developing the *Big Idea* that will strategically position the product or service into the proper market. The *Big Idea* should be developed into the language that will appeal to the market we're trying to reach.

As in Chapter two, the intensive planning session is an ideal way to run a brainstorming or creative meeting. With all of the involved personnel in a room, start the creative ideas flowing; the energy will grow as the process moves forward.

Start by asking the group members for their thoughts on how to communicate the product or service to the market place. What is the first thing you want the prospect to know about the product? What is the headline? In other words, how can you approach someone with your product or service, and what are the first words that you would use to get their attention?

The creative people can develop these original thoughts. The initial concept will give the creative organization a starting point. From this starting point, with all the involved personnel contributing their thoughts, a great deal of time can be saved. All of the people involved in the project have contributed to the project from the germination, which will save a lot of sign off time later on.

Brainstorming Sessions

The real challenge is getting the non-creative people to participate in the creative process of generating the *Big Idea*. The brainstorming session is an organized, structured approach to having everyone actively participate in creating ideas. All of the individuals involved in the project should be asked to participate in the session. The session should be conducted in a conference room, classroom or office large enough to allow everyone to be comfortable.

The following guidelines will help you to run a more successful brainstorming session:

1) No negatives. No one can say anything negative about any idea offered by any member of the group. The session moderator should make sure this rule is adhered to. A negative can seriously stifle the creative process.

2) There are no rules of communication. A group member can express himself verbally, in written words, graphically (even if he/she can't draw well -- nobody cares -- it is the idea that is important) or by acting out an idea. The formal decorum that is normally part of the corporate culture should be suspended. All group members must be able to move about freely. Oftentimes, when the energy level is high and people get excited, it is difficult to stay seated.

3) Nobody is more important than anyone else. No matter what the pecking order of the organization, in the brainstorming session, all participants are equal.

4) No interruptions. Once convened, the group should not be interrupted for phone calls or any other reason. Interruptions divert energy of the group and often stop the flow of ideas. For this reason, brainstorming should be scheduled for and limited tor one to two hours. In less than one hour it is difficult to get the ideas flowing. After more than two hours, individuals begin to get concerned about their work and are no longer thinking of the project at hand. For major efforts, the group may meet off-site or

during non-working hours. This tends to limit interruptions and will help maintain focus.

The session can be broken into several sessions. This will make continuity of thoughts difficult, and it will take some time to re-establish the energy level of the previous session. We don't suggest multiple sessions, but some business situations will leave no alternative.

5) The group leader is responsible for writing all of the ideas on a board or flip charts. Flip charts are ideal because as pages are filled up, they can be removed from the easel and taped to the walls allowing all generated ideas to be in constant view of the group.

As the *Big Idea* is developed and evolves, it should be reviewed in light of the objectives.

Group members are welcome to have pads but they are discouraged from taking notes. This is an excuse to bring structure back into their lives and restrict the freedom being sought. Pads can be used to jot down thoughts to be introduced later.

6) Once a *Big Idea* is generated, all members should state their views. This is a forced communication to allow each member to support, enhance or challenge the *Big Idea*.

If this step is deleted, disgruntled group members will go back to their responsibilities with the thought of killing the *Big Idea* down the road. If the *Big Idea* cannot stand the the test of all of the members of the group, then it needs to be revisited in another brainstorming session.

When planning a brainstorming session, consider the value of the management time it will require. It may be impractical to have the company president involved in a session that pertains to decisions that have not been clearly delegated and identified.

The brainstorming session can be run more effectively by someone from outside of the company. This is the off-the-plane syndrome. For some reason, people who are brought in from the outside, particularly if they travel from out of town, have greater credibility then people from within one's own organization. These outsiders may not have any more knowledge or experience, but they are considered experts and can be helpful in developing the *Big Idea*.

The outside person can be especially effective if he/she is perceived as a creative type. Employees are often constrained by the formal and informal pecking order within their company. Employees are also interested in their own personal situation within the company. They may have a tendency to control the discussion to their own benefit; this is a natural human reaction. An outsider can keep the session impartial and moving forward.

Once the *Big Idea* is generated, the creative group can explore versions of the idea. They can also put the idea into a form that satisfies the technical requirements of the promotion.

Brainstorming is your chance to be a kid again. You are still just as creative as when you played with the box instead of the toy bicycle. The toy was structured, the box wasn't. Have some fun; let fly with a few wild ideas from time to time, even if they're not part of a brainstorming session. You may be surprised by how many other people might join your brook and journey to the the sea. You may find that that your little trickle of an idea creates a flow that turns into a river. The energy you create, like a river, can move mountains over time.

Take the no negative reaction to ideas rule of brainstorming, and try it in your office for one week. You'll be amazed at how many ideas will be offered up on almost every subject. Creativity is just the free flow of ideas. Everyone has ideas, therefore everyone is creative. The real creative challenge is finding an environment that enhances the free flow communication of ideas.

Testing

The creative process will often produce more than one *Big Idea.* The problem then becomes determining which concept will produce the best results. Even with a single *Big Idea,* there may be alternative ways to implement the idea. For example, the *Big Idea* may be to send a special offer to the president of prospect companies and several formats and packages are suggested that can all satisfy the concept. How do you determine which concept will produce the best results? Which *Big Idea* is really the best for the company?

Direct marketing allows you to test many approaches and scientifically determine which is best. To test, you exert one or more marketing efforts to small, representative samples of your market. Then you evaluate the responses to determine which marketing effort yielded the greatest for the marketing dollar. The representative samples should be statistically significant, and the market conditions should be identical at roll-out as during the test period.

The biggest problem in testing is that the forces causing a market to act and react in a certain way are out of your control. In consumer testing, there is a better chance of testing a representative sample because a lot more is known about the people making the decisions.

In consumer testing, you know the following:

1) The person receiving the message is either the president or chairman of the household. Most married men believe they are the president, and know they must report to the chairman of the board who is the chief executive officer of the relationship.

2) When mail is used to deliver the message, the target reviews it within five minutes after arriving home from

work, while standing in the kitchen. The mail is not read at that time, but only reviewed as part of "the kitchen cut," to see if it will be read later or thrown directly in the trash. When phone is used, the target is generally in and available between 5 PM and 9 PM on weekdays and during the day on weekends.

3) Houses buy people, people don't buy houses. The economics of a house select who will live in that house. With census, list, database and all the fancy overlays available in the consumer universe, you can pinpoint which houses meet certain criteria. The demographics and even the psychographics of the occupants of houses can be established prior to attempting a direct marketing contact. When the occupants move, you will want to follow them to their new location, which will be approximately the same demographically as the old location.

You will also want to contact the new occupants of the first home; they will probably have the same characteristics as the original occupants. They will probably have the same disposable income as your customers. You can create need and desire, you are talking to people with authority and if they are interested in your offer, money is probably available.

The biggest flaw in this approach to consumers has been the elderly market, where small retired incomes and houses in less expensive areas have masked people with large cash reserves.

The consumer environment is considerably easier to target than the business universe. Businesses also have some common characteristics:

1) There are a finite number of businesses. While there also are a finite number of households, that number is in excess

of 90 million. These are conveniently structured into ZIP codes and will eventually be even more exact with ZIP +4.

There are only a few million businesses in the United States. Does it make sense to develop a test program, train your organization and then test 50 companies?   If the stakes are high, yes.

Generally, there isn't time for this kind of luxury, so the test is an effort to the entire market. Also, inherent in the smaller market is the fear of upsetting the apple cart. You are less likely to test a wide selection of offers because you fear that prospects may learn of them through their independent interaction with others. Test variations are seldom a problem for consumer marketers. If a consumer becomes angry and stops buying, there are plenty of other prospects to sell to -- but even this philosophy is changing. In the business arena, losing a customer could represent a significant amount of total business and the risks need to be more carefully evaluated.

2) When promoting to a business, you are never entirely sure who will make the buying decision. You cannot be sure what the process of reviewing your offer may be or to whom you should speak. In today's corporate world, the decision maker will get the blame if something goes wrong. On the other hand, if the decision proves to be good, at least six people will take credit. Politics are always present in the business world and can have a significant impact on your selling efforts.

3) You must overcome two sets of reviews for each person you reach in the business world. First, you must overcome the emotional, personal bias of the person. Then you must overcome the logical, role-playing process that the same person fulfills as an employee.

4) Response in the consumer world can and usually does mean an order. In the business universe, response is often the first step of the selling process, particularly when selling capital goods. Response rates are important but should not be the primary measurement vehicle used to determine the success of the direct marketing program. Establish a chain of events or activities that must happen to generate an order. Each link of the chain will probably represent a contact with the prospect or customer. Each will have a cost and a success rate for moving to the next link. When the process is complete, you will be able to measure sales results and compare them to the investment.

A 0.01% response rate could make a lot of money, and a 50% response rate could lose money. The key to measurement and testing is to structure the project so you can measure the actual sales, cost per order and profitability of the project. Don't fall short by only measuring the initial response rate.

With all of the problems in marketing to the business world, is it worth doing any testing? Yes. You can and should test marketing concepts to determine the best and most profitable approach. Test the big things first: those areas that can have a big impact on costs, results and ultimate profitability of the project. The elements you test should be those changes that have the highest probability of improving final results, not just the initial response rate.

The elements that can have the greatest impact on the success of the program, are exactly the same as the areas discussed earlier:

List
Offer
Format
Copy

The rules for constructing tests are fairly simple. Start at the top of

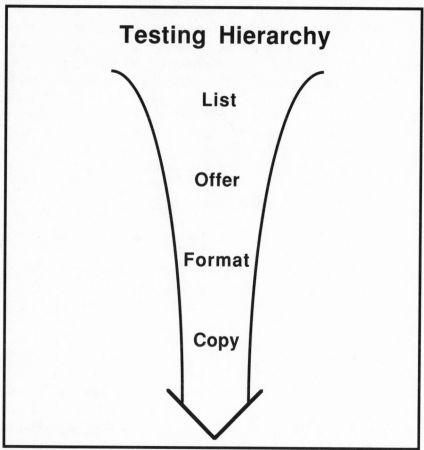

Testing Hierarchy

List

Offer

Format

Copy

Illustration 5-11: Testing Hierarchy

the list and work you way down. Illustration 5-11 shows the hierarchy of the variables.

The corollary is never start at the bottom, with the copy, and work your way up. Never, never test more than one variable at a time. If you do, you will not be able to determine which variable influenced any change in the results. The size of the group you're selling to will limit the amount and types of testing you will be able to do.

If you have a large universe to select from, you can design tests that are fairly complex and complete. If you only have a few thousand names and you're planning to use only direct mail, testing more than one variable may prove impossible. Whenever you construct a test, you should test against a control package that has a proven history of response and sale results. This will allow you to measure the success of your new approach at the start and throughout the program.

Let's assume that you have a fairly large universe, and you are going to test five different lists (L1-L5), five offers (O1-O5) and five formats (F1-F5). You will not test copy because while a four dimensional test can be calculated, it cannot be easily illustrated.

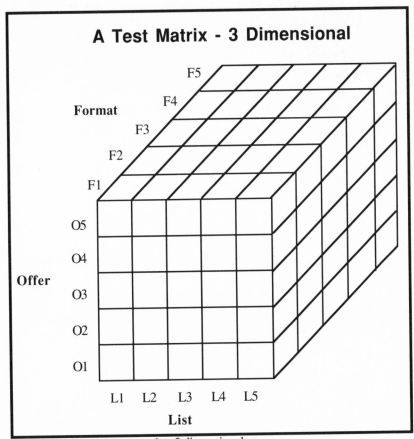

Illustration 5-12: A test matrix - 3 dimensional

As demonstrated in Illustration 5-12, the intersection of each variable must be filled with a representative group of your market in order provide reliable results. Each test group or cell will be assigned a code to identify which list, offer and format that were used. This code will be used to measure results and determine the best programs.

Assigning the test cell codes can be an important part of the your direct marketing program. If you want your codes to make sense, you can build intelligence directly into the codes. In this example, the first cell could be L1O1F1, next L2O1F1 and so on. Or you can assign codes in sequence from 001 to 125, representing the number of test cells (5x5x5=125). It will be a lot easier for analysis and communication if you don't build intelligence directly into the codes. For some reason, intelligent codes tend to become the masters of the program they represent in order not to violate the intelligence they represent. In addition, intelligent codes can be more difficult to handle for data entry. Numeric information is much easier to enter into a computer and is less prone to transcription errors.

Unfortunately, the lack of uniformity in company names and abbreviations makes complete and accurate measurement almost impossible. In addition, no matter how diligent you are in coding solicitations, 25% to 50% of responses may not be able to be tracked. This is because some respondents do not use your response format or vehicle. The only consolation in this area is that the lack of measurement is uniform and consistent across the entire program and therefore it is predictable.

The test looks like a box with 125 cells inside. This means you must have 125 separate promotional efforts. If you need five sales per cell to have a large enough sample to evaluate results and you anticipate five sales per 1,000 people contacted, you need 125,000 prospects. This maybe a reasonable test concept, but it is not necessary if you are willing to evaluate the results and not just the numbers.

You can easily eliminate every second cell in the test and still have enough information to judge the best list, best offer and best format.

If all remaining cells perform equally well, the cell with the lowest cost would be the best direct marketing program.

Very often in business-to-business selling, the sale is more complex than one contact and may take a prolonged period of time. If the selling effort is traditionally a four month effort, you will be unable to evaluate results for four to six months. This depends on how long it takes to get a prospect to respond to the direct response effort. This time delay is frequently not accepted by upper management and becomes a primary reason for not testing. There are some techniques that can be used to give preliminary indication of the success of the program, but you have to track the results to measure the ultimate success of the test.

If you try to test using the strict rules and evaluation techniques required for statistical accuracy, you may never get anything implemented beyond the test stage. If the sell cycle is long, your odds of statistical measurement will be reduced even further. You can also over test as demonstrated by the 125-cell test discussed earlier. In many situations you'll have to use your instincts and prior selling history to construct stages of the sale that can be measured as you move through the process.

Your customer file and prior selling experience should be helpful in determining the best arena for your marketing efforts. Don't spend time and money majoring in the minors.

If you have a product that can be consumed by many businesses, test lists that will give you a representative result for an industry segment and company size (if this is a key variable). Don't test two similar lists from different suppliers unless you're sure that the industry is good for you.

One test effort should be aimed at the people by name and another group targeted by title. When you rent a list of stapler buyers, Jim Smith, stapler buyer may have left the company for which he is listed. Your promotional effort does not reach Jim because he is no longer there. If you had aimed your effort at the "person who buys staplers," you would have a better chance of reaching Jim's replacement. You always have to evaluate whether to name or title address your mailings; understand the differences in response and order rates.

Once you know your arena, try different types of lists -- customer, compiled, responder and subscription -- to discover which type gives the best results. In some consumer promotions, some lists are too small to test because they don't have a large enough universe to roll out. There is no business list too small if it happens to yield the results you need. If there are a limited number of prospects in your universe, you may have to use a variety of small lists.

Repetition in the business universe is normally successful. You can and should go back to the same businesses every time you change your offer, format or copy. If a promotion is successful, you should go back with the same effort as soon as you can. In fact, you should continue to reuse successful lists until they no longer work.

A common mistake is to discontinue a successful program because personnel have become bored with the campaign. Personnel assume that the market is also bored with the promotion. Let the results tell you when the program is no longer effective. When you think a promotion is no longer effective, test a new format or offer against the existing approach. The results will determine which program to continue. You should always be trying to "*beat the champ*". Create a program that outperforms your best existing program.

When testing offers, test significant differences. Don't test a free pen against a key chain as a premium for attending a seminar. Test a free pen against a free car. You may have seen an offer to buy 100 pens for only $39.95 and get 400 free . It's more than likely that the selling price for 500 pens is $39.95. It has been determined through testing that this offer called the most people to action.

Limiting the time of an offer can build a sense of urgency into the mind of your prospect. Time limits can be effective motivators. Be cautious to have the offer expire as indicated by the time limit.

Free gifts work better in business offers than discount pricing does. Prospects like to receive something they can enjoy in their personal lives for purchasing things at their place of business. Look at the offers from airlines and hotels to encourage frequent use, family travel and lodging as a result of company expenditures. Consider these offers as executive green stamps that can be used personally. Powerful, wealthy executives who can afford to pay their own way are taking advantage of these offers. You may want to examine these frequent user programs and attempt to emulate them to build ongoing relationships with customers.

The offer should promote the next link in the chain that ultimately leads to the sale. If you try to sell the product too soon, you could lose the prospect or the opportunity. Sell the next contact at each link in the chain.

The formats most frequently tested and used in the business marketplace are print advertising, direct mail and telemarketing. Since most businesses use communications to generate leads for their sales force, the formats are used in combination with each other as part of the chain of contacts needed to accomplish a sale. The cost comparison of the various media is described in illustration 5-3. In lead generation, there are no rules as to which format is the best to use first. Test where in the process you'll need phone, mail or whatever.

In testing formats, it is important to know the personality of the people you are trying to reach. You spend a great deal of money training your salespeople to understand the type of individual you're trying to sell. If you're uncertain about who you're trying to reach, test formats that relate to various personalities.

Refer to the earlier discussion on business-to-business personalities. A model for stereotyping people is found in Illustration 5-6. Each general type of personality can be found in each person at any time at work or home. People are, however, generally constant in one quadrant and tend to move only to adjacent quadrants. People seldom move to non-adjacent areas.

Format and copy will reach out to the people that identify most with its approach. You will probably have to create different formats to reach different parts your market. Let's use the stapler example. Since the pragmatic only want to know product, price and guarantee, the promotion could be a picture of the stapler, price with a little print about our guarantee and printed on inexpensive uncoated stock. The promotion doesn't have to be personalized.

On the other hand, the extrovert wants to know the benefit of using the stapler and how it relates to them personally. You want to convince the prospect that your stapler is of the highest quality and will make him/her look better. Rich photography on quality coated stock enrich the image of the product.

The amiable will want to know that everybody that uses the stapler will be happy and content. Graphics showing happy people printed on rich stock will support the sale.

The analytic will want to know the specifications of the stapler: metal content, mean time between breakdown, weight, staples per minute potential, etc. Inexpensive paper with massive copy and small photographs will get the message across.

Which approach will work best can only be determined through testing and evaluating the results. Copy testing is seen in part in the format testing above. You can take the exact same layout for an space ad, mail effort or phone script and revisit the four main personality stereotypes. Your copy can be tailored to target different personalities and then test the results.

Format Selection

Now you have enough information to get yourself into real trouble. The big question after you digest all the previous material is: What is the right format and medium for your needs?

Format selection is directly related to your total budget and how much you can spend to acquire an order. For example, if you can afford to spend $100 per order and need 25 orders, your total budget is $2,500. You can't afford national TV on this budget, even if it could produce a cost per order of less than $100.

Chain Analysis

Assumptions: Historical performance data is available
            Existing customers will contribute $3 million in sales
            Product is sold by face-to-face sales representatives

Sales Goal	$6,500,000	
	- 3,000,000	(Sales to existing customers)
Net Goal	3,500,000	
	÷ 15,000	(Average order from new customers)
New Customers	= 233	(# new customers required)
	÷ 20%	(Sales rep closes 1:5 proposals)
	= 1,165	(# of proposals required)
	÷ 30%	(3:10 appointments end in proposal)
	=3,883	(# of appointments required)
	÷ 60%	(6:10 leads secure appointments)
	= 6,472	(# of leads required)

Leads from Advertising
Leads	3,000	
	x $80.00	(Average cost/lead, space ads)
	=$240,000	(Space ad budget)

Leads from Direct Marketing
Leads	3,480	(Remaining required leads)
	÷ 3%	(3% response rate)
	= 116,000	(# of direct mail pieces required)
	x $900/m	(Diret mail cost)
	= $104,400	(Direct mail buget)

Lead Generation Budget
Space	$240,000	
Direct mail	+ 104,400	
Total budget	=$ 344,400	

Illustration 5-13: Chain Analysis - determining volumes and budgets required prior to testing.

The other consideration is how many leads or sales you can handle. This will lead you to analyze the quality of the inquiries and not just the quantity. Too many leads is worse than not enough.

Timing is another consideration. You can generate telephone and local media placements much more quickly than a direct mail program or national publication advertising.

The major factor in determining the format you'll use is the target audience. If you're trying to sell office supplies to purchasing agents, it probably won't make sense to use broadcast media to reach them. Direct mail catalogs have proved effective in this arena.

Illustration 5-13, demonstrates one approach for setting up a model to evaluate the available funds for your promotion efforts. The model should review the entire process from initial contact to the ultimate order. This approach can be helpful in determining where to spend money in order to have the greatest result.

Evaluate the prospects you're trying to reach and the ability of certain formats to contact that particular group of people. For example, the cost-per-contact in a specific magazine may be attractive, but only a small percentage of the readership is a part of your prospect group. The cost-per-contact of your prospect group in this scenario could be higher than having a salesperson call directly on the prospect.

The more expensive the cost-per-contact the more directed and targeted it can be. You'll always be trading off costs and the ability to reach a specific market segment. The smaller a group of specific prospects, the harder they will be to reach. Direct mail and telemarketing are ideal vehicles to contact precisely targeted audiences.

Unfortunately, there is no magic formula or easy method of selecting the appropriate format or media to reach a specific target. It is easier to eliminate certain approaches because of expense and results considerations. The planning and creative brainstorming sessions are going to be critical in the selection of format and media.

Even after you have identified an approach, you should identify at least two alternatives and test both to see which is best. A direct marketing agency can be helpful in evaluating and creating different approaches to fulfill your requirements. After discovering a format and media that works and produces an acceptable cost per order, don't rest on your laurels. Look for other approaches that may improve on your in-place effort.

The old adage "We've always done it this way" can cost a lot of money. Looking for efficiencies in the relationships you have with your customers and your potential customers can be fruitful and exciting. Being completely sales force-oriented or channel of distribution-oriented is myopic.

The high technology industries are faced with an unusual problem: The prices of the products they sell are coming down while the cost of selling is going up. Companies in these industries which are not continually looking for better ways to sell and market their products will not survive.

A format or media that is successful today will not necessarily always be the best approach. Continually identify and test alternatives with the objective of *beating the champ*.

Formats obviously lend themselves to a given media. For example, catalogs are most often used in direct mail, however they can be inserted in newspapers or delivered by salespeople and can also be used as a handout. A advertisement will be used in a print format but has also been used as a reprint and sent as direct mail. Our definition of direct marketing demands that we continually seek to produce a lead or an order and that we use specialized promotional material. Trying to use a format that was designed for a different medium with a different objective can be far more expensive than creating the format for the medium.

In direct marketing, everyone can have a good idea. Evaluate the format and media creative alternatives in light of the financial implications. The best formula to use is: If the effort looks like it can meet your cost-per-order requirements, find a way to test it.

Multimedia Synergy

The combination of one or more formats or media can have dramatic effects on results. The use of a combination of media can be planned or accidental. For example, participating in a trade show at the same time as you are using direct mail in a particular market can boost direct mail results three or four times. In addition, the traffic at the trade show booth could be lifted. This response is most likely to occur when large companies have separate groups responsible for direct marketing, sales and trade shows.

It has been proven time and time again that there is a dramatic synergy in combining direct marketing promotions to substantially increase results. If planned properly, the combination of mail and telephone produces three to five times the results of either program individually.

If you are executing telemarketing lead-generation or sales programs, you should also use direct mail. This may not be immediately apparent, however telemarketing prospects will ask for more information as often as they accept the offer. The direct mail material used to fulfill this request for information will force you into a combined phone and direct mail program. The same scenario also applies to space advertising unless you are selling a product directly from the space ad.

These synergistic approaches may not be planned but required as you begin to implement any direct marketing promotion. Deal with prospects who request additional information as people who are beginning to close and not just another rejection. Often, particularly in telemarketing, prospects will request information simply to end the dialogue. The prospect does not want to be rude, so he/she requests additional information as a put-off. However, about 25% of this group of people can be converted to orders and sales if handled properly.

You may not consider this a synergistic promotion; you may look at it as simply linear common sense. Don't be misled; if you're using multiple formats and multiple media, there is a synergy in the promotions. Without proper planning and execution of the *Big Idea*, synergy can be reduced and sales opportunities lost.

These are the types of questions that are most often asked concerning multimedia:

- What happens when you use mail prior to telemarketing?
- What happens when you use direct response print advertising in a market at the same time you are doing a direct mail promotion?
- Does awareness advertising have any effect on the success of your direct mail or telemarketing programs?
- How important is the timing of direct mail followed by telemarketing?

There is a significant increase in response rates when mail is used prior to telemarketing. In Chapter six, we will discuss several specific programs that used mail and phone combined. There is a definite correlation between the time the mail is dropped and when the phone call should be made. When examining the results of mail and phone together, use the combined totals for the promotion as compared to the individual results of either medium alone.

An example: A direct mail program by itself might produce a 2% response rate. Telemarketing of the same product and no direct mail might produce a 6% response rate. While you might think that the combined media of mail followed by telemarketing would produce a response rate of 8% -- we have seen the combined program as high as 20% and 30%!

Timing is one of the major issues of the synergy of media. You may not be able to wait for the responses to finish from one medium before you implement another medium within the same program. Since telephone is ideally placed about two weeks after the mail is dropped, you may have to start the telemarketing program before you are able to receive all of the mail response.

We have all seen the effectiveness of the book and record clubs in using newspaper inserts and TV advertising to work together to produce higher results. Remember those "secret gold boxes?" The synergy of direct response TV advertising and space or direct mail continues to be cost effective.

We have conducted direct marketing campaigns for cellular telephone companies and high-technology companies while they were also using awareness ads in the same markets. We have also performed the same direct marketing campaigns in different markets with no advertising support. There was an increase in response rate in the markets with the advertising, but it was difficult to determine if the advertising cost provided enough increase in results to pay for itself. The fact that the campaigns were in different markets could distort the results.

We have frequently tested mail followed by telemarketing and found there is a definite correlation between the time the mail is dropped and the time to be on the phone to the prospect. Telemarketing response rates seem to be at their highest between 11 and 16 days after the mail is dropped.

Media synergy does not always have to be a major program. An example is the use of two 30 second TV spots on the three network morning programs in the same market as we are participating in a trade show. The day this was done, the traffic in the booth was three times as high as any other day. The total cost for the advertising was under $3,000.

You have now gone full cycle. The media selection and synergy flow from format and media selection. These issues flow from your *Big Idea*. Your *Big Idea* came from your brainstorming session. We cannot say enough about the planning phase and brainstorming phase of the development of your direct marketing program. Don't be afraid to go back and have additional brainstorming sessions if you are working too hard to make the *Big Idea* a reality.

Promotion Summarized

Promotion is defined as the further development and encouragement of prospects to purchase one's products or services. It has two aspects: creative and technical. The creative elements are the *Big Ideas* that are used to present a product or service to the marketplace. Technical promotion has four parts:

List - the customers or prospects to whom you plan to target marketing effort.

Offer - The proposition you are making to your customers or prospects in order to get them to respond.

Format - The vehicle for delivering the offer to your market: mail, phone, print or broadcast.

Copy - The words you use to communicate your offer to the market.

The four parts of technical promotion were explained and the relative importance of each part to the ultimate success of a direct marketing program was discussed. List is 50%, offer is 25%, format is 15% and copy is 10%.

List selection is the most critical element in the process of developing a direct marketing program. Determining the elements that can be used for better target identification is more difficult in business marketing. Information is not as readily available as in the consumer world. Abbreviations and a lack of standards in company name and address information further complicate the selection process. In addition, the high degree of change in business titles and functions makes contacting the correct decision maker to purchase a product or service difficult. List selection and testing are critical and should not become an after-thought in direct marketing program development.

Offers were discussed in detail and over 100 offer techniques were described. Business offers can appeal to the individual as a business person or a consumer. As a business person, you have to appeal to his/her professional motivations. As a consumer, the appeal can be on how the offer will yield the individual personal gratification. Both approaches should be tested to determine the best alternative for your company.

We discussed formats and reviewed how to select the most appropriate for your needs. The cost per contact and personalization of each type of contact were contrasted to help evaluate the best approach to reach your prospect or customer. A detailed description, along with the advantages and average cost per contact, of many types of formats was discussed.

Direct marketing copywriting was discussed. Several formula were reviewed to help you develop a hard-hitting explanation of your product and offer. One formula, AIDA was discussed in detail. Several approaches to reviewing copy to insure that you are taking your best shot at success were also discussed. These approaches also focus on the AIDA formula for copy development.

Targeting the correct individual in business marketing is probably the most difficult challenge you will be faced with. A complete review of the types of personalities involved in the business world was discussed. There are four personality stereotypes: analytic, pragmatic, amiable and extroverted. Each personality stereotype has different likes and dislikes and should be approached separately. You should determine the personality type that is most closely aligned with the environment you're trying to sell to and develop the direct marketing program around that personality.   We discussed the do's and don'ts in marketing to each of the personality stereotypes to make creating the direct marketing program easier.

Creating the ideas behind the direct marketing program can be the most fun and most difficult aspect of the entire effort. Everyone has a certain amount of creativity and can help in the creative process.

There are several approaches that have proved successful in creating the *Big Idea* behind any direct marketing effort. Brainstorming sessions that are designed to foster ideas and get the creative process started, are an excellent method for creating the *Big Idea*. Regardless of the creative approach used, a simple rule of no negative reaction to ideas is required to allow a free exchange of information.

The creative process will normally develop more than one approach. Direct marketing testing allows you to determine the most effective approach. Developing tests and measuring the results are critical to the ultimate success of your efforts. We discussed how to set up and measure testing different concepts for your programs. Business-to-business direct marketing often involves longer selling cycles and multiple contacts. The testing and evaluation techniques must also address interim measurements to evaluate the program as it progresses. When testing different concepts, focus on testing the big things: those areas that can have a big impact on costs, results and the ultimate profitability of the project. Don't spend time and money majoring in the minors. You should always be trying to "beat the champ." Create a program that outperforms your best existing program.

Selecting the best format for your direct marketing program is difficult. One technique and formula was reviewed in detail. An example was used to demonstrate how to establish the minimum required results for a format to be effective. Some of the variables you will need to consider were also discussed: timing, target audience, costs and available budgets. It is easier to eliminate certain approaches because of expense and results considerations than to determine which format will be best for you.

What happens when you use more than one format in the same direct marketing program? Will multiple contacts improve results? Is there synergy in using multiple formats at the same time? Does one format require the use of another format? These questions and there answers were reviewed in some detail.

The question on how to best reach the prospect with the offer is never going to have an easy answer. As time changes so does the best approach to promotion. What is effective today may not be effective tomorrow. You will have to continually evaluate the success of your programs and seek new and better ways to promote your products and services. One of the beautiful things about direct marketing is its testability. This chapter gave you a foundation to build upon.

If you're already using direct marketing, try a brainstorming session to see if you can create a better way to approach your market. Use the testing techniques to determine if you can "beat the champ".

If you're just starting direct marketing for the first time, test multiple approaches to determine the best promotion techniques for your company. Don't rest on your laurels; continue to look for better techniques to improve the results.

Chapter Six - Telemarketing

While the database concept discussed earlier is too new for its definition be found in every dictionary, telemarketing is so new, as a word, that to date it does not even have a dictionary definition. In this chapter we will establish a definition for the concept of telemarketing.

Many companies believe that they are using telemarketing, when in fact they are performing telephone selling. There is a substantial difference between the two.

<u>Telephone Selling</u>

The increasing cost of making a sales call in person has created a need for less expensive methods to:

a)   handle the smaller customer and
b)   set up appointments for the salesperson.

Many companies take some of their outside salespeople and convert them into telephone salespeople. They're paid commissions on their sales and are making sales calls on their customers and prospects by using the telephone.

This "Telesales" concept can be very worthwhile but it is not telemarketing. Telesales or telephone selling does not conform to our definition of direct marketing because it may or may not be measurable in its cost and results.

As you may recall from our discussions in Chapter one, we believe that direct marketing:

Explores, tests and substantiates methods of accomplishing:

- *Prospecting*
- *Qualifying*
- *Closing*

Exclusive of a Face-to-Face contact by a salesperson.

Although the salesperson is using the phone, he/she in reality is still making a face-to-face sales call via the telephone. The key to direct marketing is its measurability and predictability. As you form an activity and determine its success, you can plan on similar results if you perform a similar activity again.

The Definition of Direct Marketing

- **An organized and planned system of contacts**

- **Using a variety of media -- seeking to produce a lead or an order**

- **Developing and maintaining a database**

- **Measurable in cost and results**

- **Works in all methods of selling**

- **Expandable with confidence**

Illustration 6-1: The definition of direct marketing

Using Illustration 6-1, let's review telesales in light of the definition of direct marketing.

Telephone selling is really not an organized and planned system of contacts using a variety of media. In most cases, the salesperson is allowed to schedule and execute the telephone selling on his/her own. The average salesperson will attempt about 25 telephone calls in a day's activity in this kind of an environment.

We're never quite certain of the objective or results of the telesales function. The salesperson is not scripted and may or may not record the results from the sales call. Telesales is like sending a different letter to each customer. It may be a good idea and have very positive results, but it is not measurable direct marketing. Because each contact is personalized and specific to that customer, there is no common standard that is necessary for the measurement or predictability of performance.

Some companies have become fairly sophisticated and will allow the tele-salesperson to interact with a computerized database. The database may or may not schedule the telephone selling activity, may or may not record responders, and may or may not record purchases. In essence, it is probably not a direct marketing database.

Measurement of cost and results of the telesales operation is problematic. We can probably establish the costs (in most case they are seriously understated) but measuring the results can be difficult. Since the offer and actions of the salesperson are not controlled, a true measure of his/her results will be hard to determine. Again, the same problems identified in Chapter three on lead programs and interacting with a sales force are present when dealing the telesales personnel.

The telesales activity may or may not work in all methods of selling. And, the ability to predict similar results and expand the project is impossible. Telesales is based on the effectiveness of the individual salesperson. There will be a wide disparity between good and bad salespeople. Results are based on the individual, not on the list, offer, promotion or activity.

We are not discouraging the use of telephone selling or telesales, but it is not telemarketing as part of the direct marketing effort. We have developed lead generation programs where true telemarketing has been used to generate sales leads to be followed up by a telesales call. You have probably received calls from brokerage and insurance companies, where telemarketing is being used to screen the list for a qualified salesperson to execute a sales call to you on the phone. This approach can be a very cost effective way to sell products and services but since it is not direct marketing, therefore it is not true telemarketing.

Telemarketing Defined

If telephone selling isn't telemarketing, how do you define this powerful concept?

Telemarketing is a medium used to perform direct marketing.

- *It is controllable, measurable and not dependent on the individual for its success.*
- *It can be used as support of direct mail or advertising or as a stand alone campaign.*
- *It is a planned series of contacts, using a constant message, seeking to produce a lead or an order.*
- *It builds and maintains a database and is completely measuable in its cost and results.*
- *It can be outbound or inbound telephone calling .*
- *It can be used to either sell to consumers or to other businesses.*

Telemarketing uses a scripted or message controlled communicator to deliver a direct marketing message over the telephone.

Telemarketing incorporates two different approaches:

- Inbound Telemarketing
- Outbound Telemarketing

Inbound telemarketing involves the systematic servicing of a call from a prospect or customer that results from a message seen in another other medium. The person initiating the call has taken the initiative to start the sales cycle.

Inbound telemarketing is not controllable since the volume of telephone calls will occur whenever the prospects or customers determine it is in their best interest to call. Thus planning and controlling the inbound telephone effort is difficult due to this unknown variable.

When an inbound call is accepted, we're usually not certain what caused the call or the actual reason for the call. If the call was prompted by a direct response message, we'll want to determine the specific source of the call in order to calculate response measurements by source. However, a prospect or customer often will say that his/her call is a result of an advertisement read, saw or heard from a medium in which we never ran an ad. So while the accuracy of sourcing the inbound call is always suspect, it is still a basis to help evaluate the effectiveness of the advertising.

Inbound telemarketing can occur at any time. Therefore, how and when the telephone must be manned, plus the number of inbound phone lines needed are all tough variables to determine. If available, prior response history is most valuable in evaluating the level of activity to anticipate as a result of new ads or mailing programs.

Frequently, the advertising department will forget to tell the people responsible for handling the inbound telephone calls that a new ad has been placed. It is not unusual for the inbound telemarketing people to be handling calls for which they had no warning. It can be most embarrassing and damaging to the company for prospects and customers to call in reference to an offer only to catch the communicator flat footed, not knowing a thing about the program.

Outbound telemarketing is more controllable. You can plan and execute the telemarketing effort at your leisure. You will know who to call, when, how to deal with almost every selling situation. The best way to view outbound telemarketing is as a direct mail message being delivered through the telephone.

The outbound call can be timed to take advantage of the synergy that occurs between the various media. If direct mail produces a 1% result and telemarketing produces a 5% result, the use of both media together will produce at a higher than 6% response. In fact, it is not unusual for the total to be twice the combined results. There is a critical time frame when the phone call should occur after the mail has been dropped. This same kind of synergy is also possible when space ads and other media are used in conjunction with mail and telemarketing. Only by testing will you determine what is the best balance of the various media for you.

Within each area of telemarketing are two sub-categories of targets that you can reach. These are the consumer, a person who will be contacted at his residence, normally during evening and weekend hours -- or the business person, who will be contacted at his office or place of business, normally during the business day. The time of day and week that you are attempting to place or receive calls has a major impact on your telemarketing efforts.

Inbound Telemarketing

To effectively coordinate and control inbound telemarketing, a number of steps must be taken. Inbound telemarketing can never be used by itself. It is the response vehicle used for some other direct response media. A detailed media plan must be developed that projects the number of responders anticipated. If direct mail or an advertisement with a coupon is used, project both the total response and the response via telephone.

Every program is different, but in our experience the best, and most valuable, responder will come through inbound telephone. This makes a lot of sense if you consider that the prospect went out of his way to take an immediate action and call the number provided. Therefore, you want to ensure that your response to that person is of the highest quality, anticipates his needs and is complete in fulfilling the promise of your offer.

The use of a toll free 800 number will make it easier and more attractive to your customers and prospects to overcome their resistance to call you. Several companies we have talked to are against using toll free numbers because they feel it makes it too easy for people to call and gripe or comparison shop. Evaluate the reason you want people to respond to your company. The toll free number can be an effective tool to help overcome fear of responding.

Think of how you react when you see an offer to call to respond to an ad or promotion that you've received. You probably conjure up an image of someone who is waiting for you to respond and is prepared to take your order or answer your inquiry. Your challenge is to fulfill this mental picture.

When direct mail offers an inbound telephone response as an option, typically between 5% and 20% of the total response will come via inbound telephone. Prospects are frequently reluctant to call because they don't want to be aggressively sold at that particular time. They may only want to receive information to evaluate at their leisure and then make a decision to purchase or see a salesperson. The group that does respond via telephone probably represents the cream of the crop and should be handled accordingly. Responses from advertising offering mail and phone options tend be behave similarly. About 5% to 20% of the total response will come from the telephone. This is not a hard and fast rule; your product or service offer may react differently.

Knowing that your best responses will probably come through inbound telephone activity, you must ensure that they are handled in a timely and professional way. If you don't plan, the worst will happen: the prospect will be ignored, handled discourteously or not handled at all. You must plan how you'll deal with responders during peak and off peak hours, how you'll ensure that the telemarketing communicator is prepared for the calls and how you'll deal with the responder in a timely and professional manner.

Whatever media you've used, you should plan for about 15% of the total response to come via the telephone. This may be more than you'll actually receive, but planning for a higher response rate will ensure that the calls are handled in a very professional way.

If you're using a broadcast medium (TV, cable or radio) to drive response, it will normally cause almost all the response to occur within 15 to 30 minutes of when the ad was run. This naturally requires a larger number of communicators available to handle the volume of calls for a very short period of time. In consumer advertising, thousands of calls can be received in 10 or 15 minutes when a national direct response ad is run on network or syndicated television. This normally doesn't apply to business-to-business direct marketing, but with the increase of successful national cable business programs, it could become a consideration.

A number of considerations are in motion when your prospects call your phone number. If it is a toll free number, they may have to decide whether to respond to an interstate or an intrastate number. The phone companies have made it much easier and less expensive to have one number for both intrastate and interstate activity. You will have to evaluate your needs and decide on the best approach for your company.

Some companies prefer to have their local offices handle the inbound telephone response. They feel that the local number makes the responder more comfortable in responding to someone who is local as opposed to an unknown location at the end of the 800 number in "never-never" land.

Bear in mind that you will have no control over the quality of the response that will be provided at these remote local locations. Plus you'll have difficulty communicating to everyone when your ads are run or your mail was sent. You also will have a great deal of difficulty measuring the response and the success of your direct marketing program. We have tested both scenarios and found no difference in the level of response between local numbers or 800 centralized facilities. But the centralized facility gave us a lot more control and information about the program.

When the prospect responds, he/she will either hear the phone ring or get a busy signal. This ties directly to the number of 800 trunks you have available to handle the incoming calls. A trunk is the line connecting your business to the phone company. A telephone line is the extension or instrument connected to the telephone system within your business. Normally, a company will have 8 to 10 times more lines than trunks. Most phones are not in use all day long so they do not have to be connected to the external telephone network at all times. Many companies install a *telephone switch* to handle the switching of the network or trunks to the appropriate line.

Telephone capacity planning is more difficult when evaluating inbound telemarketing. You must plan for the high volume peak. If you do not have enough inbound trunks assigned to the 800 number or other inbound numbers, your prospects will receive a busy signal. Hopefully, they'll attempt to call back. But about half never bother to according to a recent AT&T study on inbound calling patterns. Your phone bill for the 800 service will confirm how many calls were attempted to your 800 number but ended in a busy signal.

As you probably are aware, you are charged for 800 service similar to other WATS (Wide Area Telephone Service) type coverage. The heavier the usage on each line, the less you pay per minute of usage. If you put in excess trunkage to handle the highest volumes you anticipate, you will pay substantially more per minute of actual usage. In addition, you'll also pay a monthly access charge per line. Your phone company representative can be of great help in evaluating and recommending the appropriate number of lines. You'll always be comparing additional costs against the need for customer/prospect service.

Since the phone company will take about one month to install additional 800 trunks, you should do a relatively good job in anticipating your volume requirements. Initially, consider putting in more trunks than you really need and then evaluate the usage. There is an added cost to this safe approach since the phone company will charge to install and remove the lines.

Busy signals may not achieve the results we want, but at least the prospect may call you back and probably will get the impression that your offer must be pretty good if others are also calling. Not having the phone answered at all can never be perceived well. Let's review the situations that can cause the phone to ring but not be answered:

1) The prospect is calling when your office is not open for business. As we indicated earlier, you can't control the volume or when inbound activity will occur. You should anticipate that there will be activity beyond your normal business hours and establish some form of coverage.

   Use a message machine to announce to your prospects that you're closed, give your normal business hours and ask them to recall. Better yet, also ask them to leave a message and then have them re-contacted through an outbound telephone call.

   Have the number automatically switched to an answering service. This will give you coverage but may not ensure the consistency you desire.

2) If you have more trunks than people to handle the activity, the prospect can call and not have anyone available to pick up the traffic. The same result can occur if you're using a PBX and have not programmed the system to handle overflow traffic.

   If your inbound lines terminate individually at a unique telephone, take the empty phone off the hook to send a busy signal to that number. A busy sugnal is a better situation than a no answer.

If it is outside your normal business hours, consider using the tape machine mentioned earlier.

If you're using a telephone switch, you should ensure that it is programmed to overflow to a tape recording when all lines are busy. If you anticipate higher inbound volumes, consider adding some form of automatic call director to ensure the calls are handled in a professional way.

3) You may have a trunk that is not working properly and is not ringing through to your company. Test your inbound lines frequently and have the phone company check them as well. If your phone bill indicates lines with no usage activity, investigate to determine if the line is operating properly. As an aside, if a line is working properly and it has no usage, you have too many inbound trunks and should cut back.

Now that the call is properly coming into your inbound telemarketing operation, make sure that each call is handled in a professional manner. Publish a letter to all employees that tells them of your activity and that inbound calls are expected. Make sure that all of your remote locations also are informed.

As we mentioned earlier, in order to conduct true direct marketing your telemarketing program must operate independently of the personalities of the personnel and be measurable in its cost and results. To ensure that each call is handled similarly, you must script or provide a call outline for each communicator to use.

In the business-to-business selling environment, you must identify the individual calling, his/her company , title and business phone number. No matter what the reason for the call, always try to capture this basic information before answering any questions.

When a prospects call any inbound number, including yours, they expect to be asked for some information. Prospects tend to be fairly tolerant during an inbound call and normally will answer most reasonable questions. Use the prospect's tolerance to your advantage. Unlike outbound telemarketing, the call has not interrupted the prospect and he/she normally has more patience.

Prepare a form for your communicator to fill out to give you the following basic information:

> Contact Name
> Contact Title
> Company Name
> Company Address (2 lines)
> Company City
> Company State
> Company ZIP
> Contact Phone Number (during the day at their business)

Also try to source the media and specific ad or mail piece that caused the prospect to call, but this can often prove to be difficult at times. Never lose sight of the fact that your primary objective is to sell something by getting hung up on trying to generate information. If the prospect is uncertain or can't answer the question, quickly move into your sales presentation.

Once you establish a uniform front end for handling an inbound call, it will be easier to train people. In addition, if a problem occurs during the call, you'll have all the information to re-contact the prospect. Getting all of the name and address information at the beginning of the call makes a lot of sense. It isn't very difficult to ask a series of non-threatening questions that will serve to relax the responder. Even if the prospect or customer is calling to complain, it is easy to explain that you're capturing this information in case you're cut off and need to re-contact them.

Design a form that follows the script so your communicators have a call guide that is also easy to follow. Keep this form the same, regardless of the type of response, so it will be easy to train your people. By forcing a uniform approach to handling every inbound call, you are

Good AFTERNOON/MORNING -- Thanks for calling ABC Company. My name is _____ (use your full name).

Can I have your name and your company name please?

And your company address?

And the ZIP code?

Mr(s) _____ (use full name from above) can I have your title, please?

And the phone number that can be used to contact you during the day?

And finally, can you tell me what prompted your call today?

Illustration 6-2; An opening for an inbound telephone call

Date __/__/__   Time __:__   Communicator _____

Contact name   _____
Title   _____
Company   _____
Address   _____
                _____
City   _____ State _____ Zip _____
Telephone No. (___) ___-_____

Reason for response _____

Illustration 6-3; A sample form for handling inbound responders.

fostering good call quality and professionalism. You will also have a basis to build a database for the future.

Prospects who do not give a company name or phone number are usually of lower quality. They may be good leads or referrals, but your company probably doesn't operate during the hours that these prospects are available. If you're sending a responder to your sales force without a company name, the odds are pretty good that the salesperson will not even attempt to contact the prospect.

We have seen situations where prospects will respond either by mail or phone and give their name and company address but no company name or phone number. There is no way to establish the phone number for these prospects and contact them in the future. In the business-to-business arena, if respondents don't give you a company name, just send them literature (as inexpensively as possible) and consider them suspects.

Because the prospect has taken the initiative to call you, he/she will be *more tolerant in allowing you to ask questions. He also expects you to be able to handle his queries in a professional manner.* If your communicators cannot answer every question, they should be up front in admitting that to the prospect. Establish procedures for more qualified personnel to return calls to prospects who asked difficult questions. If varying levels of prospect qualification will prompt different kinds of fulfillment, ask these types of qualification questions during the phone call. These calls should be scripted and the answers entered on the form used to record the call information.

Don't forget our discussion in Chapter three concerning lead qualification -- establish money, authority, need and desire. Don't get trapped into market research type questions. These responders are of the highest quality; don't run the risk of turning them off. They may be more tolerant of questions, but don't lose sight of your objective to generate a sale or a lead. Only get the information necessary to establish the best way to handle the prospect.

Keep a copy of all inbound responders to develop a database. As we said earlier, these tend to be your best qualified responders. They called because they wanted to be handled quickly. Put them into your fulfillment system within 48 hours of their call. Consider sending them a letter thanking them for their response that further describes how their inquiry will be handled. If you've ever been treated this way, you know how powerful a letter like this can be. One note of caution: Keep the promise delivered in the letter or it can create a terribly negative situation.

Inbound telemarketing is a very powerful response tool. However, whenever you offer a phone response, you should always also offer the opportunity to respond through the mail. Some people feel threatened, inhibited or incapable of using the phone and will not respond if only a phone option is offered.

If you anticipate a very high volume of responses to your program, consider using an outside telemarketing service bureau that specializes in inbound capabilities. Another reason to consider an outside service could be your company hours of operation. If you're doing business across the country and only operating for eight hours a day, three hours of your non-business hours are business hours for your customers.

The make or buy decision for inbound telemarketing is complex:

1) Your company management may be very nervous about the quality and customer service issues in sending the inbound activity to a service bureau. Company management can force the activity in-house when a better alternative may be a service bureau.

2) Unless you're selling commodity type products, the service bureau will probably not be able to handle detailed questions. The inbound responder is your best and hottest responder. You may want to strike while the iron is hot. This is a strong argument for keeping the inbound activity in-house.

3) The volume of activity may require a large staff to handle inbound activity only for short periods of time during the day. Even with part time personnel, this manning problem can be difficult to deal with.

4) Non-business hour activity could require you to operate your telemarketing operation at odd hours. This can create management and staffing problems.

5) Scripting and call control tend to be more difficult with in-house staffs than when using an outside service.

6) Trunk availability is difficult to plan. You're not in the telemarketing business and planning for telemarketing is probably new to you. An outside service has the experience and expertise to guide you through the planning process.

Inbound telemarketing is very complex and difficult to plan for. It becomes even more complicated if you are targeting the consumer universe as well as the business-to-business arena. The best advice we can give you is to try to provide the same kind of response you would want to receive if you were calling another company.

Establishing the Costs of Telemarketing

Whether you're planning inbound or outbound telemarketing, you must be able to evaluate the true costs and results of your efforts. The costs for telemarketing are more than just the communicator costs. If you're evaluating whether to keep the function in-house or go to a service bureau, you must know your cost per hour of telemarketing.

Three broad areas should be considered when evaluating the total expenses associated with telemarketing:

1) The cost of operations - Telephone
2) The cost of operations - Clerical Support
3) General and Administrative Expenses

Within the cost area defined as cost of operations - telephone, are all the labor expenses. The cost of phone center management should be included. If this function will only occupy a percentage of time for an

	Annual	**Monthly**
Hours of Telemarketing	_____	_____

Cost of Operations - Telephone

Labor - Mgmt $_____/yr	_____	_____
% of Mgmt needed ___%	_____	_____
Labor - Supv $_____/yr	_____	_____
% of Supv needed ___%	_____	_____
Labor - communicators	_____	_____
Payroll taxes	_____	_____
Fringe benefits	_____	_____
Temporary - outside labor	_____	_____
Telephone equipment	_____	_____
Telephone network - inbound	_____	_____
Telephone network - outbound	_____	_____
Telephone network - local usage	_____	_____
Telephone installation	_____	_____
Total cost of operations - phone	_____	_____

Cost of Operations - Clerical

Labor - Mgmt $_____/yr	_____	_____
% of Mgmt needed ___%	_____	_____
Labor - Supv $_____/yr	_____	_____
% of Supv needed ___%	_____	_____
Labor - Clerks		
Look-up	_____	_____
Maintenance	_____	_____
Tabulating	_____	_____
Sorting	_____	_____
Payroll taxes	_____	_____
Fringe benefits	_____	_____
Copy machine rental/depreciation	_____	_____
Copy machine supplies	_____	_____
Telephone equipment	_____	_____
Total cost of operations - clerical	_____	_____

	Annual	**Monthly**
General & Administrative		
Rent		
Heat & electricity	____	____
Insurance	____	____
Equipment depreciation	____	____
Furniture & fixtures depreciation	____	____
Telephone equipment	____	____
Telephone network	____	____
Receptionist/secretarial support	____	____
Data processing	____	____
Data processing supplies	____	____
Repairs & maintenance	____	____
General office supplies	____	____
Travel & entertainment	____	____
Dues & subscriptions	____	____
Training & seminars	____	____
Advertising & public relations	____	____
Bad debt/bad pay/returns	____	____
Total cost of operations - G & A	____	____
Total Costs	____	____
Cost per hour of telemarketing	____	____

Illustration 6-4: Telemarketing Expense Worksheet

individual, the total cost should be included and then the appropriate percentage applied. Supervision and communicator cost are obviously an important part of the labor costs.

Use the Telemarketing Expense Worksheet to help you establish your cost per telemarketing hour. Before you get started, try to determine the amount of telemarketing you're planning to perform. This quantity will be critical in all of your planning and evaluation. We have provided areas to establish both the annual and monthly costs. In many cases you'll find it easier getting either the monthly or annual expense. You can convert either by dividing or multiplying by 12. This will give you a methodology to evaluate all of your costs.

Outbound Telemarketing

Outbound telemarketing can be used by itself or in conjunction with other methods of direct marketing. It is a medium to deliver a message over the telephone. Unlike direct mail, telemarketing is interactive and allows you to quickly alter one or more variables while you're still conducting your campaign. You can plan and control outbound telemarketing better than you can control direct mail.

The first element in planning and executing outbound telemarketing is similar to any other direct marketing effort...the **List.** When selecting a universe to use for telemarketing, you will need to establish the availability of telephone numbers.

Businesses are in a constant state of change. People are constantly changing jobs and responsibilities. The larger the company, the more likely the mailing list contact will have changed. You can anticipate about a 30% change in contact and other information each year. Depending on the age of your list, the odds are pretty good that you'll be reaching a different target than you initially went after.

When you use direct mail to contact businesses, if no contact name is available, you can use title and function addressing. This type of mailing will normally prove successful and not substantiality alter the results. When you consider the relatively high degree of turn over, title addressing can be almost as effective as personalized, name directed mailings. Each company is different and the only sure way for you to establish the difference in title addressing versus name addressing, is to test both and evaluate the results.

Many compiled and response lists have phone numbers. However, most lists do not include phone numbers. If you plan to use outbound telemarketing as a stand alone medium or in support of direct mail, you'll need to make sure that you can use the list for telemarketing. Many list owners are reluctant to allow their lists to be used for telemarketing because:

1) They have a negative attitude about telephone selling. Many have received unprofessional and poorly executed calls at home and in their offices. They don't want to have their lists subjected to this kind of activity.

2) List ownership is a major concern. Many list owners have heard of telemarketing response rates of 20% to 40% and are concerned about losing their list to the telemarketer.

If the original list doesn't contain phone numbers, typically you'll only be able to secure about 60% of the numbers through most phone number appending services. Then through the telemarketing effort, you'll be able to reach about 65% of the list that has phone numbers to make your offer. If even 40% accept your offer, a great response rate, the net acceptance against the list you started with is only 15.6%. Yes, this is still a high response rate, but not so overwhelming as to worry the list owner that he/she will lose his/her list. We must educate the list community regarding the true nature of telemarketing and its impact on their lists. It will take time.

1,000	Names on original list with no phone numbers
60%	Obtain phone numbers
600	Net names for telemarketing
65%	Are reachable on the phone
390	Net offers made
40%	Accept the offer
156	Net acceptances
15.5%	Response Rate

Illustration 6-5: An example of Telemarketing Response Rates

As you are probably aware, you normally rent lists for a single usage. Any responder who accepts your offer, or asks for additional information, becomes yours for future activity and action. In direct mail you're only allowed to retain the names of your actual acceptances. In addition, you may have an opportunity to learn about the quality of the list if you elect to have the non-deliverable (nixie) mail returned to you. The acceptances and nixies are all you ever receive back from any mailing.

In telemarketing you'll receive information not only from the acceptances and nixies, but also from other segments of the list. If someone refuses your offer, you can still learn a great deal about their business. You clearly will own the data captured, which is valuable market research information. However, in most cases, you can't keep and re-contact any name that doesn't accept your telemarketing offer. Review this situation with the list owner prior to starting your campaign.

Many list owners are now renting their lists for annual or unlimited usage, to allow you to make multiple contacts via mail and phone. Some contracts allow you to use the list for a mail and phone contact. If you rent a list for a single contact, and plan to use mail followed by a telephone call, that is two contacts. Make sure you review your plan with the list owner.

Outbound telemarketing creates many segments to the original list that must be dealt with independently. The most familiar and obvious segment consists of those who you were able to contact and made a decision concerning your offer.

Let's look at all of the ways a record can be used:

1) On the original list but no phone number is obtainable when the list is sent to an outside service. This record is never used for telemarketing.

2) The phone number is obtained and we attempt to contact the prospect;

   A) It is a wrong number. You reach a company, but it isn't the correct one. Your prospect may have moved on to a different company. If you attempt to contact his successor, then this record would not be consumed as a wrong number.

   B) The call results in a tape recording indicating that the number has been disconnected. This is a non-reachable technical difficulty.

   C) The company is moving or going out of business and can't make a decision about your offer.

   D) Completed Call

   • Refused to talk to you and aborts call in the middle. In fact, this prospect made a decision concerning your offer and rejected it.

   • Accepts Offer. There are a number of possible ways to accept your offer. These can include a request for literature or a later contact.

   • Rejects Offer. A prospect who is unsure about your offer can be coded as either rejects or accepts your offer. You should determine the appropriate disposition prior to starting your program.

   E) Not reachable after a pre-established number of attempts.

   F) Not a decision making location. This happens from time to time in the business world. You can consume the record or attempt to get the phone number and appropriate contact at the decision location and then contact via telemarketing.

When measuring telemarketing you should evaluate the number of dialings made in a specific time frame, normally an hour. In addition, you should also measure the number of completed calls (D), and the number of acceptances of your offer in that same time frame. When people discuss outbound telemarketing performance standards, many confuse apples and oranges. A constant set of definitions needs to be established that will allow everyone to compare the same thing. Business-to-business calling complicates the situation because additional dispositions are added by the nature of the calling.

In the consumer universe, you normally get through to the prospect or spouse. There is no one screening calls and no switchboard to have to deal with. The prospect is normally the decision maker and most lists. used for telemarketing are name directed.

The business universe is totally different. In most cases, the phone is answered by a receptionist or switchboard operator. The list may not be name directed, or the name may be wrong. In either case, you'll have to establish through the switchboard your individual prospect's name and title. This prospect probably has a secretary, whose whole mission in life is to prevent calls like yours from reaching her boss. When you finally get to your prospect, there is a good chance that he/she is not the person responsible and you'll be referred to someone else within the company.

If this occurs in one call you'll be very lucky. Normally it takes several calls to reach the original prospect and perhaps just as many to contact a referred name. Obviously, the calls tend to be longer due to the multiple level of contacts required to reach your prospect. In addition, it will take more dialings that have to be rescheduled in order to ultimately consume the record.

Bertha Barrier, the secretary assigned to the mission of screening your calls from her boss, complicates business-to-business telemarketing even further. She must be dealt with to allow you to make your presentation to your prospect. She also performs the same function when she screens face-to-face salespeople and direct mail. She can't be ignored.

In the consumer world, it is fairly common to attempt to reach each record four times before considering the record not reachable. The timing and way you make these attempts can change but four attempts seems fairly common. Because of multi-contact problems, the business universe requires a higher attempt threshold. Six attempts is average and it isn't unusual to see the attempt level set as high as eight.

Every program and list differs on anticipated results. In our experience about 25% to 35% of dialings made to the business universe will end in a completed call. This is substantially less than the 40% to 50% completion rate of dialings in the consumer world.

Depending on the type of product and the list being used, whether the list is name directed or not name directed and the length of the script, the number of completed calls per hour ranges from five to 13. Dialings range from 20 to 35 per hour. These are not hard and fast standards, but production results that most business-to-business programs seem to operate within.

As part of your business planning process, establish goals that allow you to measure the program at all times. Set dialing, completion and acceptance objectives for each hour of telemarketing. Once you've established your cost per telemarketing hour, it is easy to evaluate your cost per lead or cost per order.

Illustration 6-6 shows how a typical outbound telemarketing plan might appear. This plan assumes that we are starting with 1,000 records. Only 65% of the records will be contactable, because many records will either be wrong numbers, not be decision making locations, going out of business or records that reach the recall limit after a predetermined number of attempts.

About 30% of dialings will result in a completed call or contact. This plan assumes that we will dial the phone 25 times per hour of telemar-

Total records	1,000
% of records contactable	65%
Total records contactable	650
% of dialings that are able to be contacted	30%
Dialings per hour	25
Contacts per hour	7.5
Planned response rate	10%
Acceptances per hour	.75
Total telemarketing hours for project	86.7
Total acceptances	65

Illustration 6-6: A Typical Telemarketing Plan

keting, with 30% or 7.5 completed calls per hour. The plan also assumes that 10% of the completed calls will accept the offer, or .75 acceptances per hour.

The number of hours required for this project is 86.7 hours. This was derived by dividing the total number of records that were contactable by the number of completed calls per hour. The total number of acceptances was established by multiplying the number of hours by the planned acceptances per hour.

With the cost per telemarketing hour we established earlier, we can develop the cost per responder and the cost per order.

This type of planning gives you measurable objectives to evaluate the success of your outbound telemarketing project each hour of the project. The model can also be used to measure the success of different lists, offers and products being sold over the telephone.

Each communicator should make the same presentation to each member of the list to whom you're marketing. This is one of the basic criteria to telemarketing as opposed to telesales. We recommend the use of scripts that control the complete flow of the telephone call. The communicator is even provided pre-scripted answers to questions and objections.

There are a number of script techniques that you can employ.

1) A script outline. This approach uses an outline of the structure that you want the communicator to follow. Every word is not scripted and the communicator has a great deal of flexibility in what is said. Normally a record or form is provided to record the responses from the phone call. The form should be the outline for the call.

   The script outline approach is easy to use, and not cumbersome during the phone call. It has a stronger dependence on the individual communicator and you're never absolutely certain of what was said on the phone. The communicators have to be well trained to handle questions and objections.

2) A script on pages. This is a typed version of the script on several pages of manuscript. This approach scripts virtually every word that we want the communicator to use. It is an easy and quick way to introduce short easy to learn scripts into the phone operation It also uses a record or form to record the responses from the phone call.

   The script on pages approach is easy to introduce and change in the phone operation. Typically the communicator will memorize the script and then never use it during the phone call. After a period of time the script becomes personalized to the individual and really isn't a script at all. As in the outline approach, the record ultimately becomes a call guide and controls the call.

3) A script on flip cards. This script has one or two statements on a flip card. Based on the interaction during the phone call, the communicator is instructed to which card to proceed to next. In Chapter three, we used an example of this type of scripting during the IBM project. It is a complete script and controls every action and reaction during the phone call. The communicator says the same thing all of the time. It also uses a record or form to record the responses from the phone call.

The script on flip cards approach is a little more difficult to create and introduce into the phone operation. It takes more to produce. You might consider using a photo album with flip windows that are staggered so you can see the base of the next window. This type of scripting is dynamic and can change by simply changing one or two of the cards. Your communicator will still memorize the script and eventually use it less and less, but the script on cards approach makes handling questions and objections fairly easy.

4) Computerized scripting. This approach has a computer terminal in front of each communicator. As the call progresses, the reactions to various questions are entered into the computer and these answers determine the next part of the script that should be read by the communicator. No paper record is used in this approach as the information is entered directly into the computer system.

The computerized approach is great but expensive to implement and difficult to make changes to. The communicator may memorize the script but really has no alternative but to read and view the computer terminal during the phone call. This is probably the most reliable approach to ensuring that the same message is delivered to every person on the list.

Telemarketing is an effective and proven media to ask for an order or commitment from a prospect or customer. However, it is very difficult to sell unfamiliar products or services via telemarketing. The products sold on the telephone almost always must be commodity or well known items.

A telephone call is disruptive. Think about the calls you've received either at home or in your office. The call probably interrupted something you were doing. You may have been tolerant or even interested, but your patience probably wore pretty thin in a relatively short period of time. This reaction is fairly typical and is the challenge you're faced with in your telemarketing call.

Most people will not allow you to sell a product to them over the phone. If they already are familiar with the product or a similar product, they may agree to try yours. You only have between 25 and 45 seconds to generate interest and get your prospect involved in the phone call. The key to the phone call is the offer you make up front to interest the prospect in allowing the call to continue.

This means that you must make your offer easy to understand, risk-free and easy for your prospect to decide on . Multiple offers and choices are difficult to sell over the phone. However, you can make a single offer and then an additional offer after the initial offer has been evaluated and accepted or rejected by the prospect.

If you're selling a product directly, consider a trial or money back guarantee. Remember that, you're asking a prospect to purchase something without seeing, feeling, touching, smelling or tasting the product. The prospect has to evaluate your offer with no sensory support. If the product is a known commodity, depending on the offer, the prospect is more likely to be able to make a buying decision. The less known the product is, the more difficult, and less likely, the buying decision.

When using direct mail or direct response advertising, you can write longer copy to describe and inform the prospect. If they're interested, prospects can read the material provided and then evaluate and research the information to reach a buying decision. Although you are still asking prospects to make a decision without actually seeing the product, they have more time to consider it.

Telemarketing asks the prospect to make a decision immediately. Because you don't have a lot of time to explain your product or offer, your scripted copy must be short and to the point. On the phone, people do not have time to internalize the words presented. They may not form the word pictures you are trying to convey. Decisions are threatening to most people and they look for reasons to avoid uncomfortable situations. As you are making an offer on the phone, your prospect will be searching for reasons to reject or object to the proposition. They probably will not hear a lot of what you might want to present.

Does this mean that you can't sell over the telephone? Absolutely not. But we have found that you really won't have a lot of time to convey your message. If you're trying to sell a more complicated product or service, a combination of direct mail and telephone will probably be more appropriate.

If you're using the telephone to qualify leads and offer the prospect an opportunity to see a sales representative, similar rules on the offer and length of the message apply. Explain to the prospect why seeing a salesperson will be good for him/her or his/her company. This message also must be delivered in a very short and to the point presentation. Again, words and copy that work well in other media may not perform as well on the phone.

When designing a telemarketing script, try reading something out loud for 30 to 45 seconds. You'll be surprised how long a period it is. Your prospect will have to be hooked very quickly to allow the call to continue. If you're asking for information to evaluate qualification, you still must get the prospect interested in continuing with the call.

In many cases, the prospects will ask that additional information be sent to them so they can make a decision. Many telemarketers view

prospects who request literature as disinterested people simply looking for an easy way to get off of the telephone. Most people do not
like to be rude. By asking for additional information, they are defer-
ring the decision and they don't have to be rude to the communicator.
A good percentage of these people in fact are simply doing it to get
off the phone. However, some of these prospects are legitimately
interested in the offer. You must deal with the interested group in a
very professional and effective way.

When conducting lead qualification telemarketing programs, we tend
to see more prospects requesting additional information than agreeing
to seeing a salesperson. And depending on the offer being made in
the direct selling programs, they also can have a large number of literature requestors.

As you may recall from Chapter one, promotional material must be
designed to deal with prospects who ask for additional information. It
must be designed with the specific mission of creating a lead or an
order. You can't use a promotional piece that was designed to be left
behind by the salesperson after his/her sales call and expect it to perform the direct marketing mission. Trade show literature won't work
any better. What should become obvious is that when you start your
telemarketing campaign, you will also need to create some direct mail
follow-up.

You might think that it is easier to treat literature requestors as rejec-
tions of your offer and not care about the material, if any, that you
send them. If you're generating enough activity from the prospects
accepting your telemarketing offer, this might be a good decision,
particularly if your universe is large enough to support your sales and
lead requirements for the foreseeable future without dealing with
prospects who want additional information.

We have found, however, that when literature requestors are re-contacted by telephone about ten days after the material was sent to them,
approximately 25% will convert into a solid lead or an order. The fulfillment material used was specifically designed to move the prospect
further along the buying decision.

Evaluate the financial impact to create, produce and fulfill literature. The cost of the second phone call also must be evaluated against the anticipated results to ensure that the program is profitable. If you decide to re-contact the literature requestors, you will be starting down the road towards database marketing.

We are obviously recommending the use of direct mail to support your telemarketing efforts. Telemarketing works best when it is used in conjunction with direct mail. Direct mail followed by telemarketing will normally yield better results as a combined effort, than when either media is used separately.

We have tested the use of mail and phone separately and then tested mail followed by phone and the results were very different. The mail produced at 2% and the phone produced at 7.5%. You would therefore expect the combined results to be about 9.5%. The actual result of the combination of the two was almost 13%.

We also tested to determine the best time to follow the mail with telemarketing. We began telemarketing about five days prior to the mail. The first scripted question asked was, "Do you recall seeing the information we sent you ?" Even before the mail was dropped, about 30% of those asked indicated that they could recall receiving the mail. This may sound amusing, but some people will respond positively so as not to appear ignorant. After the mail was dropped, we continued to track the answer to this question. The favorable response peaked at almost 70% from day 11 after the mail was dropped and remained there through day 17. The response rate then began to drop. Within 30 days after the mail drop, the favorable response rate dropped to 40% and stayed there for the next 15 days. It ultimately went back to the 30% range.

Answer rates to this question by itself were interesting, but the front end results were even more informative. The response rate followed the awareness of the mail fairly closely. There was an increase of almost 25% in response rate when the awareness of the mail was at its peak.

Mail and phone work exceedingly well together. To maximize the combined effect of the two media, the phone call should be timed to follow the mail from between ten to 15 days after the mail is dropped. We have been involved in programs that delayed the phone call to allow for all of the mail responses to be returned. This may make sense, but the results should be carefully evaluated. Test both approaches to determine the best results for your company. If your mail response rate is anticipated at about 2%, you'll only be calling and contacting a very small group who would have or already responded by mail. Remember, you will achieve only about a 65% contact rate of all of the records that have phone numbers. Therefore, given a 2% mail response rate you will only duplicate about 1.35% of the list. The only way to find out the impact of phone and mail together is to test... test... test.

Outbound Telemarketing Results

Every direct marketing and telemarketing program is different and it is dangerous to apply hard and fast rules to all programs. However, we will try to give you some guidelines to help you do a reasonable job in estimating results. We have found that after about 100 hours of business-to-business telemarketing with a list and script, the results will not deviate substantially (more than 10%) for the balance of the program. This assumes that the list, script and offer remain the same. Consumer calling results also will level off, but after about 250 hours of calling.

If the list is sent to a computer service bureau, normally we have experienced about 50% of the list is successful in having a phone number added. This can vary depending on the quality, age and techniques used to compile the list. You can establish additional phone numbers (about 15%) by sending the remaining unmatched names to a manual telephone look-up service. This tends to be more expensive and take substantially longer. Evaluate the complete information you require on your list prior to sending it to the service bureau. It is possible to have S.I.C. and other sizing information added to your list at the same time as the phone number.

Now that you have the list ready for telemarketing, what kind of results can be expected? Our experience says -- it depends. Not a comfortable answer but really true. When you're calling different industry groups or different size companies the results will vary greatly. It is fairly difficult to get a doctor on the phone, but fairly easy to reach office managers and purchasing agents. The single biggest factor in altering the calling results will be whether the list is name directed or not. If you don't have the contact's name, then you really must make multiple calls to the same company to first establish the contact, and then to make your presentation.

Long scripts with lots of market research questions can also alter the results significantly. The more questions and the more prospects or customers have to think about their answers, the longer the call will take.

The number of phone attempts made to particular name on the list can also alter the results significantly. We suggest that the average business-to-business contact should be attempted six to eight times and then considered not reachable.

With six attempts the average list will yield about 65% of the records as able to be contacted. In addition, assuming cross industry calling, about 20% of dialings will result in a contact during the first three attempts, 15% will result in a contact in the next two attempts and then 10% or less will result in a contact after six attempts. About 10 to 15% of the list will be not contactable because of wrong number and out of business statistics and these will normally be found during the first dialing attempt. Let's examine 1,000 records and identify what happens on six attempts.

1000	Records to start
15%	Not contactable due wrong number and out of business
150	Records not contactable
850	Records contactable

20%	Contacted on 1st attempt
200	Records contacted on 1st attempt
650	Records remaining to contact (200 contacted + 150 not contactable)

20%	Contacted on 2nd attempt
130	Records contacted on 2nd attempt
520	Records remaining to contact

20%	Contacted on 3rd attempt
104	Records contacted on 3rd attempt
416	Records remaining to contact

15%	Contacted on 4th attempt
62	Records contacted on 4th attempt
354	Records remaining to contact

15%	Records contacted on 5th attempt
53	Records contacted on 5th attempt
301	Records remaining to contact

15%	Records contacted on 6th attempt
45	Records contacted on 6th attempt
256	Records remaining to contact and will be treated as not contactable.

As you can see, we will contact 599 records of the original 1,000 or about 60% of the records we started with. Eight attempts will bring the total to about 65%. It gets very expensive to contact records as more attempts are made. A certain percentage of the records will never be reached and they will make up a larger portion of the remaining records after each attempt. You must evaluate the number of attempts you'll make and the results you anticipate.

The dialings and contacts per hour will vary depending on each program. Business-to-business programs average about 20 to 30 dialings per hour and about 20% to 30% as completed contacts. Therefore the average business program will result in about five to eight completed calls per hour. A good planning number for most business programs is about seven to 7.5 completed calls per hour. If your list is not name directed, you will lose about one completed call per hour.

When executing lead generation programs, we have found for every person that accepts our offer to see a salesperson, about the same number of people request additional information. This group of literature requesters, when followed up with a phone call after the information was sent, converted into a lead about 25% of the time. This seemed to occur in almost every lead program we executed using phone follow-up to the literature requests.

When planning a follow-up call, within 90 days of an earlier phone contact, you can expect to contact 90% of the list in four to six attempts. This is true because the list is name directed, and we have established a correct phone number and a prior relationship of some sort with the prospect. In fact, you can use this prior relationship as a method to overcome "Bertha Barrier". You can start your call by telling Bertha that you're calling about some information that Mr. Contact asked for.

Your response rates will vary significantly based on your offer and script. As you establish your business plan, the required response rates will be established to determine whether your program is successful.

The Telemarketing Plan

Like any other direct marketing program, outbound telemarketing has to have a detailed plan prepared prior to the start of the program. After you develop the business background and the strategy for your direct marketing program, you should review the use of telemarketing. If outbound telemarketing is an appropriate medium, then you'll have to develop a detailed flow chart and business plan for the use of outbound telemarketing.

As you'll note from Illustration 6-7, the flow chart will start with the

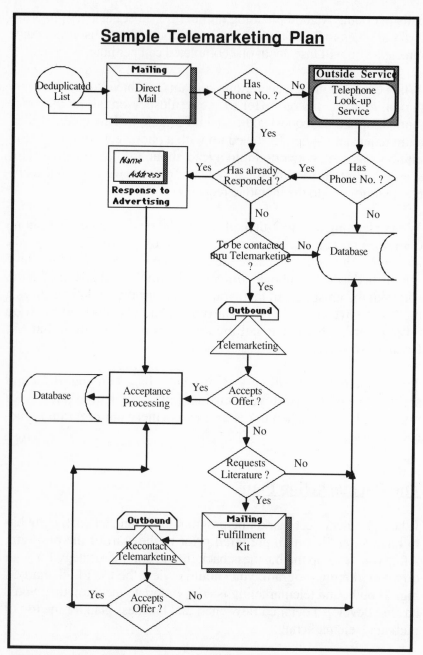

Illustration 6-7: A Sample Telemarketing Flow Chart

tape of records that are being used for the direct marketing effort. We assume the tape was deduplicated against the existing customer file and within itself to ensure that there are no duplicate records.

Frequently, you'll acquire lists that contain several names of people within the same company. Although these can be correct and appropriate names, you may find that all of the records must go through the same switchboard. We have experienced that when you call the same switchboard with a production telemarketing approach, you may overwhelm the attendant. After a number of calls, you may encounter a reluctance to switch the call to the appropriate person. If your list contains duplicate phone numbers, evaluate mixing the records throughout the calling period or only selecting one record to contact.

Now that you've established the list that you'll use for telemarketing, you may want to eliminate the responders from direct mail prior to starting the telemarketing. As we mentioned earlier, the number of responders will be a very small part of the total list. You should evaluate the cost of eliminating the responders and the additional time it will take before you can start telemarketing.

As the telephone calls are made, you will determine if the prospect accepts your offer. Acceptances will be processed similarly to other acceptances from direct mail and inbound telephone. With the telephone program, we will generate another group of prospects who will request additional information. This is due to the immediate decision requirement of outbound telemarketing.

Don't lose those prospects who request additional information. Although most are asking for information simply to get off the phone, in our experience about 25% can be converted into a lead or an order if re-contacted after the material is sent. You should test this concept with your product in order to determine the number of prospects that can be converted to an order or lead.

This sample flow chart, as illustrated in 6-7, is a simplified approach to a telemarketing program. However, it introduces some interesting concepts in using telemarketing and will give us a practical example to develop a business plan and measurement plan.

The Sample Telemarketing Business Plan

Product Information

Total Revenue per Acceptance	$750.00
% Allowable Expense per Order	10.00%
Allowable Cost per Order	$75.00

Total Records in Test   2,000

List Costs

Direct Mail @ $85 per 1000	$85.00
Telemarketing @ 85 per 1000	$85.00
Total List Costs	$170.00

Direct Mail Costs

Cost per 1000 pieces of Mail	$750.00	$1,500.00

Phone Number Look-up

% of records that find number	50.00%	1,000
Cost per Record for Look-up	$0.15	$150.00

Telemarketing Costs

Total Telemarketing Hours	92.3
Cost per Telemarketing Hour	$38.00
Total Telemarketing Costs	$3,507.00

Direct Mail Results

Total Direct Mail Costs	$1,585.00
Total Acceptances Required	21
Required Acceptance Rate	1.10%

Telemarketing Results

% of Total Records Contactable	65.00%
Total Records Contactable	650

Dialings per hour	25
% of Dialings that are contact	30.00%
Contacts per hour	7.5
Total Initial Call Telemarketing Hours	86.7
Total Telemarketing Costs	$3,530.00
Total Acceptances Required	47.07
Required Acceptance Rate	7.20%
Required Acceptances per hour	0.54
Planned Request Literature Rate	7.20%
Request Literature per hour	0.54
Total Hours	86.7
Total Acceptances	47
Total Requests Literature	47

Send Literature Follow-up Call

% of List Contactable	90.00%
Total List Contactable	42
Contacts per hour	7.5
Total Hours	5.6
Follow-up Telemarketing Costs	$212.80
Literature Request Fulfillment Costs	$70.50
Total Literature Request Costs	$283.30
Required Acceptances	3.8
Required % of Follow-up Calls that Accept	8.1%

Total Direct Marketing Costs

Direct Mail	$1,585.00
Initial Telemarketing	$3,530.00
Request Lit Fulfillment @ $1.50 each	$70.50
Request Literature Telemktg Follow-up	$213.00
Total Direct Marketing Costs	**$5,398.50**

Acceptances

Direct Mail	21
Initial Telemarketing	47

Request Lit Fulfillment @ $1.50 each   4

Total Acceptances   **72**

Required Response rate of 2000 records   **3.6%**

Cost per Acceptance   **$74.98**

Like most business plans or pro-formas, the revenue and expense that will be allowed for direct marketing needs to be established. In our example the average order is $750 and the allowable sales expense is 10% or $75 per order.

For the telemarketing test, we will acquire a list of 2,000 records. This list will be sent to a service bureau for phone number look-up and we anticipate that 50% of the original names will be returned with phone numbers. The list is being rented for two contacts, a mail and a phone contact. Therefore, we will have to pay the list owner for using his list two times. The cost for the list is $85 per 1,000 records, therefore our total list costs are $170. Many list owners have minimum charges and small quantities may not meet the minimum charge requirement. You will have to discuss your unique list requirements with your list vendor.

The cost of direct mail is completely variable and will depend on the quantity of material printed, quality, the type of postage and a number of variables that can only be established as you develop your own requirements. Obviously, the more expensive the mailing piece, the higher the results have to be to cover the additional expense. For our example we used $750 per 1,000 pieces mailed as our direct mail costs. We are planning to mail all 2,000 names on the list, even though we will not be able to call all of the names. The mail costs are $1,500. We assumed that the fulfillment kit for people requesting additional information would be more expensive and estimated them at $1.50 per package.

The telephone phone number look-up service will only charge you for those records that match and are able to provide a telephone number.

The telephone look-up services also have minimum charges that you may have to contend with. The price per phone number look-up record will vary depending on the quantity and turn-around you require. The smaller the quantity of records sent to the service, the higher the cost per look-up. For the small quantities we used for this test we estimated the look-up charges at $.15 per record. This probably will not meet the minimum charges at most service bureaus. We estimated, in our example, that only 50% of the records would be found during the phone number search. Therefore, the total expenses are $150.

The cost per telemarketing hour will vary significantly for each company. You can purchase a telemarketing service bureau calling hour from $35.00 to $60.00 per hour depending on volume and the level of support you require. We have used $38.00 as the cost per hour in our example. As an aside, we have rarely seen the average business conduct in-house outbound telemarketing at $38.00 cost per hour if all of the costs are reviewed. You should find the telemarketing cost worksheet discussed earlier very helpful in establishing your cost per hour. As you'll see, the total hours required to make the initial calls and perform follow-up calling to the literature requests amounts to 92.3 hours at $38.00 per hour for a total telemarketing cost of $3,507.00

We have encountered many techniques people use to estimate the results expected from direct marketing programs. Most of the time the expectations are unreasonable or are just guesses as to what people would like to have happen. As the first step in our business plan, we established the revenue per order and the allowable sales expense per order. With these "tools" you can establish the required response rate to have a successful program. By establishing required response rates for each step of your program, you'll be able to measure results as the program is being executed.

If you take the mail and list expenses and divide them by the allowable cost per order, you'll establish the number of orders required for the program to be successful. The total required orders divided by the quantity mailed will give you the required acceptance rate.

Establishing telemarketing results is probably a new experience for you. Remember, we only anticipated that 50% of the records would come back from the service bureau with a phone number. Therefore we'll only be starting with 1000 records for telemarketing. As you may recall from our discussion earlier, the number of attempts you plan to make to each record, the composition of the list and the length of the script can all significantly effect the results you'll experience in telemarketing.

For this business plan we have assumed eight attempts per record and anticipate 25 dialings per hour with 30% of the dialings concluding with a completed call. We have assumed that 65% of the records are contactable. This means that we will complete 7.5 completed calls per hour of calling. This is arrived at by multiplying the initial records starting on the telemarketing list by 65%. In this case we started with 1000 records in telemarketing and 65% of this list equals contacting 650 records. We then established the number of calling hours required by dividing the 650 records by 7.5 completed calls per hour and arrived at 86.7 hours required for the initial call to the prospects.

Now that we have established the number of calling hours, the costs for telemarketing are derived by multiplying the hours by the cost per hour. In our example, 86.7 hours x $38.00 per hour = $3,530.00. As you know we have allowed $75.00 per order in sales expense. We divide the total costs by the allowable sales expense per order and establish the number of orders required in order for this program to be successful. It will take 47.07 orders to have a successful program.

Establishing the required response rates seems pretty easy at first. However, how many records did you really start with? If you assume the 2,000 records that were on the original list we acquired, the required response rate is 2.35% (47.07 ÷ 2,000). The percentage of the 1,000 records available to telemarketing is 4.7% (47.07 ÷ 1,000). The percentage of the 650 records able to be contacted is 7.2% (47.07 ÷ 650).

We suggest you do your planning using both the records available to telemarketing and the records that are contactable. The original list that included names without phone numbers doesn't help measure the program. Our plan reflects the percentage of completed calls. This allows us to focus on the per hour results and measure the program while it is in progress.

We established the acceptance rate per hour by dividing the number of acceptances required by the number of hours. In our example this was .54 acceptances per hour (47.07 ÷ 86.7).

We have assumed that for each acceptance we will also generate another person who will request additional information. Therefore, we will have .54 literature requesters per hour in addition to the .54 acceptances of our offer. Literature requesters are important because we plan to fulfill their requests with information and then make an additional phone call to follow-up and attempt to generate them into a lead. We will have additional expenses to fulfill the literature requestors of $70.50 in mail expense (47 x $1.50 fulfillment kit expense).

The additional phone call will be made 10 to 15 days after the mail is sent. We have planned a 90% contact of these prospects at the same 7.5 completed calls per hour. Therefore we anticipate 5.6 hours of telemarketing (47 x 90% = 42.3 completed calls) (42.3 ÷ 7.5 = 5.6 hours). The total cost for the literature fulfillment and follow-up calling is $283.30 ($70.50 mail costs + $212.80 phone costs). For this part of the program to be successful, we need 3.8 acceptances ($283.30 ÷ $75.00 allowable sales expense). This is a required response rate of 8.1%. You could have actually planned this segment of the program at a 25% response rate because of our prior experiences. Either approach would be acceptable; if you have no prior experience, the 8.1% planning number is more conservative.

The total direct marketing costs are now easy to establish. We summarize the total direct mail, initial telemarketing, literature request fulfillment and literature request follow-up telemarketing to establish the total direct marketing costs.

The total acceptances are also summarized. The total costs are than divided by the total acceptances to establish the cost per acceptance for the program. If we had used the required 3.8 acceptances for the follow-up calling we would have only had 72 acceptances for the project. This means that we need a total response rate of 3.6% of the total 2,000 records we started with. It may seem contradictory to go back to the 2,000 original records, but this allows you to examine the entire program. We have included all of the costs and if this program performs as planned, we will have a successful direct marketing program.

Mail and Phone Synergy

Mail and phone together can together create very powerful results. Like any other direct marketing program, the results will depend on your approach, product and list. We had an opportunity to actually see and measure a program that proved how effective the two media can be together because it allowed us to break-through and reach our target contact.

Trillion was a small software company that sold a innovative product to personal computer users. The product established a common interface to several of the most popular software products operating on the PC. The company was in deep financial trouble and looking for a way to contact the major users of PC's in larger businesses.

A direct marketing program was designed to use direct mail and follow-up with a telemarketing call. The telephone call was to follow the mail by ten days to maximize the synergy of the mail and phone. A special offer was created which allowed the prospect to receive five copies of the software product for 30 days absolutely free. At the end of the 30 day trial, the prospect could keep all the copies and pay our invoice, which was substantially discounted, or return the software and owe nothing. In addition, the prospect could keep one copy of the software as an incentive for trying the product.

We acquired a list of 2,000 known large users of PC's. These were mostly larger companies and all had at least 50 PC's in use in their business. Our contact was the PC coordinator or the director of data processing. The list was name directed and fairly current -- no older than one year.

A mail-gram format was used to make the offer and explain the product to the prospect prior to any telemarketing contact. A response vehicle was included to allow the prospect to accept the offer in the mail. The free trail and free copy premium were highlighted in bold headlines in the mail-gram format. In addition a small brochure was included to give some limited details about the product. The response in the mail was under 1%.

The phone program started ten days after the mail was dropped. The telemarketing service bureau actually performed the mail creation, production and letter-shop services so we were able to ensure the proper timing of the phone behind the mail.

The results were not very gratifying. The phone produced at about 4% of completed calls and the results were not considered successful. We began to examine the phone results and found that the prospect did not recall our mailing and could not understand the benefit in trying the Trillion product. Our problem was breaking through to the decision makers and making them understand the offer. As we mentioned earlier, it is almost impossible to sell a new concept over the phone. The prospect has to have an understanding of the products for the phone effort to be successful.

We decided to send the prospect a premium that we thought would help our total effort. An inexpensive tee-shirt was designed and created that said "Be a Trillionaire". We again included a personalized computer quality letter and mailed the Tee-shirt, 1st class to the prospect. Our offer remained the same. There was almost a 30 day delay in the program while the shirts were developed. Due to timing problems, we only offered inbound phone as the response vehicle in this mailing. The outbound telemarketing program remained virtually the same.

The combined mail and phone results on this second approach was over 45%.   Almost all the executives we talked to recalled our mailing and were very interested in trying the product.

This program clearly demonstrates the powerful effect of mail and phone. It also proves that we can only get through to our targeted contacts if we create an appropriate mail and phone approach. The data processing executive is overwhelmed by mail from many sources. For your program to succeed in this environment, the creative will have to "break through" the clutter on his desk. We found that a premium (amusing and personalized) could be very effective. The mail and phone combined approach allowed the prospect to have a prior understanding of the product and accept the offer with less reluctance and fear. We had informed the prospect in the second mailing that we intended to call and ask for his acceptance of our offer.

Telemarketing Summarized

In this chapter, we tried to establish a definition of telemarketing that clearly distinguishes telephone selling or telesales from direct marketinging, telemarketing.   If you are using telesales there are some elements of direct marketing that can significantly improve results. The database and timely follow-up of information requests can substantially assist the salesperson who is selling on the telephone. However, it will remain very difficult to measure cost and results in the telesales environment.

Telemarketing removes dependency on any individual's personality for results in the marketing program. It uses a script and is controllable in both its costs and results. Let's again look at the definition of telemarketing we established earlier:

Telemarketing is a medium used to perform direct marketing.

- *It is controllable, measurable and not dependent on the individual for its success.*
- *It can be used as support of direct mail or advertising or as a*

stand alone campaign.
- *It is a planned series of contacts, using a constant message, seeking to produce a lead or an order.*
- *It builds and maintains a database and is completely measurable in its cost and results.*
- *It can be outbound or inbound telephone calling .*
- *It can be either used to market to consumers or other businesses.*

Telemarketing uses a scripted or message controlled communicator to deliver a direct marketing message over the telephone.

You will have to evaluate both your inbound and outbound requirements for the effective use of telemarketing. If you're using inbound, make sure that the communicator staff is aware of your advertising and direct mail plan. In addition, plan your efforts to deal with respondents who may call your phone number during your non-business hours.

As you evaluate your inbound requirements, examine your costs to provide the service yourself and then price outside vendors. You may find that an outside service is more economical and efficient.

Outbound telemarketing is a strong promotional format but is dependent on the offer you make. You really can't sell anything new during an outbound call and, after list selection, the strength of the promotion will be your offer. Remember, you will only have about 30 seconds to convince your prospect to listen to the rest of your proposition. Good script writing includes making a compelling offer very early in the phone call.

We examined a number of script approaches including outlines and flip cards. A complete example of a flip card script is available in Chapter two. Evaluate and decide on the best script approach for your program.

Like any direct marketing program, outbound telemarketing is controllable and measurable. You can plan and evaluate your results in a fairly short period of time. The key to measurement is the plan you develop prior to the telemarketing program.

Mail and phone are the ideal combined direct marketing program. In fact, once you commit to telemarketing you will need direct mail to answer requests for additional information. The combination of the two formats typically produces greater results than the sum of each format run independently.

Telemarketing is a powerful weapon in your marketing arsenal. It is one of the fastest growing promotional formats being used by business today. If you haven't tried telemarketing, you're missing a tremendous opportunity.

Chapter Seven - Direct Mail

Direct Mail Defined

Direct mail is the primary format businesses use to execute direct marketing. The direct mail format allows the business-to-business marketer to select from a large variety of creative options for soliciting prospects and customers. With direct mail you can select whatever environment and voice you feel is appropriate. Direct mail allows you to lead the reader through the offer and to the response vehicle using your own tempo and rhythm.

There are other media and formats that may allow similar creative flexibility (such as space advertising), however, none are as targeted as the direct mail format. Direct mail allows you to involve the reader as no other medium can. A mailing has the unique opportunity of receiving 100% of its reader's attention. A name directed mailing can be targeted and personalized more so than any other medium.

Direct mail is the most testable of media; you can vary each mailing piece. Each reader can receive a personalized mailing suited to his/her individual needs, tastes and desires. You can test the positioning of your product and provide research on how to proceed within the entire market. The same flexibility exists with telemarketing, but it is not available in print or broadcast promotion.

The advantages of personalization, targeting and copy flexibility cause direct mail to be somewhat expensive on a cost-per-contact basis. As you may recall from our earlier discussions, direct mail is just ahead of telemarketing in the cost-per-contact matrix. Illustration 7-1 re-emphasizes the personalization and cost-per- contact compari-

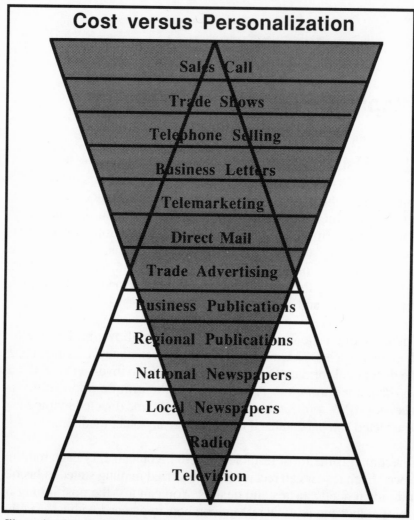

Illustration 7-1: Cost vs personalization.

son.

The additional costs mean that the response rates and closing rates for inquiries generated through direct mail have to be higher than similar inquiries generated in print or broadcast promotions.

Direct mail responders tend to be of high quality because the message they receive in the mail is clear and concise. The prospects understand the offer and are responding to something they are interested in. When evaluating the success of the direct response marketing program, the cost per order will normally prove that direct mail is one of the most economical direct marketing media available.

Creating a Direct Mail Piece

The varieties of direct mail pieces range from a simple post card to a full color catalog. Anything mailed to potential customers can be classified as direct mail, even a price list.

By definition, direct marketing is designed to produce a lead or an order. An ad run in a magazine to create awareness and a brochure used as a "leave behind" aren't designed to produce leads or orders. Don't start a direct mail program by taking inventory of existing printed material and deciding what will fit in an envelope.

Many a business managers has mailed a reprint of an ad and decided "Direct mail doesn't work!" These managers did not have a direct marketing program; they simply mailed an advertisement. Mailing an existing brochure designed as sales collateral can prove just as unsuccessful. Saving pennies in the cost of producing a mailing can cause the loss of dollars in terms of results.

The design of a direct mail package begins with the business plan you have created and the objectives you want to achieve. In the promotion chapter we discussed the four elements of a direct marketing program:

- List

- Offer

- Format

- Copy

In your business plan you defined the target universe you want to reach, focusing on their personalities and buying motivations. As with any direct marketing promotion, these personality issues will govern the format and copy. A brochure designed to be left with the president of a company should not be delivered to a specifying engineer.

The list and offer account for 75% of your success. If your existing materials do not contain your direct response offer, they should not be used. If you use existing materials to a mailing, your list may be correct but your results may not achieve your objectives.

To produce a lead or an order, make your target market an offer that will ask them to take the desired action. Making the offer a second thought will prevent the package from achieving its objectives.

Create the direct mail package as if you are writing a single letter to a well-defined individual. The goal of the creative effort is to move the target to take the action you want. During the planning process you defined an offer that, if accepted, would achieve your objectives. In addition, you have identified the personality of the target people in your market. Your creative effort should use a custom format and direct mail copy to reach your targets.

A direct mail piece created to reach an analytical individual will not be as effective when mailed to an extrovert. Such a mailing may generate results because the list is correct. However, the results may not be

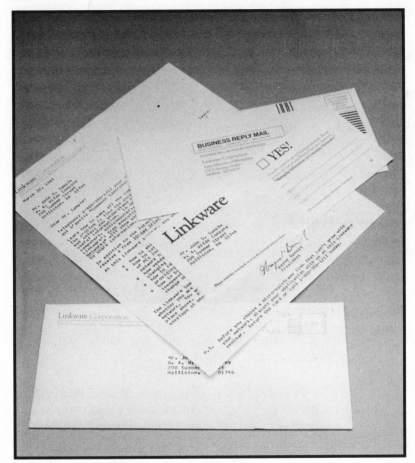

Illustration 7-2: A standard direct mail package

enough to constitute a successful program.

The standard direct mail package contains:

- an outer envelope
- a letter
- a brochure
- a response device
- a prepaid reply envelope
  (see Illustration 7-2 for a standard direct mail piece)

Except for the outer envelope and the reply envelope, each element of the direct mail package should be able to stand alone. Each element should contain the product benefits, the offer and a way to respond by mail and/or phone. A mailing may come disassembled in its target's office; the prospect may receive or save only a portion of the mailing. The letter, the brochure and the response device should all be stand-alone elements creating their own AIDA (Attention, Interest, Desire, Action). This is why existing materials may not fit your direct mail needs.

Copy and Graphics

There are two major areas of consideration within the creative process:

- Copy: The words you use to explain you offer and product.

- Graphic: The visual elements you use to explain your offer and product.

It is unrealistic to try to explain all of the rules of style that pertain to copywriting in this book. For more information about complete texts on copywriting for direct mail, request a bibliography from the Direct Marketing Association, 6 East 43rd Street, New York, New York 10017.

The point we want to make here is that copy should be written with the target in mind. The length of the copy depends on the needs of the target. When writing copy to a person working in a stand-up industry (hair stylist, gas station manager, independent retailer) copy must be short and to the point. This type of individual is not oriented to heavy reading while sitting at a desk. He will probably review a mailing package in the same manner as a consumer standing over a trash can.

If you are writing to a lawyer who is accustomed to reading while sitting, long copy can be successful. In this environment there is a bigger problem: Getting your mailing passed a secretary and to the reader. Remember, Bertha Barrier! This problem is independent of the length of copy and must be addressed in the overall strategy of the direct marketing plan.

The length of the copy can be tested. There is a perpetual battle between those who advocate long copy and those who advocate short copy. There is only one rule that applies in either case: Copy that interests the reader will be read.

We have all heard and used the term "junk mail." Mail that addresses products of interest to the reader is not junk; mail that addresses products that are of no interest to the reader is junk. If the reader is interested in the copy, its length is insignificant.

Headlines are copy set apart from text by position and size. Headlines and sub-heads are copy used as a word graphic. Being set apart and in larger type, headlines pull the eye toward them. Headlines should reach out to the reader with the strongest benefit available. Many people do not read past headlines unless their interest is aroused. Headlines are, therefore, the magnet that will draw people into the offer.

When there are too many headlines and sub-heads on a page, the overall visual effect may put off the reader. Too many headlines mean no headlines, no visual magnet that stands out to draw the reader's eye in.

Using headlines in letters reduces the similarity between promotion and a true business letter. Few people use headlines in business correspondence. Headlines create more of a promotional impression than a business correspondence impression. Headlines are fine in brochures and on reply devices, which are normally viewed with promotional eyes by the reader. If you're trying to convey the image of a standard business letter, headlines may not be effective.

In the research for this book, we found that we could not improve on Bob Stone's formula for letter writing. As found in his book, *Successful Direct Marketing Methods*, Third Edition (Crain Books, an

imprint of National Textbook Company, Lincolnwood, Illinois), here
is Bob Stone's letter writing formula:

Promise a benefit in your headline or first paragraph - your
most important benefit. You simply can't go wrong by leading
off with the most important benefit to the reader. Some writers believe in the slow buildup. But most experienced writers
I know favor making the important point first.

Immediately enlarge on your most important benefit. This
step is crucial. Many writers come up with a great lead, then
fail to follow through. Or they catch attention with their head-
ing, but then take two or three paragraphs to warm up to their
subject. The reader's attention is gone! Try hard to elaborate
on your most important benefit right away, and you'll build up
interest fast.

Tell the reader specifically what he or she is going to get. It's
amazing how many letters lack details on such basic product
features as size, color, weight, and sales terms. Perhaps the
writer is so close to his proposition he assumes the reader
knows all about it. A dangerous assumption! And when you
tell the reader what he or she's going to get, don't overlook the
intangibles that go along with your product or service. For
example, he's getting smart appearance in addition to a pair of
slacks, knowledge in addition to a 340-page book.

Back up your statements with proof and endorsements. Most
prospects are somewhat skeptical about advertising. They
know it sometimes gets a little overenthusiastic about a product. So they accept it only with a grain of salt. If you can
back up your own statements with third-party testimonials or a
list of satisfied users, everything you say becomes more
believable.

Tell the reader what she might lose if she doesn't act. As
noted, people respond affirmatively either to gain something

they do not possess or to avoid losing something they already have. Here's a good spot in your letter to overcome human inertia - imply what may be lost if action is postponed. People don't like to be left out. A skillful writer can use this human trait as a powerful influence in his or her message.

Rephrase your prominent benefits in your closing offer. As a good salesperson does, sum up the benefits to the prospect in your closing offer. This is the proper prelude to asking for action. This is where you can intensify the prospect's desire to have the product. The stronger the benefits you can persuade the reader to recall, the easier it will be for him or her to justify an affirmative decision.

Incite Action, Now. This is the spot where you win or lose the battle with inertia. Experienced advertisers, know once a letter is put aside or tossed into that file, you're out of luck. So wind up with a call for action and a logical reason for acting now. Too many letters close with a statement like "supplies are limited". That argument lacks credibility. Today's consumer knows you probably have a warehouse full of merchandise. So make your reason a believable one. For example, "It may be many months before we go back to press on this book." Or "Orders are shipped on a first-come basis. The sooner yours is received, the sooner you can be enjoying your new widget."

The old adage "a picture is worth a thousand words" is applicable in direct mail. Graphics can be in two forms: photography and illustration.

Photography is just that: pictures of the product and its use. Use either color or black-and-white depending on the overall design and budget of the package. Color can be a powerful tool to support or defeat your offer. When offering a budget priced product, color can defeat the offer. When offering color-coordinated work clothes, black-and-white can defeat the offer by not showing the benefits color coordination will bring to the buyer.

Graphics should show the reader the benefits of the product. Just showing pictures of the product, without showing a benefit, will not help the selling effort. Using photography because it already exists can do as much damage as using brochures that already exist.

Another decision you make will be whether to use photography, illustrations or both. A simple concept which can help you decide which approach to use:

- photography depicts reality

Illustration 7-3: An illustrated graphic.

- illustration depicts illusion or fantasy, the dream of what can be.

We can use a combination of photography and illustration in the same piece to generate both of these impressions in the mind of the reader.

The overall layout of any direct mail component is also a graphic. A brochure that is copy from top to bottom and from side to side, it is visually oppressive. Most people will not bother to read such a piece. Because the overall look of the piece is visually unappealing, the copy will never be read.

Graphics can also take the form of small design elements that are used as visual breaks between copy points. Such graphics, like *, give the mind a chance to breathe ^ before continuing to read.

An illustrated graphic can be used to present a product and its application. The mailing in Illustration 7-3, shows how a piece of capital equipment solved confusion in a manufacturing environment.

Many field salespeople found this illustration posted on prospects' bulletin boards with names of employees written on the illustrated people. The illustration from the mailing lived on long after the mailing was complete. The company name, product, solution and offer were continually selling the prospect.

The Components of a Direct Mail Package

The differences in direct mail packages are as varied as the individuals who create them. A package can include many different pieces. Many companies even include multiple types of components in the same mailing.

Outer Envelope

The outer envelope is the passport that will get the message to the reader, just as a salesperson's appearance is the passport that allows him/her to make a presentation. You never get a second chance to make a first impression, so do not underestimate the outer envelope.

The most acceptable outer envelope appears as a professional business letter to someone you have a relationship with. The envelope would have a preprinted *cornercard* (the return address information printed in the upper left-hand corner) with company name and logo, a personal address and first class postage. This type of outer envelope is the most expensive since the contents, (the letter and the reply device) should also be personalized where appropriate. Prospects receiving this kind of expensive looking mailing usually open the envelope. This type of personalized mailing is a tedious task for the lettershop and will increase the cost.

If you decide against the business letter format, you can try a variety of creative approaches with the outer envelope. Keep in mind that the goal is to have the prospect open the envelope and read the message.

If you decide to use window envelopes to cut costs, there is no point in maintaining the professional letter appearance. No one uses window envelopes for business letters on a day-to-day basis. With a window envelope, you can use bulk postage, oversized envelopes, graphics and/or copy on the outer envelope. You can test these variables to see which outer envelope yields the greatest results. In essence, if you are not going to use the professional letter format, you have no limit on what you can do with the outer envelope so you should experiment.

Quite often, the outer envelope is stripped from the contents by an administrator before the prospect sees it. Unlike consumer mail, Bertha Barrier may strip the contents from the outer envelope as a service to her boss. You therefore have a two-step creative challenge:

- To get the mailing reviewed and accepted by the administrator before it is passed along.

- If the mailing reaches the prospect unopened, to have it opened and reviewed.

It is probably better to use more professional envelopes when mailing to larger businesses that typically have administrators. When mailing to small businesses that do not have such a screen, a more graphic attention-getting outer envelope may improve results.

Letter

The letter should appear as though you were sending a one-of-a-kind letter to each individual, just as though you were mailing a personalized business letter. This process is expensive and may not prove cost effective.

Write your direct mail letters to someone you know, assuming they know nothing about your product or service. Follow the AIDA formula we discussed earlier in Chapter five.

The elements of the direct mail letter are the same as a normal business letter:

- Printed letterhead
- Date, month and year are fine without a day of the month
- Addressee information - name of contact, title, address. It is appropriate to title- or function-address letters when you don't have a contact name.
- Salutation
- Letter body
- Complimentary close
- Signature
- Administrative code
- Postscript

Like most written works, your letter must look readable and be attractive to your prospect. If a page is packed from top to bottom and from side to side with prose, the odds are pretty good that it will not get read. Examine the letters you read and enjoy; they are probably written with short paragraphs and contain lots of white space around the copy or prose. Use yourself as a guide and don't mail anything that you wouldn't read.

The reader's interest and eye movement will travel first to the letter-head and addressee information, next to the salutation (those parts that contain the reader's name and title), to the signature block (to see who and of what station is the sender), to the P.S. (unfortunately an uncommon occurrence in a business letter, but when used a real eye-catcher). The P.S. should contain the primary benefit and a call to action since it will probably be read before the body of the letter.

Direct mail letters can contain headlines and sub-heads to get the reader involved with your sales presentation. Be careful not to sell features but to focus on the benefits the prospect will receive from your product or service. The use of headlines and other eye-catching techniques, such as bold face type, italics and different size type fonts, set direct mail apart from the standard business letter. Unfortunately, these techniques can be over done to a point that they become a turn-off to the prospect. The best approach will move prospects completely though the presentation and have them feel as though the letter was written to them personally.

Brochure

The brochure may or may not be necessary. If needed support information cannot be put into the letter, a brochure may be required. A brochure is generally required when trying to sell a product or service in a mailing. The brochure can cover all of the information readers may need to satisfy their technical questions prior to making a purchase decision.

A brochure can be multi-color, multi-page with beautiful (and expensive) art and pictures, or it can be a single page of information about a specific product or service.

If you do require a brochure, make sure that it is consistent with the objective of the direct mail program. An over-supply of brochures from a trade show or sales force collateral material, may not be effective as a direct mail brochure. The brochure must contain all of the information about the offer and a call to action. Remember, it may be used separately by your prospect.

The brochure is also a place to sample the product or service. Prospects can see (using art and photographs) the product and receive a detailed explanation of how the product can meet their needs. Testimonials and case histories can be discussed to help overcome FUD (fear, uncertainty and doubt); and the offer can be reinforced and discussed. The brochure can be a lot more explicit than the letter. In fact, you can even reference the brochure in the letter.

A brochure is not always required or advisable. A brochure that gives an overview of the product or service, may provide insufficient information to make the sale, but enough for the reader to determine that the product or service is not for them. If you are selling a seminar that will give detailed information on a specific product or service, enclosing a brochure in the mailing can actually depress response.

Lead generation programs are designed to have a salesperson visit the prospect and review the product offering. You may not want to give the prospect enough information to determine that he doesn't need your offering. A detailed brochure could do more damage than good in this situation. On the other hand, you may want only a few good leads and offer a brochure as a fulfillment device with detailed information on your products or services. You may want to offer the brochure as an information kit if the prospect fills out the response vehicle and returns it for fulfillment.

Whether or not your mailing requires a brochure is directly related to the objective you've set for the program. If the objective is the direct sale of a product, the mailing will probably include a brochure explaining the details of the product or service. If you're trying to generate leads, the use of a brochure may be excess baggage in the mailing package.

If you determine that a brochure is appropriate in your mailing package, it may be worthwhile to test a group of prospects who receive no brochure to determine the effect the brochure is having on your program.

Reply Envelope

The prepaid business reply envelope (BRE) has become a standard. Your local post office can supply you with layouts. The preprinted portion of the reply envelope is strictly regulated by the United States Postal Service.

Since this element of the mailing is more of an administrative piece, it is probably not worth the time to overlay your creative efforts in either design or paper selection to enhance it. Black printing on white envelopes will fill the bill if you use a BRE. In fact, you may choose not to include a BRE as a part of your mailing package.

It is not unusual to use a Business Reply Card (BRC) or to request inbound telephone as the response vehicle. Reply envelopes or cards may go largely unused when you provide a telephone number for prospects to use for their response. If your budget permits, use a BRE in your mailing package.

If you are an infrequent mailer, you may not want to go through the process of getting a reply mail number from your servicing post office. You could then provide prospects with a self-addressed envelope that they could stamp and return. This could save expense, and there is no evidence that prepaid postage in business mailings is as critical as it is in consumer marketing.

The easier you make it for your prospect to respond, the better the odds are that he/she will take the desired action. If you only offer a telephone response vehicle, the prospect may feel uncomfortable with the pressure of being sold on the phone. A BRC-only response vehicle may make the prospect uncomfortable with having the information able to be read by all. A BRE without postage may turn the prospect off because of his financial doubts about your company. Evaluate your market and the prospect you're trying to reach to determine the requirement for a response vehicle.

Response Device

The most critical element of a direct mail package is the response device. In fact, you would be well advised to begin your creative process by creating the response device. By creating the response device, you finalize the action you want the prospect to take as a result of the direct mail program.

With the response device designed, you can create the letter and brochure around the action you want the reader to take. This sounds simple enough, but direct mail is not always implemented in this way. More often than not, people spend weeks on the letter copy and put together a response device as an after-thought. The situation is often compounded by a lot of time pressure, as the mailing is probably running behind schedule and has to be finished immediately.

The response device should be easy to understand. People in business are generally careful about what they respond to since they are representing their company when they act. The response device should not be a legal looking document that may frighten the reader. If you are looking for a legal, binding commitment, your response will probably be small.

The flow of the response device should be the same as the flow of the letter and brochure. Do not introduce anything on the response device that has not been covered elsewhere in the mailing. This ties in with the concept that each piece of the mailing should be able to stand alone.

The concept of no surprises as you ask for the order is not new to the art of salesmanship. Good salespeople know that once you've built your proposition with the prospect, ask for the order and shut up. The next person to talk loses. Never introduce a new idea or concept at the close that gives the prospect something he/she can question or object to. This basic approach to selling holds true in direct mail. The response device asks for the order. You may want to reestablish the benefits -- but ask for the order and shut up. Don't try to introduce new concepts on the response device that haven't already been covered in the letter and brochure.

The response device should contain your phone number in several places. If a prospect is completing the reply form and the phone number is conspicuous, he/she may decide to pick up the phone and call. The impulse decision can be important, and you want to make it easy to reach you.

If the prospect does decide to call, you can begin selling and cross-selling during the phone conversation. The phone moves you more quickly into a personal relationship with the prospect and allows you to sell faster with larger orders. In addition, if your phone number is on the response device, the prospect will have information about your product in front of him/her when he/she calls. You are on his/her mind, and he/she is in a positive mode. The prospect took the inertia to call you; this is a great time to move your relationship forward.

Many readers of direct mail breeze through the letter and the brochure and go directly to the response device. They want to determine how much money, if any, the offer will cost if they choose to take advantage of it. They look at the response device as a summary, an outline of the mailing. Many people read the response device to determine whether it's worth their time to read the entire mailing.

If you're asking your prospects to spend $2,000 for your proposition and their buying authority is only $100, you have probably lost the buyer. If they perceived a benefit and value from your proposition and response device, they may read the mailing and refer it to someone who has authority. In either case, you are not going to make an immediate sale, but the response device sure played an important role in the direction they will take.

It could be fun to test mail your response device as a stand-alone mailing package. It may work as well as the entire package at a much

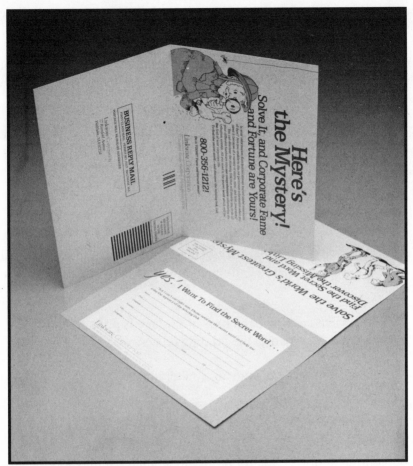

Illustration 7-4: A response device as the entire mailing.

lower cost. In this type of mailing, your offer is for a simple response only - - no money enclosed. You can offer a "Bill Me" or trial samples or free issues of a magazine. Illustration 7-4 shows an entire mailing. This is an example of a response device without a package.

Response devices take many forms and formats. Business Reply Cards (BRC) are the most common. The prospect is asked to complete the card and send it back. The BRC is frequently a self-addressed, prepaid postage mailer. Even if you have a prepaid postage BRC, you should also include a BRE for the prospect to use. Many business people feel more secure in knowing their response will be handled in a confidential manner.

When mailing packages are computer generated to take advantage of the personalization possibilities, it is fairly common to have the BRE as a tear-off portion of the document.

Response devices can be designed to get the prospect involved in the promotion and perform some task as they complete the process. There are no limits to the format of the response device. The key is involvement by the reader and, most importantly, ACTION.

Postage

One of the most frequently overlooked components of the direct mail format is postage. There are three methods of applying postage to a mailing:

- Preprinted -- where the type of postage is printed on the mailing pieces as part of the printing process.

- Metered -- where a postage meter applies postage directly to the piece.

- Stamped -- where actual stamps are affixed to the mailing.

The preprinted form is fine for promotional mail but may kill the personalized image when using the business letter format.

In the business letter format, use metered postage since most businesses use postage meters in their day-to-day operations. Stamps can be an attention-getting device on a business mailing, since stamps are seldom seeen on business letters.

Your target may never see the outer envelope, so in a lot of cases the postage decision may be moot. However, some businesses have instructed their mailrooms not to deliver third class or bulk mail. The mailroom personnel do not look at the postage actually paid, but at the mailing's nature and approach. If mail looks too promotional, it may be discarded by the mailroom staff even if it carries first class postage.

There are two basic postage rates for direct mail:

- First class - cost fixed for the first ounce, and restricted in size to no larger than 6 1/8 by 11 1/2 inches and no smaller than 3 1/2 by 5 inches. Additional weight costs extra per ounce up to 12 ounces maximum.

- Third class or bulk - cost fixed for the first 3.91 ounces with no size constraints. Additional weight costs extra per ounce up to 16 ounces maximum. A minimum number of pieces is required for a third class mailing.

Each of these two classes of postage also has reduced rates for pre-sort, tie and bag preparation before entering the mail stream. Check with your local post office for the regulations that will affect your mailing. A lettershop that prepares mailings will also be able to provide current postal information.

Postage can be a major cost element for direct mail efforts. Almost every conceivable approach to affixing postage and postage rates has been tested. There typically is little difference in response between first or third class rates. Metered mail usually pulls better than stamps, and a well-designed, preprinted permit will pull as well as metered mail.

The decision to use either first or third class postage will be governed by the speed at which you want the mail delivered. First-class mail is normally delivered within three to five days. Third class mail is delivered at the leisure of the post office but can stay in any single facility for a maximum of 48 hours. For a national mailing, it could take as long as 15 work days for third class mail to be delivered.

First class delivery costs almost twice as much, therefore you should evaluate the speed at which you need the mailing delivered in making the postage decision.

There are no rules or known formulas that can govern the best method to affix postage to your mail or determine the best postage rate to use. The way to determine which will be best for you is to test different techniques. However, this is not a major point. After establishing the best lists, offer and major formats, it may be worthwhile to test postage approaches.

Illustration 7-5: A "Pop-Up" mailing.

Breaking Through

The biggest challenge in direct mail is breaking through the clutter of mail that a prospect receives each day. As mailers use more standard creative direct mail packages that are sold by various production facilities around the country, the clutter will increase. As you economize more and more, you'll run the risk of becoming part of the clutter rather than beating it.

You can test to determine if frequency will be more important to your

Illustration 7-6: Popcorn Breakthrough Mailing

direct mail program than creative approaches. Most business publishers and seminar companies have decided that frequency, and not creativity is the key to results. If you are on any business lists you have received the 8 1/2 by 11 inch three-fold, self-mailing brochure from at least one seminar company. This format seems to be the standard.

Breakthrough creative is the development of some type of package that yields the best results for the investment. In some cases, breakthrough can mean just getting a mailing read. This can be a real challenge in markets where there are a few buyers and many sellers. For example, trying to reach MIS managers for the Fortune 1,000 companies.

To reach a difficult and highly mail cluttered prospect, it may be necessary to develop packages that get attention because of size and shape. These are called *dimensional mailings*. Dimensional mailings are generally large in a three-dimensional sense; they are packages or fat letters that have a tendency to get put on top the prospect's mail pile. Once delivered, a dimensional mailing should follow the AIDA rules.

The use of a dimensional mailing can be effective in breaking through to a prospect you have been trying to reach. The dimensional can be directly related to the offer or just a cute approach to getting the prospect's attention. Illustratiuon 7-6 shows a dimensional mailing to presidents of industrial companies in the metal grinding industry. A six gallon can of popcorn labeled with a fake OSHA placard was used to breakthrough. The purpose of the mailing was to generate leads for a $40,000 filtration system. Sales were 14% of those mailed. Even when sales representatives followed-up non-respondents (up to a year later) the popcorn was recalled.

Formats

Business Mail

As discussed earlier in this chapter, business letters are the format generally used for direct communication in business today. The business letter is a closed-faced envelope addressed from one individual to another. It has no promotional copy on the outer envelope. The letter inside is signed by the individual. A brochure may or may not accompany the letter. There is seldom, if ever, a response device. The response device is the difference between a general business communication and a direct response promotion.

Two techniques are available to produce a direct response letter that resembles an actual business letter:

- Full Print

- Match Fill

For either technique, everyday letterhead must be preprinted in sufficient quantity to satisfy the promotion. To avoid signing thousands of letters, preprint the signature on the letter in a blue ink unless the sender normally uses some black or some personal color ink as a hallmark.

Full print is when the addressee and all of the body copy are generated by the printer. There are several options on the quality and appearance of the print used to generate the letter. The more it looks like a personalized, typed letter, the more expensive it becomes. Computer printing can be accomplished with an impact or non-impact process. The non-impact techniques look close to personalized, typed business letters. Technology continues to expand the options in this area. Review the image, offer and format you are using when selecting the production technique.

Match fill means having the letter body copy typeset and preprinted by a printer, then achieving the appearance of a fully personalized letter. The address, salutation and perhaps some specific information in the body of the letter are added during computer printing. This approach is less expensive since there are less lines to print during the computer run.

Here are a few points to consider to ensure that the match fill letter resembles a full print letter:

1) The letter body should be generated on the same equipment that will be used to complete the match fill. This will ensure that the letter is not set in two different fonts-- Like this.

2) The letter body should be printed in a dark grey ink rather than black. Printer ribbons tend to fade quickly and often appear grey.

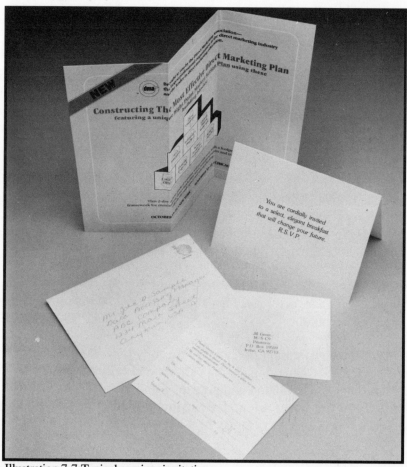

Illustration 7-7:Typical seminar invitations.

3) Printer alignment is critical. Order extra forms so the computer operators will have all they need for the alignment process.

4) When using a fill in that varies in length (i.e. a person's name inserted in the letter), write copy so the insert will be at the end of a line. This will ensure enough space for the insert, and it will not appear out of position.

In either case, pre-position the signature on the page before the letterhead is printed. This means the letter must be written before the letterhead is printed. If the letter is not written and printed in the same font and type size before positioning the signature, there may not be enough or too much space for the signature. There are situations where a whole letter was written around a preprinted signature block spaced improperly on the page.

You will need to know which type of paper your printer requires. Computer printers require either continuous form paper (paper connected top to bottom with computer pin-holes on the sides) or single sheet fed individually into the printer.

We don't believe there are such things as junk mail and junk telephone. There are poorly implemented uses of the media that get classified as junk. We hope you will think about how your promotion will be classified by your targets. Don't mail anything you wouldn't want to receive. Some things to consider:

NO LABELS. Business mail is never sent with an address label. If you must use labels, do not waste your energy on a personalized letter. The label will probably be a different color than the envelope and will probably be affixed to the envelope a little askew. The labeled envelope does not demonstrate the same care given in the preparation of a business letter. If you are going to use labels, spend your money on other elements of the mailing. It will be clear to the target that it is not a business letter, and you will have to use other techniques to ensure that it is read.

NO TEASER. Teaser copy or teaser graphics on the outer envelope is designed to get the reader into the envelope. Teasers are not normally used on business letters, so do not use them when you are trying to make an envelope look like business mail. (As demonstrated in Illustration 7-2).

Making your promotion appear like a business letter increases its chances of being read but also increases the cost.

Letter Packages

A letter package is a direct mail promotion that uses the same general size envelope used for business letters. This can range from an invitation size to a number 10, regular business size envelope. The envelope can be closed faced or have a window. A great deal of business direct mail uses the window envelope since it is less expensive to address and mail. Illustration 7-8 shows a letter package in a regular business-size envelope.

A mailing in a window envelope costs less because the target address appears only one time and shows through the window. The address often appears on the response device. Addressing on the response device allows capture of accurate information about the responder. It also makes it easier for the target to respond because he/she does not have to complete a response device.

We suggest that you personalize the response device. Business promotions are often passed on to other people, so you may receive responses from people you originally did not target. Personalizing the response device ensures that you will be able to establish the coding and source information even if the responder is different from the target.

Letter packages generally only carry personalization on one piece within the package. The balance of the mailing includes:
- the letter, which is generically addressed to Dear Executive, or Dear Associate

Illustration 7-8: Letter Package - Number 10 envelope.

- a brochure
- response device
- business reply envelope (if the response device is not a BRC).

This type of mailing can often prove to be the most productive because of its relatively low cost compared with a business letter format. The cost savings are primarily in the addressing and matching of addresses. The components of the mailing are often the same as the business letter. The personalization, high-quality print and matching of multiple elements in the business letter format tend to be expensive.

The letter package can carry a teaser on the outer envelope. The teaser can be in the form of copy or graphics intended to get the reader into the package and into the offer.

Oversize Packages

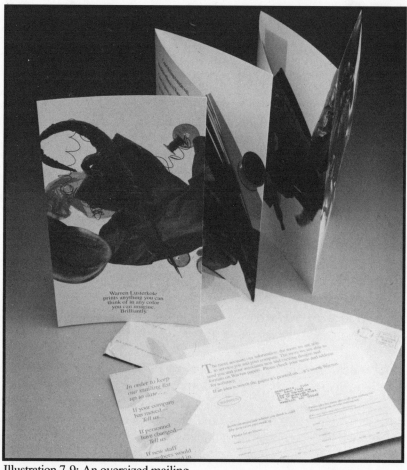

Illustration 7-9: An oversized mailing

Any mailing package that is larger than a number 10 business envelope is an oversized mailing. This is a United States Postal Service definition. Fulfillment literature sent in a 9-by-12 inch envelope is an oversized mailing. The advantage of oversized packages is that they receive special handling because everyone thinks there is extra postage involved.

This is true in mailing first class. It is not true in the bulk mail rates where the 9-by-12 requires the same postage as the number 10 envelope. This means you can use the 9-by-12 mailing to gain extra attention in a direct mail promotion. You can go larger or smaller that the 9-by-12 depending on the production techniques being used. Keep postal regulations in mind when producing an oversized package.

Check with your local post office to determine the appropriate regulations that govern the relationship of your package's height to the length. Regulations govern the ratio of height to length because of postal machines and handling. If your package does not meet the requirements of the postal service, you will be subject to additional postage even for a bulk mailing.

Teasers can be used on oversized mailings when you determine a promotional look is best. If you're not going to use teasers on the envelope, you may want to consider a business-looking label, similar to the concept of the business letter. The more a promotion looks like general business correspondence, the better the chances are that it will be opened and read by your target.

Self-Mailers

You can choose not to use an envelope at all. The elements of your promotion can be printed on a single sheet and folded to a size that can be mailed. Self-mailers can also be brochures or catalogs consisting of multiple sheets bound together and mailed.

The advantages of self-mailers are that they:

- are generally inexpensive to produce
- are easily readable
- get the target involved without opening an envelope
- allow you to quickly state your offer

The main disadvantage of a self-mailer is that the response device is printed on the same weight paper as the entire mailing, unless a heavier weight paper is bound or attached for the response device. This

Illustration 7-10: A Self-Mailer.

means you must print the entire piece on a seven point paper stock, the minimum the post office allows for a return postcard.

Your choices are:

1) Use seven point stock so the reply device can be mailed back as a card.

2) Use 3.5 point stock so a response device can be made of a sheet folded in two to yield the seven-point necessary for mailing. This requires a glue strip or some other form of closure. The post office is getting touchy about staple mail because it hangs in their machines. You could get hit with extra postage if you ask the recipient to use a stapler.

3) Request the reader to insert the reply form in his/her own envelopes. One of the basic rules of direct marketing is to make it easy for your prospect to respond. If you ask the prospect to use his/her own envelope, you've made it more difficult to respond by adding a step. Most targets will not have an envelope handy and may not make an effort to get one.

4) Ask for telephone response only. Even though you will get a lot of response by phone, some people will not call in order to avoid talking to a salesperson. If you choose this option, it is advisable to provide an address for those interested in responding by mail.

5) Require recipients to use their own envelopes and letterheads to respond. This is certainly a qualifier, since you are making it as tough as possible to respond. You will get much fewer responses because of the additional work involved. This is generally not a good idea.

Most self-mailers are designed so the response device does not carry the original address and coding information. The prospect is asked to complete a response device and provide all the pertinent information.

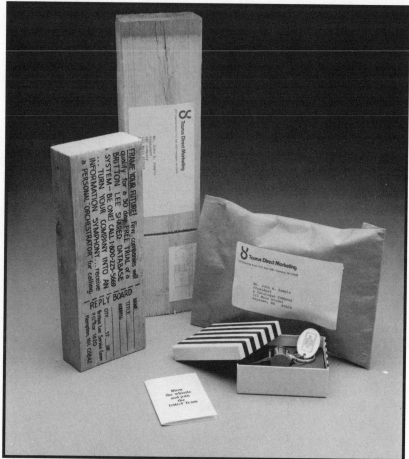

Illustration 7-11: Dimensional mailings.

Illustration 7-10 shows this approach. One format that works provides personal addressing and coding with the face of the mailing and the same on the response device. This format is generally printed on seven point paper stock. Illustration 7-3 is an example of this format.

Dimensionals

The easiest explanation of a dimensional format is any mailing that is greater than two dimensional (height and width). A dimensional mailing also has depth. While a regular letter package has the depth of a few layers of paper, a dimensional's depth is noticeable to sight and touch. A box, a tube or even an envelope containing something fat is considered a dimensional mailing.

The advantages of dimensional mailings is that they generally are not opened during the screening process and that they generally are put on the top of the mail pile when it is delivered to the recipient.

A dimensional mailing appeals to two strong motivations of your prospect:

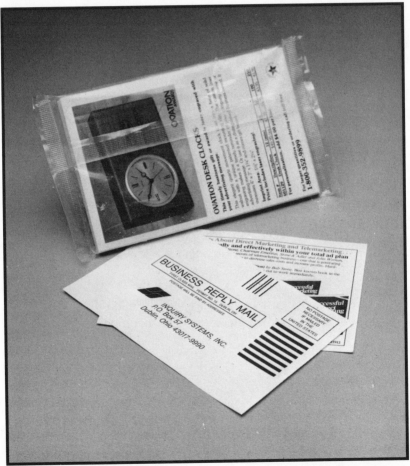

Illustration 7-12: A card deck.

- Ego. We all feel good when we receive a gift.
- Curiosity. It ultimately killed the cat.

These two motivations are the overriding advantages to the cost in using the dimensional format. Everyone loves to receive packages they can open and be surprised by. So it is with a dimensional. It will get opened and reviewed and has the highest opening rate of any mailing package. The dimensional will not ensure results; it only ensures that it will be opened. Results will be determined by the offer and list.

Card Decks

In the last few years, the card deck has evolved as a popular form of mailing. The card deck mailing began as a cooperative form of mailing with several marketers sharing the cost of production and mailing. It is still a cost-effective promotional format. Today, many multiple-product companies use card decks as a form of catalog and preclude other companies from participating in their mailing.

A card deck is a collection of 3-by-5 cards gathered in a wrap, bound together or placed in an envelope. Each card is a stand-alone sales-and-response device offering to sell or provide information about a product or service. Each participant in the card deck pays a fixed fee for each card in the deck. This form of mailing has proven to be very effective for several types of business mailers when evaluated on a cost-per-inquiry or cost-per-sale basis

The marketer supplies either camera-ready art in the sizes specified by the printer/mailer or printed pieces in sizes specified by the mailer.

Co-Ops

A card deck is a type of co-operative mailing organized by a printer/mailer to generate a profit. Another form of co-operative marketing is when two or more marketers get together to share expenses and lower the cost of marketing to a common market.

This approach has become common in the travel and entertainment markets. Airlines, hotels and car rental companies will often get together and promote their individual products in a joint mailing. They may even share offers or the mailing piece with the creative effort unified to improve the overall impression of the mailing package.

The reduced cost and improved results of this type of marketing is being repeated in other markets. Companies dealing in the same vertical markets are beginning to work together to improve their promotional position. For example, service contractors, equipment suppliers and finance companies will all promote in the same package.

Inserts

Inserts are more a process than a format. The process is when one business uses another business' publication or product fulfillment vehicle to carry its promotion. This process delivers the first company's offer to recipients of the host's product. The most frequent use is the consumer application of inserting a promotional flyer in the Sunday newspaper. Another application is placing promotions in invoices for your credit cards and utility services. A fundamental difference between a co-op mailing and an insert is the user of the insert will pay a fee to the mailer. This fee will be in addition to mail costs and preparation of the mailing material.

This same approach is being used in selling to other businesses. Insurance companies will allow non-competing companies to insert flyers in their mailing packages. The frequent-flyer program mailings from the airlines are often filled with inserts.

The insert process can generate cost-effective leads and sales. However, it can also be uncontrollable and unreliable. For example, if you're paying to have your product promotion inserted in another company's product packages, you are relying on the inserter's shipping department. The insert program in this case is an additional duty for which the shipper's production people are not normally compensated.

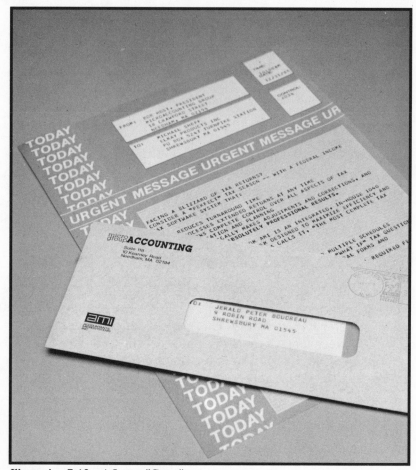

Illustration 7-13:   A Letter "Gram".

Insert programs can be limited in scope. The customer list of most businesses is limited in size. This type of a program may not achieve the contacts you want.

Letter "Grams"

The familiar yellow format of the Western Union Telegram has high delivery and readership because Telegrams were the original important or urgent format for delivering information. This format has been copied, expanded and used by many mailers to achieve a variety of objectives. All of the objectives capitalized on the opening and reading rate of this format.

Inserting a brochure decreases its effectiveness because it makes it more of a letter package. Copy is generally computer generated on a continuous form colored stock.

Copy for this format is written in an abrupt form in order to simulate the by-the-word cost of a Telegram.

This format, which once ensured high readership, is now experiencing a reduction in readership due to overuse.

Catalogs

Since catalogs are a unique way to sell products, this form of direct mail is covered in depth in Chapter eight.

Frequency

Successful salespeople will tell you one of the keys to their success is never letting go of a qualified prospect. They constantly stay in contact with known qualified prospects through personal contact, telephone selling and the mail. The salesperson believes that over time the prospect will understand his product or service and will ultimately agree to investigate further. The concept of repetitive contact is also effective in direct marketing techniques.

Frequently in business-to-business selling, products can be sold only when the customer or prospect has an immediate need. A demand cannot be created in all cases. For example, if you are selling light bulbs and the prospect had just purchased a three month supply you want to position your company and products to be the alternative the prospect considers the next time he is acquiring light bulbs.

Consumable products will often only be acquired when there is a need within the company. Sustain your marketing effort so you will be on the prospect's mind when the purchase decision is being made. Being thought of at the time of the purchase decision does not guarantee an order, but not being thought of guarantees no order!

In fact, the selling of consumable products is a major area of business-to-business direct marketing today. Consumables generally carry margins and volumes too low to support the use of a field sales force. The challenge is to be in front of the prospects when they are making a buying decision.

If you are selling a capital product, which is acquired infrequently, the decision process is prolonged. Successful salespeople of capital products use frequency techniques to move with the prospect through the decision process. They *condition* the prospect to move closer to their product. People cannot grasp many concepts at one time. A frequency or conditioning program will allow the salesperson to gradually move the prospect through the selling process.

The lessons the salesperson has learned through experience about multiple contacts and frequency should be applied in direct marketing. The promotional approach you use may vary depending on what you are selling. However, the concept of frequency and multiple contacts will improve results.

To gauge frequency, evaluate cost versus the results achieved. In face-to-face selling, you can't measure the effect of multiple contacts. Because every salesperson does their own thing, you may never know the detail of the contacts. You do know they occurred, but you don't know when, how or the ultimate results of each contact.

Direct marketing allows you to control the contact, content, method used and measurability of each contact made. With this in mind, you can continue to contact a customer or prospect until the frequency does not provide a return on the investment.

There are several different issues in frequency:

- The number of times you contact a prospect

- The timing between contacts

- Format of contact

There is no magic formula to determine how frequently to contact a customer or prospect or the timing between contacts. Each situation is unique. During the planning phase, determine the level of investment you can make in acquiring a lead and/or a sale. Your algorithm for required response will dictate the success you require for each contact.

The format of your contact will vary. However, we suggest you continually test your most successful promotion against any new format. In capital goods selling, it may be worthwhile to develop three different formats delivered over a three-month period. On the other hand, catalogers have found that they can mail the same catalog to the same group 14 times per year and still get acceptable results on the last mailing.

The key to determining the effect of frequency is to test. You can perform multiple tests fairly inexpensively when you combine mail and telemarketing follow-up to establish readable results in small samples. To effectively measure the results of frequency you will probably require the use of a marketing database.

Each contact you make will condition the prospect to have a better understanding of your company and its products. The conditioning process can be particularly helpful if the prospect is part of a decision-making team. You may even consider mailing to a number of contacts within a single company to help sell your products.

The sales force has learned that people cannot absorb a lot of different points at one time. The salespeople will frequently focus on a key point in each of their contacts. Hopefully, they are relating the features of their products to the benefits that the prospect will achieve.

Your multiple contacts should also stress a limited series of points. Don't try to take a prospect completely through a complex product and all of its benefits in one mailing. Focus on the primary benefit that will help the prospect relate to your product. Don't lose sight of your objective: to create a lead or an order. If you awaken desire and convince the prospect there is a need, you don't have to fully explain all of the features and run the risk of confusion. Use frequency to help educate, but don't forget to continually ask for the order.

There are some promotions that, by their very nature, are frequency programs. These programs will use the formats discussed earlier but are planned for more than one contact.

- **Continuity Programs**: As the name implies, these continual or on-going contacts to a group of customers or prospects. Book or tape clubs and magazine subscriptions are examples of this type of program. The definition of this type of program requires that the marketer continually contact the prospect or customer; the frequency and type of contact may vary.

- **Catalogs**: The economics of catalogs demonstrates that the profits from them will come from the follow-up catalog sales. A catalog marketer will frequently break even or lose money on the first catalog sale, in order to acquire that customer for future programs.

- **Newsletters**: Can be sent to prospects or customers. This communication is not often viewed or used for direct marketing. If you are using a newsletter or periodic contact to your marketplace, it should be used to help sell products and services. This is an excellent opportunity to use frequency to your advantage.

- **Frequent-user programs**: Are the "Executive Green Stamp program." To be effective, you will want to frequently tell your prospects about their accrued benefits and the opportunities available for additional usage.

- **Showmanship mailings or super-premiums**: Are a form of

dimensional mailing that are so expensive you are compelled to follow-up the original mailing with additional contacts.

Schedule

There are a number of factors that have to be considered when planning and scheduling a direct mail program. The most obvious is the time necessary to execute a program. Illustration 7-14 shows a schedule of rough time estimates needed to move through a mailing project. This 14-week schedule shows the steps to be gone through. Your actual time frames will depend on your own program and the capabilities of the vendors you select.

Campaign planning and development is covered in the Chapter two. It is critical to spend enough time to developing a written plan. If you move directly to the creative step without planning, you may exclude proper list and offer development. Without these two elements, the creative execution will probably not achieve your objectives.

Creative execution is covered in the Chapter five, as well as in this chapter. Your creative staff or outside creative vendor should have a working knowledge of the capabilities of your computer service and your mail house. It is quite possible to create direct mail packages that cannot be assembled by the mail house's machines. This means that the mailing may have to be assembled by hand, causing time delays and substantial increases in mail house charges.

You should do a complete list analysis prior to ordering your lists. Since 50% of the success of the direct mail program depends on the list, you should be comfortable in the lists available before finalizing your target audience. When ready to order lists, be sure to provide written instructions to the list vendors including the specifications on list variables plus the technical requirements of your computer service company. There are far too many variables in list ordering not to document your instructions.

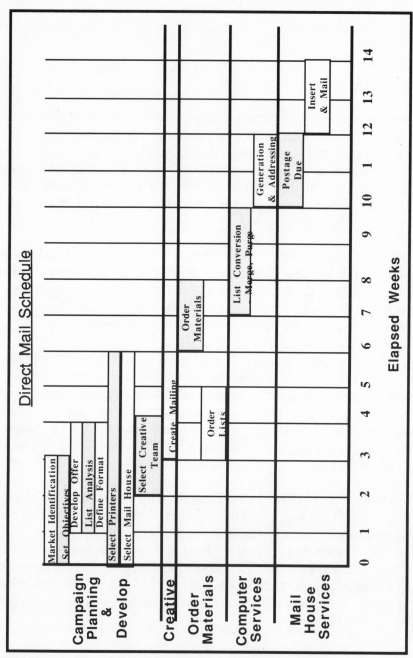

Illustration 7-14: A direct mail schedule

Printed materials may be ordered from several printers. There are three major types of printers:

- Continuous form printers. Check with your computer service to see whether they require continuous forms or can use sheet fed materials.

- Commercial printers that print from one color to full color materials. These printers will provide brochures and other non-continuous form materials to insert in the mailing.

- Envelope printers that provide the specialized printing necessary for creating envelopes. This printer will have the longest lead time for delivery, especially if you order custom envelopes. Beware of envelope lead times.

Computer-generation and mail house service may be offered by a single vendor. More and more mail houses are providing computer-generation services. If you are planning to do a merge/purge, query your mail house to see if they have this capability.

After the mail has dropped, request a Postal Form 3602 if it mailed third class or a Form 3606 if you mailed first class. These forms, prepared by the mail house and then verified by the post office, are your receipt and proof of the mail quantity. Verify that the actual quantity mailed is consistent with the materials and names you provided and the postage you have paid.

Direct Mail Summarized

Direct mail is the primary tool in business-to-business direct marketing. Direct mail is used as a fulfillment vehicle for other media and formats in direct marketing promotional efforts. It can't be overlooked and should be an important part of campaign strategy.

Once you have established the list and offer you plan to use, you should begin to consider the format and copy to deliver the message. Direct mail is flexible and the most testable of all media. It is easy to control and to evaluate.

You must have a well-defined set of objectives before you create your direct mail package. The personality of the individual you're trying to reach can substantially alter the creative strategy used. Although existing materials may save expense, the objective and target of the direct mail program will probably preclude their use.

The offer, audience and format you use will dictate the copy and graphics used in the direct mail package. A photograph depicts reality, and an illustration depicts a dream. The combination can be an exciting visual experience for the reader and an effective support vehicle for the package.

Whatever components the direct mail package contains, all should be able to stand alone. If the package components become separated, you don't want to lose the selling opportunity. The flow of the mail package should continually ask for the order. The old sales adage "close early and close often" applies to direct mail.

The target audience and offer may dictate the use of a special direct mail format, such as a dimensional. These promotions are more expensive, typically take longer to implement and have greater success in breaking through to the target. Carefully control and test each element of the direct mail program. When working with a small universe, direct mail coupled with telemarketing can be an effective combination to test and evaluate the success of different direct mail formats.

Multiple contacts and the use of a frequency program can significantly increase the effectiveness of your direct mail efforts. Evaluate the techniques being used by the salespeople in your industry. Frequent contact will probably be the key to the success of the better salespeople. Direct marketing also improves when used in a sustained program. Evaluate, test and measure the effectiveness of multiple contacts.

The Achilles Heel of direct mail is the time it takes to execute a program. It is not unusual for a program to take 10 to 14 weeks to develop and implement. Trying to short-cut the time frame can negatively affect the quality and increase the costs.

Direct mail is an important and dynamic direct marketing promotional format. You will use direct mail whether you want to or not. If you plan your direct mail program, it will be more successful.

Chapter Eight - Business-to-Business Catalogs

<u>Business Catalogs Defined</u>

The business-to-business catalog is probably one of the most widely used and least understood of the many business-to-business media. While there are approximately 6,000 consumer catalogs in the domestic United States, there is no definitive source for how many business-to-business catalogs there are.

Let's establish a definition of a catalog:

> *A catalog is any device that offers a potential buyer (customer or prospect) the choice of more than one product or service at one time in the same promotion.*

This definition differentiates catalogs from solo direct mail, where only a single product or service is offered. One example of the difference between a catalog promotion and a direct mail effort is the multi-magazine sweepstakes offered by several subscription agency companies. This promotion offers the purchaser the opportunity to acquire a number of magazine subscriptions in one promotion. While the magazine publisher uses direct mail to solicit a potential purchaser to subscribe or renew his/her subscription, the catalog mailing offers a number of product alternatives to the purchaser. Again, direct mail is specific in offering only one product, while a catalog offers more than one product or service in the same promotion.

A catalog does not always have to be a fancy, full color magazine looking format. Card decks are a form of catalog marketing. This is where many dissimilar offerings are gathered together in an envelope or cellophane wrapper and mailed to a potential purchaser. The mailing provides ease of response because each card carries its own business reply device.

A catalog is a shopping vehicle while direct mail is a targeted sales call. Any time you gather several products together in any format, you can call it a catalog. Most companies prepare some type of sales literature. It may be in the form of product fact sheets for each item offered by the company. If the company provides a vehicle to gather these product fact sheets together, such as a binder, they have in essence created a catalog. If the company doesn't provide the vehicle to gather the material together, the field sales people are probably performing the function themselves just to organize their presentations. Many companies are in the catalog business and don't even know it.

You probably provide a binder to help organize the product fact sheets. Therefore, you're into catalog selling in some form. You may not be mailing your catalog, but instead have it delivered by your sales people. This is the most expensive delivery system for your catalog, so you may want to reexamine your catalog effort.

We worked with a company that was generating sales through a catalog and didn't even know they were in the catalog business. The company sold office furniture designed for computers. The company used a field sales force that called on end users and sold the potential purchaser on the benefits of their products. The salesperson carried an extensive set of promotional materials, including a series of product fact sheets on each of the company's products.

A fairly industrious member of the company's advertising staff thought it would be helpful to send out product sheets to the company's customers and prospects who had inquired about its products as a result of trade advertising. Over a period of six years, 1976 to 1982, the sales from this direct mail (catalog) effort grew from $0 to over $45 million. This direct response sales growth greatly contributed to the success of the company since it experienced overall growth in sales to over $80 million.

Since the company's accounting systems assigned all sales to a specific sales territory and field representative, the sales people were making great commissions. This accounting system masked the effectiveness of the catalog operation; it appeared that all of the sales were coming from the sales people because the company didn't even know it had a catalog operation.

In fact the sales force wasn't very effective when you removed the sales made direct. We suggested that the company reexamine its approach to catalog sales and establish a reasonable measurement and control system. The company now has an established catalog group with a mission and budget. The catalog now carries the company's normal merchandise as well as items purchased outside when they prove profitable.

The acquisition of additional products to sell through your catalog can increase the profitability of the catalog operations. Once you make the decision to have a catalog as a profit center, you may want to consider allowing it to grow by selling any product that makes sense because it is profitable. But first a basic question has to be resolved: Should the catalog exist as a profit center or as a support vehicle for other sales activities?

The answer to this question lies in the mission of the department that is handling the catalog. Historically, printed materials are within the domain of the advertising department. Because the budget for the catalog is controlled by advertising, a cost center, the catalog is typically viewed as a cost item.

Two things happen when you send out a catalog:

1) You affect your current customers. We are assuming that your customers will get mailed the catalog, which we strongly recommend -- this should be your most profitable available list .

2) You will generate orders and sales. If you do not intend to sell products, you're doing direct mail advertising or public relations and not direct marketing.

These two activities traditionally have been the province of the sales force. Customer contact and sales are the activities we expect from our field sales force. Based on the functions being performed by the catalog, it seems more appropriate to align the catalog operation with the sales activity than with advertising. Because the catalog operation is also producing revenue, it makes good business sense to convert it to a profit center from its current cost center role. You may even want to consider moving the catalog operation to the sales organization.

Catalog budgeting is very different than traditional sales budgeting. Annual budgets usually allow for a fixed amount of money to be consumed. The consumption of the budget will normally coincide with the end of the fiscal year. If the money is spent sooner or at a greater volume than the budget, the manager responsible is usually penalized. The catalog activity should be budgeted as dynamic activity, similar to a cost of goods accounting concept. If the sales are higher than anticipated, additional dollars should be allowed to increase the promotion of the catalog. The catalog should be allowed to flow with the dynamics of the market.

If the catalog is not successful, the budget should be reduced and moved to other more successful channels of distribution. Good catalog budgeting should be based on the percentage of sales allowed for promotion through the catalog. If the catalog is very successful and ahead of the plan, additional dollars should be allowed for catalog efforts. If the catalog is less successful, less dollars will be available for catalog efforts.

Catalog Missions

In order to properly measure your business catalog, you must understand and develop your catalog's mission.

1) The most basic mission a catalog will perform is that of a sales aid, the visual documentation a salesperson uses during a face-to-face sales situation. This documentation can take the form of typed materials, printed material, audiovisual aids or even videotape. If the sales representative is giving the prospect the opportunity to purchase more than one product through the material, it is really a catalog. This form of catalog activity doesn't require any change to your existing organization.

2) Another mission of the catalog is to support a telephone contact with the ultimate objective of spurring a face-to-face contact by a sales representative. This type of catalog is frequently used to help qualify responders from other trade advertising.

   Before a prospect or responder becomes a referral, some type of information is normally provided. Generally, more than one product or service is offered in the material sent to the responder. This means that the material is actually a catalog. This can be counter-productive, since the catalog is a shopping vehicle and too much information can actually confuse the prospect. It is similar to being a kid in the proverbial candy store with only limited time and money. There were so many options that the kid couldn't decide what to do. Ultimately, the kid will run out of time and may buy nothing or something just out of desperation to make a decision.

If you confuse your prospect with too much information, you run the risk of the candy store syndrome. Review the information being sent to your prospects. We have seen situations where so many different product sheets and brochures were being mailed, they were actually packed in a box. This volume of material is so overwhelming that the prospect may not read any of the information.

3) The catalog may have the mission to replace the field sales representative in situations where the product sale is relatively small. In other words, the sales potential is too small to warrant wasting a salesperson's time to make a face-to-face sales call or even a telephone contact. These catalogs are most often used in the role of customer support. The most common use for this catalog is to offer purchase of periodic consumable support products to a customer who has made a large capital expenditure.

Computer supplies are a classic example of this type of catalog effort. The sales representative is interested in selling the computer but really doesn't want to spend the time to sell the customer each $20 consumable item needed in the future. This doesn't mean that sales representatives aren't interested in supporting their customers, but rather that selling low priced consumable items may not be a good use of their time.

This type of selling really works well through a catalog. The catalog frees the time of the salesperson to work on bigger opportunities and allows the vendor company to still generate the revenue from the consumable items. This same approach can work for repair parts, add-on products and even new additional major capital equipment items. This type of catalog is well suited to provide customers with products and services that enhance your product, even if you don't normally offer these enhancements through your sales force. You can realize additional sales and revenue because:

- Your customers already have credit with you.

- They have a relationship of trust and confidence with you as a vendor.

4) The catalog is used to replace the field or telephone sales representative. This type of catalog is often introduced with the sales force's support, because the company will continue to pay commissions to the sales force even if the sale is consummated via the catalog. When the catalog has become firmly established, the company may decide to reduce or eliminate the commission structure.

The elimination of the sales force channel of product distribution to a catalog must be very carefully planned and executed. Customers have to be weaned from their dependence on the field organization for ordering. Plus, the sales force must be convinced that they can still earn at least the same amount or more once commissions are reduced or eliminated for these products.

In short, the field sales force can make or break the catalog effort.

These are the basic missions catalogs can be designed to fulfill. A catalog may be used to perform more than one mission at a time.

Another group of catalogs have a different set of mission statements. These missions are not related to the true mission of the catalogs described earlier, but focus on managements desire to use the catalog to perform other functions. Let's look at these peculiar missions:

1) *Catalogus Junkus*. This is when management decides to take all of the great products the company has made over the last several years, in spite of the fact that they were

never sold successfully by the sales force, and put them in a catalog. This mission will cause you to dust off your resume the quickest. Unless you can identify and correct the major reasons why the products didn't sell in the first place, you are guaranteed a disaster. Not only will you need a new position, but your customers will receive a lot of wrong signals about your company being in the "dog product" business.

2) *Catalogus Maximus.* As the name implies, this catalog will do it all. It will attempt to satisfy certain specific needs of your customers while also being the showcase for everything you make from your largest product to your smallest replacement washer.

You will have created the tome of your company. Properly indexed, this type of catalog can be valuable to you and your customers. You will, however, produce very few of these type catalogs.

First, it seldom will get into print because there is always something new to add to the book, or something that needs to be dropped or changed. Creating new photographs and prices will also cause constant delays in printing this catalog. This tome involves every product manager's sign off and quickly becomes the nemesis of your department.

Second, the tome catalog is very expensive. When management reviews the cost of producing this type of catalog, you will have a great deal of trouble justifying the investment. This catalog will serve as an advertising vehicle to help the sales force sell products. It will be difficult to track sales specifically to the tome catalog. ROI will be very difficult to evaluate.

3) *Catalogus Mistakus.* This catalog is generated without any support from the organization. It has no budget or

management commitment. You can generally squeeze a few bucks from various sources. Even if the catalog is produced, it will rarely succeed. If management doesn't provide financial support to the catalog effort, moral support is probably also lacking. As you generate orders, there will probably be difficulties with shipping and billing.

It is very difficult to develop a catalog and have it succeed by trying to squeeze resources from other areas of the company. Each area that is asked to contribute to the catalog effort will be asked to participate by sacrificing something from their own primary areas of responsibility. It is possible to succeed and become a hero, but the odds are against it.

Consumer and Business Catalogs

Business-to-business catalogs have increased tremendously in the last few years. Many catalogs are being established completely independent of the sales force. The field sales force is intentionally left out of the development process. The mission of this catalog is to create customers that will only be serviced by phone or mail. These types of catalogs have proliferated as the cost of selling face-to-face has increased.

The growth of the consumer catalog arena has helped to increase interest and activity in using catalogs in the business arena. This propensity to order products through the mail based on a picture and a brief description has flowed over into business.

The business catalog is proliferating because it may be the only place to get information on certain products and services. For consumers, the retail store employee traditionally has been helpful in explaining and demonstrating the products you want to buy. With the increasing use of technology in business and the lower costs of high technology products, business people typically have no one to explain products.

There are not enough sales people to satisfy the questions being asked by all levels of business.

Business oriented retail stores, like computer stores or office supply stores, are frequently staffed by little more than cash takers. The norm is not enough information givers available to satisfy every question, simply because the number of products available in the business oriented store is so large that no one person can know every product.

As in the consumer catalog, the business catalog must provide plenty of clearly written information about the products. The payment and return policy offered by the business catalog should be as powerful as any consumer catalog. One of the primary reasons attributed to the initial and sustained growth of the Sears and Roebuck catalog was its unwavering policy of a no questions asked money-back guarantee. It allowed the customer to purchase products with little concern about quality or applicability. The same kinds of techniques will help the business catalog become effective.

In both realms the customer must perceive that the products offered are not readily available elsewhere in order for the catalog to succeed. He must at least perceive that the product is a good value and that it will be easier to purchase through the mail than other methods. Buying toothpaste by mail is not normally a cost effective way to distribute the product, unless you can sell it in quantity. Most people won't buy and store large quantities of toothpaste when it is easily available at a reasonable price. In business, we may only need one printer ribbon at a time, but we are not uncomfortable buying 12 or more at a time. Businesses are fairly comfortable carrying an inventory of consumable products while consumers are not.

As we discussed in Chapter one, consumers are spending their own money and are very concerned about quality and price. The business person is spending company funds, and although price and quality are issues, time and availability can be even more important.

The major difference between consumer and business catalogs is the basic design. The consumer catalog is designed as a shopping vehicle. The design is developed to interest the reader to make several trips through this paper and picture store. The business catalog is designed to be a reference document. It should be well indexed so that the purchaser does not have to shop through the book in order to find the item he/she is looking for. The difference between the two types of catalogs is beginning to change, but it will take time.

Consumer catalogs must develop a style that is attractive, in the graphic and order generating sense. The catalog is competing with retail stores that offer many similar, if not the same, products. As business catalogs grow more numerous and competitive, they too must develop an attractiveness that is enticing to the potential buyer.

Probably the best way to present your business is with an editor's eye. Don't look at yourself as a supplier of widgets requiring an inventory of 1,200 stock keeping units. Consider yourself a publisher of a special interest magazine that your readers will enjoy reviewing. You want your magazine to be a book that will deliver some enjoyment to your readers.

The editorial approach uses both copy and graphics to give information that is helpful and interesting. Your reader can move through the book quickly to get an overview of the contents through headlines and graphics. They can go deeper into the book for more details on the products being offered when time allows or the need arises.

Consumer catalogs have a shelf life dictated by the consumer's interest in the products and attractiveness of the book. Business catalogs often enjoy a much longer shelf life if the buyer has perceived the need for the products being offered and the buyer is attracted by the presentation of the book. Research has revealed that most business catalog buyers keep a primary and secondary catalog by type of products the catalog offers. If you can attract the attention of the buyer, you have a chance to become the first or second catalog retained by the potential buyer.

The high and long retention rates of business catalogs provides powerful reasons to try to offer complete product lines in the catalog. If your customer wants an obscure item you dropped from your catalog, that customer could go to a competitor's catalog and it will replace you as his primary or secondary catalog.

Consumer catalogs add and drop products all the time. This keeps their books fresh and new to their customers. Consumer products have a high and fast fatigue rate because they tend to become over-sold and therefore must be replaced by new items that will cause the inventory to turn. On the other hand, business books should not drop a product just because it is not pulling its space right now. Only cus-tomer research into sales patterns for each product will tell you if a product is turning into a dog or if it is just in a sales valley.

Editorial Techniques

In order to keep the same products interesting, here are some editorial techniques you might experiment with:

1) Personalizing the content. Present the products and their explanations like you are a salesperson talking to a buyer. Don't be afraid to include pictures and information about the people that are supporting your catalog. We are all comforted when we feel we can pick up the phone and call someone if we need help.

2) Repeat the name of the company on every spread so the the reader can identify the source of the products. This is a regular technique used in the publishing industry.

3) Sidebar stories. General information that might pertain to a product or group of products or a company philosophy can be highlighted. A sidebar story is then used to empha-size the point and develop a theme just as this technique is used in magazines.

4) Feature products. Feature certain products on a two-page spread to draw attention to that product and to provide a variety of rhythm throughout the book.

5) Group products by theme. Grouping the products by theme like a newspaper does in its various sections will add continuity to the thoughts of your reader.

6) Use headlines. Use headlines to call attention to the product groups or new products.

The Business Catalog Process

There is no easy track to follow when putting the catalog together. There are, however, some steps which follow others on a linear basis. That is, you cannot go to the next step until you finished the previous one. But there are some steps that can be accomplished simultaneously. We will discuss all of these steps so that you will understand what needs to be done to get a catalog in the mail.

The first step in the creation of a catalog is the most important, the conceptual step which provides the foundation for the future development of the entire catalog. So that a great deal of time is not wasted later, convene a meeting of all the managers that will be involved with and responsible for the catalog. This group should agree on the theme and image that the catalog should project as well as the objective statement of the catalog.

This first step is so important because as the development of the catalog progresses, it is increasingly difficult to make changes. Changes to the catalog are much more expensive than the execution of original ideas since they are generally executed on rush schedules. If all of the key players are not involved at the outset, changes become the norm rather than the exception as each manager not present at the conceptional stage tries to redirect the objectives of the catalog.

This group should understand the budget for the the creation of the catalog as well as its profit and loss objectives. The conceptual committee sets the strategy for the catalog so that the organization cannot play its normal games of redirection for the benefit of different self-interest groups within the company. Strategic statements this group might prepare read as follows:

- Catalog Z is being developed on a modest budget of $50,000 in order to provide support to the field sales force, in the sales of products that cannot support a personal face-to-face call. This catalog will be developed primarily from existing product information and photography. All sales from Catalog Z will be credited to the individual sales representative areas.

  Sales for Catalog Z are forecast at $3,000,000 with a contribution to marketing and profit of $1,000,000 based on our dealer wholesale pricing of 66.6%.

- Catalog M is being developed as a direct sales catalog with a budget of $200,000. This catalog will represent our state-of-the-art products in order to generate sales from current and new customers. New product photography will be taken whenever existing photography is not in keeping with the overall design concept of the catalog.

  Sales representatives will receive commissions on sales they write as a result of leads rather than sales generated by the catalog. Direct sales will not be commissionable.

  Sales for Catalog M are forecast at $10,000,000 over the 12 months following mailing with a contribution to marketing and profit of $5,000,000 based on dealer wholesale pricing.

These are highly abbreviated statements and financial projections. They are intended to provide a basis for the preparation of a more detailed business plan. These abbreviated definitions are excellent tools to communicate the mission and plan of the catalog to others within the company and senior management. The preparation of a mission statement is also politically important; its existence makes it more difficult to have the strategy or budget changed.

The next step is determining the space allocation for the catalog. Each product manager is sure his/her product line is the most important to the company. There are several ways to set parameters for the usage of space within the catalog:

1) Profitability. Feature those products which provide you the greatest profit per unit of sale.

2) Visibility. Feature those products which generate the highest number of units sold per year.

3) Importance. Feature products which are the hub of all other sales. That is if you sell the hub products, you will sell the spoke and wheel products.

4) Appeal. Feature products that will keep readers interested so they will shop the catalog and see other products.

5) Dogs. *Do not* feature products that are losers. Products that do not sell currently will probably not sell when offered in a catalog. This argument does not apply to products that have not had visibility.

6) Overstock. *Do not* feature products that you happen to have a lot of unless you are offering them as a loss leader. Manufacturing may have overproduced an item because they were easy to produce. This is a good product because it is probably very profitable. If an overstocked item is a dog, do not feature it, even if you are going to reduce the price.

7) New. Feature products that are new to your markets, not just new to you. Your markets do not really care if you

have a new product that everyone else has had for a year, unless you can offer a benefit that differentiates your new product from the competition.

8) Weighting. This process incorporates all of the above based on whatever qualitative and/or quantitative information that is available. Each product is given a weight on a scale of 1 to 10, or 1 to 100 (you decide the measurement system). This approach gives your designers the greatest level of information when they are laying out the catalog.

The term feature, as it is used above, refers to giving a product more room on a page or on a spread than the other products. It is boring to a reader to shop a catalog where everything is pictured the same size. You should, therefore, give the reader some graphic variety in your presentation. These products are what is referred to as "featured". If you do not select the weighting approach for all the products of your catalog, it is important to use a modified version of this approach to give your designers the relative graphic value of each item you have selected to feature.

When you are allocating space, it is easier to identify your featured products first. Once these are identified and specified, the remainder of the catalog can be designed.

Creative Process

The most frustrating and time consuming part of creating a catalog is dealing with the general lack of understanding by non-creative management regarding the processes that must take place. This lack of understanding causes most tardy catalogs.

Once the strategy of a catalog is established and agreed to by everyone, catalog creation becomes largely mechanical. Designers and artists are technical crafts people that engineer the desired theme and image into a catalog. While the artists normally prefer to put one item per page, they can design in whatever format they are instructed.

You will direct them to achieve your objectives within the number of pages and complexity the budget allows.

If you are not specific with the designer and artist, you will actually hurt the end product, your catalog. With complete information, the artists can create your book within your guidelines. Any lack of up front information and direction from you will generally result in a catalog that is late and over budget. Initial vagueness will lead you to be continually revising or changing the creative concepts delivered by the crafts people. Create a written document for your designer and artists that detail your complete instructions including the concept and objectives of the catalog. In addition, share the budget and size limitations you have established for the catalog.

At same time, you must also manage the product managers to ensure that they supply product information and camera ready samples according to the catalog production schedule. When this is not done, the artists and designers cannot do their work. They can design leaving empty spaces for products not yet specified only to find out when these products are finally specified, they cannot be shown in the space provided.

When the catalog'evolves' as the creative process is being performed as opposed to specifying the complete content up front, it inevitably-forces a page, a spread or an entire section of the catalog to be redesigned. If photography has already begun on the known products, it could be necessary to re-shoot part of or the entire section, because a product(s) originally shot is wrong for the revised catalog. This normally causes time delays and cost over-runs.

Incomplete catalog definition is a simple example of only one area of irritation to the creative staff. The following list will give you an idea of some of the pitfalls you might be able to avoid when you manage the overall catalog process:

> 1) *Product managers are allowed to write copy.* Product managers should be good at their job of evaluating and selecting product. They may even have a good under-

standing of the market and marketing requirements. However, they are typically features-oriented or specification-oriented and are not benefit/sales oriented. As we discussed earlier, people respond to benefits, not features. In addition, product managers typically have no professional experience in writing or selling. They should not be allowed to control the copy or creative concept in the catalog.

2) *Products are not selected and made available to the creative staff on schedule.* This is the primary issue we discussed earlier. You can't be too specific or too early in the information provided to your creative staff. **Put it in writing**.

3) *Samples provided are different than the actual product.* Sometimes buyers and product managers will provide samples that are similar to the actual product being offered, but not the actual item. When the item does arrive it can be significantly different than the sample. This can cause a major revision of that product's page or even the entire section.

4) *Only one sample is made available for photography.* If the sample contains a blemish it may have to be photographed in an alternate way that is not consistent with the design of the section. You should supply more than one sample for photography.

5) *Copywriters are not given type size and typeface specifications.* This can frequently cause the copy to be too long or short for the space available throughout the catalog on all products. Make your type decisions before you begin the creative process.

6) *Several photographers are used to expedite the work.* This will cause different lighting presentations or lighting values throughout the catalog. Different lighting values

can be disconcerting for your readers to adjust to, and projects less than a high-quality or professional image. Try to limit your photography to one shop.

7) *Manufacturer's supplied photography is used in lieu of original photography.* As we just mentioned, this will yield many varied values of photography. Although you may save on photography expense, the overall quality of your catalog can suffer. We suggest you limit the use of manufacturer's supplied photography.

8) *Blow-ups of 35mm photographs are made larger than 1/4 page.* If you do blow-up a 35mm photo, it may become grainy and fuzzy (two very exacting words). How large you can blow-up a shot depends on the quality of the original photo. Don't try to use a poor quality blow-up. Re-shoot the item to give you the quality you are looking for.

9) *Final color and type are not proofed before you go to press.* This means that you may have to correct your color on the press, the most expensive place to do anything. And, where you have the least control. See a color proof before your catalog goes to press.

10) *The order form is not the first mechanical completed.* Generally, your catalog printer is not the printer of your order form. Since the order form is the most complicated mechanical to complete, it is often avoided until the 'pretty pictures' are complete. This is a mistake. The order form carries all of the ordering information your customers will need to buy from you. If you complete the order form first, your copywriters will have a chance to use the order form information when they are writing product copy.

Producing the order form also forces you to solve all of your business questions early:

- credit cards
- 800 #'s
- customer service information
- shipping and handling charges
- guarantees
- taxes, etc.

This will improve overall understanding of the catalog for everyone involved.

11) *Customer service is excluded from the creative process.* When you do not include the people that frequently talk to your customers, you are not taking advantage of the visceral feel these people have for your market place. For example, the product manager may feel that an item's color is its most important feature. Your customer service people, however, have learned that your customers are more interested in how this item is packed or the number of units per box. If you listened to the product manager alone, you would not have shown the key feature your customers are truly concerned about, but rather the color array.

12) *Shipping is excluded from the creative process.* This is only a problem if your product managers are not required to provide shipping information as part of their product specifications. If shipping information is not provided, someone from shipping should be involved early in the creative process.

13) *You don't include you color separator and printer early in the process.* You can wait until the catalog is completed before your include your separator and printer. But, you are making two mistakes:

  1. Their experience and wisdom can save you both time

and money.
2. Their involvement creates a cleaner transition between the steps.

Never, never restrict your separator from talking to your printer. These professionals will communicate at a level that you may not understand but that is necessary to get the job done right.

14)*You delegate your responsibility to produce the catalog.* This is the kiss of death. If you do not stay actively involved in the process you will not get a satisfactory result. You may delegate the responsibility to a manager who may not have the authority to keep the process rolling on schedule. This is not to say that you must cross every "t". You must, however, let the organization know that the catalog has your attention and you expect everyone to give it their full support to meet your schedule.

The creative process includes many aspects of your business and is coupled with a variety of external suppliers. For this reason, it is impossible to outline everything you need to be aware of throughout the ordeal of creating a catalog. The best advice we can give you is to encourage you to familiarize yourself with the nuances of every step you will take.

Ask questions and try to anticipate any potential problems in order to prevent them from occurring. Meet with the managers and suppliers that will be involved so you will understand their needs. Be particularly aware of how each participant in the process wants to receive materials . To use a football cliche, you need a "clean hand-off" at each step in the process. If hand-offs are not clean, the down-line manager or supplier will point the finger at the previous step. When the catalog doesn't come out as planned, it is difficult to establish where the problem occurred. In addition, you will not get the catalog in the time frame or quality you anticipated. Don't focus on blame, focus on getting good hand-offs.

Scheduling

There is no magic in any fixed schedule; you can always shorten a time-line with money. A wise man once said that in any creative or production process there are three variables:

- Price
- Speed
- Quality

Pick two of the above. If you buy speed your price goes up and your quality suffers. This is not a mathematical formula; however, it seems to be a heuristic model.

Let's look at the steps you must go through in order to create and print your catalog.

- Product Selection - this step is self explanatory. As we discussed earlier, if you do not have the products you want to sell you cannot begin. The product selection should be complete, or as complete as possible, before you begin the next step.

- List Selection - you cannot begin too early to select your lists. As we mentioned in an earlier chapter, the list you use for direct marketing is the most critical variable in the process. If you haven't selected your list, which identifies the target and market your selling to, it is impossible to create an effective catalog.

  If you are only mailing to your customer files, it is wise to schedule your requirements early with your computer service. If you are renting lists and plan to do a merge/purge, starting early will facilitate your mailing.

  You can order too far in advance due to the rapid aging of rented lists. To avoid getting stuck with an old list, check the update schedule of the lists you want to rent and compare them to your schedule to see which lists you can order and still get the most current update. The earlier you can order a list, the easier it will be to meet your schedule dates.

Another intrinsic problem to catalog scheduling is that you are always waiting to get more definitive results from the last catalog before you order lists for the next catalog. Do not wait too long; having your catalog sitting on skids with no one to send it to will not sit well with your boss.

- <u>Printer Selection</u> - when selecting your printer you will become aware of the different size catalogs you can print; at what price; and with what trade-offs. When you have made your selection, immediately provide your creative staff with the exact specifications of what they must provide to the printer in writing. This fundamental step will avoid many future headaches.

- <u>Layouts</u> - this next step occurs by the copy and graphic teams collaborating to generate rough sketches using pencil on tissue paper. General outlines of the products, headlines and blocks of copy will begin to appear. Often this step is done in miniature (approx.1/8 scale) and is called a 'thumbnail'.

Thumbnail versions of the catalog be done quickly in order to communicate various approaches to an entire layout concept. Thumbnails can be done by page or by spread (two facing pages) depending on whether you use pages or spreads as the creative unit. This first step shows the interdependence of the products as they will appear in final printed form.

The approved thumbnails are then expanded to full size. This is why you should know how large your finished page size is going to be before you begin the creative process. A 1/2 inch difference in page size on the printing press can turn a well executed creative product into a mess.

The full size layout will show the products expanded to rela-

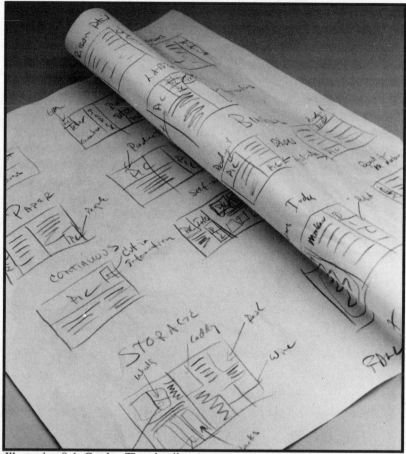

Illustration 8-1: Catalog Thumbnail.

tive size and position on the page. Headlines will be in place
and copy blocks will be aligned to show relative copy size.

Layouts are the blueprint for the construction of the catalog.
At this point, your product managers have the greatest flexibility and least painful opportunity to make inexpensive
changes. The problem is that most non-creative managers
look at the layout as some sort of kid game. They do not take
the layouts seriously because they appear so basic. Give your

product managers instruction on the timing of the creative process so they will understand what they are looking at when they see layouts.

After your first round approval of layouts, you may decide to have color added using pencils and markers. This is a time consuming and expensive step which may prove to be unnecessary if your managers can visualize color on the original layouts. However, if you are dealing with managers that seem unable to "get the picture", color layouts or comprehensive layouts (comps) may be a worthwhile step.

- Copy and Photography - these are simultaneous activities and are not mutually exclusive. It might prove helpful to your copywriters to touch base with your photographer. The preparations for a photo might yield some feature of the product that the writer missed. The writer can also share the highlighted benefits of the product with the photographer, so that a shot could be enhanced with a prop to illustrate that benefit.

Both copy and photography should be reviewed and approved on a dynamic basis. That is, do not wait until the catalog copy and photography are complete before you circulate them for approval by product managers. If you send the entire catalogs copy and photography at one time, you will overload your product managers and their attention to detail will decline. The approval process should include a copy of the layout, the copy and photo to establish the complete presentation of the product in that section of the catalog.

If you are still considering holding approvals and reviews until the entire catalog is complete, another negative factor is the inevitable time delay. The catalog will not move forward while waiting for approvals from different managers. Some managers will not move as quickly as you would like and the catalog will be further delayed. To keep the catalog moving you should insist that such a linear process is unacceptable to all of the managers. As an alternative, you could allow a single block of time where all of the product managers could review everything in one place when the catalog is complete.

- <u>Tracings</u> - this step is a creative option. If you are working with outside suppliers, you should provide them with an exact layout of the catalog. This tracing will show the exact position of type and photographs.

The steps after tracings are production oriented and they gen-

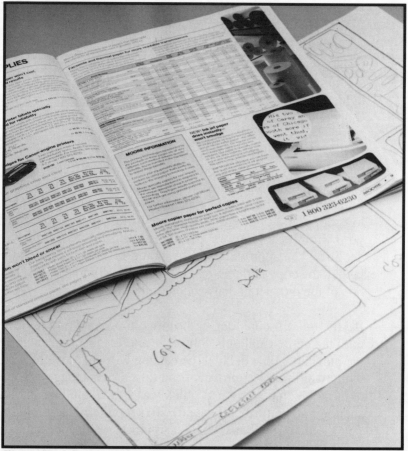

Illustration 8-2: A catalog tracing.

erally function without the necessity of your constant feedback. Tracings allow for multiple copies of the catalog to be made and distributed to various suppliers in order to control the technical steps.

- <u>Mechanicals and Typesetting</u> - this is where base boards for the catalog are prepared and the typeset copy is put on the boards in their exact position. You will be able to see photos and type in position as they will print. Color backgrounds that will be assembled into the catalog will be attached as overlays so you can see the color breaks.

  If you are creating a black and white catalog, you will go directly from this step to printing. If you are mailing a color catalog, you will move through the next two steps before going to printing.

- <u>Assembly/Stripping</u> - this technical stage is where all of the photography is cut and assembled so that color can be separated for the printing process.

- <u>Separations</u> - this is the process that prepares your photography and other color backgrounds. The color is separated into four primary colors: black, red, blue, yellow. They are represented in the form of dots, so that the primary color inks can print the respective dots and recreate the color. If you use a magnifying glass to view any color printed piece, you will see the pattern of dots used to create the color. Black type can be mounted on the black plate of the press without being separated.

  There are two ways you can review your color separations:

  - Some color separators have a proofing press. This allows you to actually receive printed samples of your catalog.

  - Several manufacturers provide equipment that uses color powders in lieu of ink to photo-electrically create color

Illustration 8-3: Baseboard mechanicals.

proofs.

When you review the color proofs, it is is your last opportunity to make any changes. Changes from this point on
are very expensive and time consuming.

- <u>Printing and mailing</u> - many printers provide both of these
  steps and some provide in-line addressing. This means that
  you can address the catalog while it is being printed. This
  allows you to address your catalog and order form at the same

Illustration 8-4: In-line addressed catalog and order form.

time and bind them together.

In-line addressing allows you to establish codes that will be returned with the order form that will make your response analysis much easier. Determining the cost justification of this process depends on how many orders you receive by mail as opposed to telephone. It is fairly difficult to capture the coding information from telephone orders.

At this point, any prior sins of list selection and/or order form neglect will become apparent. Without your list and order form at your printer/mailer, you are not ready to mail your catalog.

• Timing - how long you allow for each step in the process depends on:

  • how many products you are introducing into your catalog;
  • the timeliness of your merchandise (seasonal or non-seasonal).

Calendars, for example, must be sold prior to the year in which they will be used.

For discussion purposes (Illustration 8-5), we will review a catalog production schedule that takes one quarter (13 weeks). You can compress, expand, realign or do whatever you want to this schedule depending on your situation.

Our schedule is based on work days. Keep this in mind when you

---

Catalog Schedule

Activity-	Work Days to Complete
Layouts	13
Copy/Photography	12
Position Stats/Tracings	5
Mechanicals/Typesetting	10
Assembly/Stripping	7
Separations	12
Changes/Approvals/Revisions (throughout the process)	6
Total Work Days	65 (13 weeks)

Illustration 8-5: A typical catalog schedule.

set-up your own schedule. Weekends and holidays are very expensive days to have work done by suppliers. Your people will not be happy if you regularly make up time using week-end and holidays, but it is a management choice.

The starting point for the process begins when the products are selected and the samples are received. The more you stray from this policy, the more confusion you will have in later stages of the catalog's development.

Back-End Fulfillment

We have just spent a great deal of time on the front-end of the catalog. The strategic and creative decisions that get your catalog to the printer comprise the fun and glorious end of the business. However, the real key to your catalog's success is how well you deliver your products to your customers. People will not remember all of the little creative details you put into your catalog. Yet, they will never forget if your product arrives damaged; if you have substituted products; voided products; or if you mess up the billing charges.

The major areas of fulfillment you should be aware of are:

- Order receipt - this can be by mail or phone. Review returned mail order forms to see if order forms are easy to complete. You can determine the difficulty or ease of the order form by how many marginal notes the customer makes. A purchase order with your order form attached will still allow you to capture your coding information if you performed in-line addressing. If you just receive a purchase order without your addressed order form it will be difficult to trace your ordering information and should be treated like a telephone order. Don't get too hung up in coding, take the order.

  Hopefully, your phone orders will out-number your mail orders. The phone provides you the opportunity to upgrade and cross-sell the customer. We have already mentioned that it will be difficult to source your telephone orders. Spending time sourcing orders on purchase orders or telephone is not worth while because you must remember that your objective is orders, not sourcing.

However, telephone orders are good occasions to do a little research by asking one or two questions. For example, you may be able to find out information like number of employees or industry type. This information might help you determine your future list rentals. But do this after you have taken the order. We keep stressing that your objective is to get an order. Why run the risk of irritating your customer for the sake of market research?

After you get the order, ask the customer if he/she would mind reading the code on the address label, assuming the customer has the catalog handy. It is easy to add an afterthought question like,"Would you mind helping us understand" or " By the way, would you mind telling me.." Limit the questions you ask and always be sure not lose sight of your objective -- to take an order.

Test whether a toll free number is cost justified. Unlike a consumer who pays for his/her own home phone bill, a business manager generally has access to lines to make long distance calls without being responsible or even seeing the charges. Several business catalogers have determined that a toll free is not cost justified. We believe you should make it as easy as possible to order. A toll free number overcomes the obstacle of cost, whether it is in fact a deterrent or not.

• Credit checking - if you are extending house credit or taking credit cards, you should use a credit service that can support your needs. The major business catalogers have as much as a 15% credit rejection rate and still have 2% bad debt.

You must decide your acceptable credit risk; the cost of the services; and weigh them against your cost per order.

Offering credit in some form is definitely to your advantage. Remember, the easier you make the ordering process, the more orders you will receive. If you require cash with order, or even a purchase order, this will create fewer orders. The problem of getting a check or P.O. from the prospects accounting department can easily stop someone from doing business with you .

• <u>Processing the order</u> - the temptation is to use low priced clerical people for this function. It is not the best place to economize. This will probably be the highest volume area of customer contact within your company. The perception of good customer service or customer apathy will be determined by your order processors. Information incorrectly handled at this point will probably have the most far reaching and expensive repercussions later.

It is easy to make mistakes. How well you deal with errors and satisfy your customers' concerns could be the key to the success of your catalog. Errors fall into any one of three categories:

	Right product	Wrong Product
Right person		X
Wrong person	X	
Wrong person		X

This matrix demonstrates that you can send the wrong product to the right person; the right product to the wrong person; or the wrong product to the wrong person. There are other administrative errors that deal with pricing, quantity and customer service that complicate the matrix and increase the opportunity for error.

Review your mail or phone orders with skilled, talented and committed people. Establish some form of meaningful quality control measures to evaluate how well you deal with customer service calls. Publicly recognize and reward outstanding employee performance. Quietly remove chronic underperformers.

- Inventory - you cannot ship what you do not have. Whenever you back-order an item you increase your cost through increased handling and shipping. This also will effect your cash flow. Be frugal in your inventory management but not at the expense of customer satisfaction. The opportunity cost of a lost customer who does not get the products ordered can be higher than all of the cost savings combined and multiplied by ten.

- Order filling and shipping - this is the true nuts and bolts of the catalog operation. The warehouse people are responsible for receiving products; keeping track of them; and picking, packing and shipping them when orders are processed.

Someone must also make hundreds of decisions a day regarding the shipping carton to be used for a given order. This person is your last link with your customer. If a carton is selected that is not strong enough to protect the customer's order and it arrives damaged, you have probably lost a customer.

Take a little walk around the shipping area with a foreman. Let the people know how important they are to the success of the business. Tell them not to skimp on shipping materials. The difference between bad and good shipping amounts to pennies per order in costs, but dollars in customer satisfaction.

- Billing - always include your bill with the shipment. If you cannot, bill as quickly after you ship the order. This will help your cash flow. It is easier for your customer to get an invoice approved when the memory of the product is still fresh in their mind.

You should not bill prior to the product being shipped. This can cause irritation and a dissatisfied customer. The only exception to this rule is if you told the customer that this is part of your terms for the order.

- Problems - no matter how hard you try, you will have some complaints and returned goods. Your customer service department can expect contact with 2-8% of your customers. Problems should be handled as quickly as possible. Refunds or credits should also be handled quickly. If you are responsive, you will keep your customers. If you hold a refund for an extended period of time, you will lose a customer.

Controls

In order to monitor your fulfillment operation and ensure competent service in all areas, a few simple "red flags" should be established. Some examples are:

- Inventory in-stock conditions - monitor by keeping a percentage calculation of your items back-ordered. Track this calculation by product manager or category, by vendor and overall. You should also know the total number of orders with a back-order and the percentage of total orders that have a back order.

- Order turn-around time - the number of days from receipt to shipment of all orders received. Slow order fulfillment could indicate too many items due-in; inadequate staffing in the warehouse; a back-log in order processing; or some combination of all of the above. Set a target of x days to fulfill an order. All orders falling outside the target should be reviewed to correct the cause of the hold-up.

Many catalogers have tested order fulfillment times to determine the effect it has on customer re-orders. The faster the order is fulfilled the higher the customer re-order rate. You should attempt to fulfill your orders in one or two days after receipt.

- <u>Response time of complaints</u> - this is also a time critical situation. It does not matter as much whether you actually solve the problem, but rather that you are trying to resolve the situation quickly. Even if you do not resolve the situation totally, you will be more apt to keep these customers for future orders if they know you are paying attention to their concerns. If you do not respond and show interest, you will not have the customer in the future.

- <u>Returns</u> - a daily log and a period-to-date log of returns tell you a great deal about your products and promotion. High returns for any item can indicate that you over-presented the product in your catalog. It may also tell you that a product is below your normal level of quality. If the items are being returned because they were damaged, perhaps the packaging is inadequate for delivering the item.

- <u>Confusion rate</u> - this is a comparison measure of the number of times you communicate with a customer about an order or item. You should be tracking the number of customer contacts you have per order. If the number increases for a specific product or customer support person beyond your norm, you have a problem. You could have a product problem or a customer service personnel problem.

Stanley J.Fenvessy, CMC, president, Fenvessy and Associates,Inc., New York, NY, wrote in a manual release for the Direct Marketing Association (Release:500.1), ten suggestions on How to Avoid Fulfillment Problems. Even though this was written primarily for consumer products in all areas of direct marketing (not just catalogs), the points certainly apply to business-to-business catalogs and mail order.

The ten points as they appear in the manual release are:

1. *Clarify your promotion and offerings.* Be sure the customer understands what you are offering. Do not oversell. Explain the customer's obligations and the nature of your continuation program. Explain clearly return and refund privileges and who pays the postage. Provide a simple order form or coupon. Design the form with the customer in mind -- not your own fulfillment operations. Be sure it is of workable size with plenty of white space. Help the customer through the form by numbering the steps that must be followed. Ask for a telephone number so that he or she might be contacted if there is a question.

2. *Don't promise service you can't deliver.* Measure service from the customer's standpoint -- from the time he or she telephones until he or she actually receives the merchandise. It is misleading to advertise that orders are *handled* within 48 hours, when it may take days longer for the customer to actually receive the merchandise.

3. *Date and control all incoming customer orders and correspondence.* In the case of orders this is done by batching orders or payments in groups of 50 to 100 as soon as they are received. These batches are frequently identified by the different colors for each day of the week and are controlled throughout their processing. The original orders are eventually filed in their original batch envelope.

   When correspondence is received, a color-coded date tag is stapled to the top of the letter. The indicator shows the day of the month the letter was received. With this system a clerk can quickly arrange an accumulation of mail into sequence, either for processing or an aged inventory count.

4. *Exercise care in billing and collection.* Do not bill mer-

chandise before it is shipped. If possible send the bill
with the merchandise. Structure your dunning cycle so
that payments and bill will not cross in the mail. Be judi-
cious in employing outside collection agencies.

5. *Do not abuse the back order privilege.* If you must back
   order, cancel back orders after four weeks unless the customer specifically requests you to hold the order.
   Acknowledge the status of back orders every four weeks.

6. *Instruct your customers on how to complain and how to
   return merchandise.* Years ago it was considered contrary
   to sound sales policy to mention complaints or returns in
   any sales material or order papers. Today, well-run direct
   marketers include instructions on how to return merchandise on the back of the packing list enclosed with each
   shipment. The result: no added returns or complaints and
   those that are received can be processed easier and quick-
   er because the customer has instructions to follow.

7. *Use the telephone.* With the high cost of the three R's of
   correspondence handling -- Reading, Researching and
   Responding, telephone communications prove less costly
   in the long run. Further, the goodwill generated is simply
   amazing, and the company saves money -- even after
   paying the telephone bill.

8. *Follow the maxim "the customer is always right."* That
   retail maxim applies to direct marketing as well. Too
   many firms waste time and money and aggravate the customer by requiring additional information, particularly
   cancelled checks or order acknowledgements before making an adjustment. If the amount is small -- $10 to $25
   depending on the merchandise offered -- make the adjustment immediately.

9. *Test your own service* (and that of your competitors).
   This involves two approaches. First, install effective qual-

ity control procedures *within* your own fulfillment operation. Quality control inspections should be conducted at all key points in the fulfillment cycle and should include the opening of a meaningful sample of both packages and correspondence ready for mailing to the customer. As a result, individual workers should be evaluated by applying a quality control rating to the work sampled.

Secondly, a regular and continuing program of test ordering should be undertaken. The results of these tests will give you valuable information about delivery, item conditions of merchandise on arrival, and the accuracy of the actual order fulfillment.

10. *Accumulate data concerning the nature of customer calls and correspondence.* Management should regularly review the nature, volume and disposition of consumer complaints. This review should specifically include samples of actual complaints and some personal contact with consumers and grievances.

Changes of pattern in customer contacts and complaints provide valuable hints on weakness in deliveries, deteriorating merchandise quality, confusing sales offerings, poor packaging, computer errors and other areas which obviously need improving.

Measuring Profits

It is relatively easy to measure the profitability of a stand-alone catalog. Either you are making it or you are not.

The mail order catalog that is only one part of a business that has multiple channels of distribution may make it more difficult to determine if the catalog is profitable. This often happens because the catalog is considered a cost center within the company using existing staff to develop and operate the catalog. The profitability of a catalog embedded amongst several departments within a company is difficult to measure. This confusion can be solved by setting up the catalog as an operating subsidiary.

It is not difficult to measure direct sales that result from the catalog. Establishing who is responsible for creating the order is another area of confusion. There will always be a conflict between the catalog and other sales approaches as to who should get the credit for sales. The sales force will claim that there would be no direct sales if it were not for their efforts. The catalog managers will always claim that the catalog is stimulating the customers to buy from their assigned sales representatives. This is a never ending dilemma, one which you cannot solve. There is no easy answer. Your control stops when you decide whether to pay the assigned salesperson commissions on orders generated by the catalog.

One point to consider about commissions: If you pay commissions to sales people for catalog sales in their territories, your catalog has an additional expense and may not appear to make money. You will be subsidizing your sales force with additional unearned income. You can reduce the salesperson's commissions to improve the catalog's apparent profitability. Or, you can eliminate commissions on direct sales from the catalog. The action you take depends on your catalog strategy. If you want the catalog to be a stand-alone activity, you must separate it from field sales control.

If you are just starting a catalog and already have a sales force responsible for the customers, you must also evaluate how you will introduce the catalog. All sales currently made to the customer are done by the sales people. They are paid commissions and depend on these orders for their income. Eliminating this source of income can prove to be a serious mistake in launching the catalog. We suggest you implement a strategy that compensates the sales people at a rate that reduces over time. In addition, management must determine how the sales force will recover the lost income opportunity the catalog can create. The fastest way to fail with a catalog launch in the business-to-business area is to disregard its impact on other existing sales channels.

In addition to the sales force, a larger issue is how you allocate the company's general support overhead to your catalog. You will have a difficult time measuring profitability if you have company wide services supporting your catalog operation. Accounting departments tend to load unfair overhead onto the catalog which seriously impacts its profitability.

The following are some identifiable expense and overhead items:

- Phone line charges (if they are separate from company lines).
- Square footage utilization (for warehouse and other identifiable activities that are only used for the catalog. If the same inventory is used for all activities, it is impossible to separate this and other shared activities).
- Promotion costs are easily identified because the catalog costs are normally separate.
- Creative costs, when purchased from outside suppliers. Creative costs transferred from inside tend not to be accurate. If you are uncertain about creative costs, get an outside quote.
- Postage is measurable and assignable.
- Direct labor expenses for catalog creation, operation and management should be easy to identify. Any allocations of personnel expenses other than those reporting directly to the catalog will probably be inaccurate.

Keep in mind that a catalog operation can be very profitable. Higher margins draw the attention of top management. As a result, your finance department and other managers may attempt to overlay additional expenses on to your operation.

One approach to managing the overhead problem is to sell items to your catalog operation at your regular wholesale price. Using your wholesale price of goods assumes that overhead is fully covered in the selling price. It is far easier to charge your catalog operation at the same cost of goods as charged in other parts of your business than it is to try to allocate expenses that are not directly related to the catalog operation.

An important point to consider is that your company cannot show the profit on wholesaling of an item until it is actually sold and billed to an external customer. Just transferring goods on paper will not make a profit for your company.

Another way to handle the confusion of allocating your overhead costs is to work on a contribution to overhead and profit basis. No matter how many operating divisions you have, you can compare each division's ability to make a contribution to the overall company . By using the contribution measurement, you can compare activities and design compensation packages that do not include any arbitrary assignment of costs. The method is easy to understand and implement. For example:

> NET SALES (Gross less returns and allowances)
>
> less Cost of Sales
>
> less Direct Costs
>
> = Contribution to Overhead and Profit

As you can see, once you have deducted the direct associated costs and expenses, the remaining revenue is a contribution to overhead and profit. This type of measurement system eliminates one department trying to allocate its overhead expenses to another. Politics don't become as important. After you set profit objectives, the balance of the contribution of all the divisions must equal overhead. If your overhead expenses are higher, you only have two options: reduce profit expectations or reduce overhead.

A point of caution: Don't look at a division's contribution, decide it is not enough and eliminate the division. Add back the profit and see if it is now making a contribution that is acceptable. If you close the division, you will not have any contribution to absorb company overhead. Think before you cut.

If a division is not making any contribution to overhead and profit, it may be time to take some aggressive action to eliminate that division.

Customer Acquisition Costs

A prudent way to calculate how much you should spend to acquire a customer is to look at the life cycle of a customer. Over the life of a customer, you can anticipate or forecast some revenue stream. To be prudent, you should factor the gross contribution using present value techniques to establish the life time value of that customer in today's dollars.

Year	Customers	Rev.@$600	Cont %	Contrib $	P.V. 10%	Total
1	100	$60,000	35%	$21,000	.909	$19,089
2	65	39,000	35%	15,650	.826	12,927
3	49	29,400	32%	9,408	.751	7,065
4	39	23,400	30%	7,020	.683	4,795
5	31	18,600	30%	5,580	.621	3,465

Thus, total present value contribution of 100 customers discounted using 10% cost of capital......................................$47,341

The amount of investment to make in present dollars to acquire a customer is calculated by dividing the total present value dollars by the original number of customers:

$$\$47,341 \div 100 = \$473.41$$

This model makes assumptions on the contribution, average sale per customer and the rate of customer loss. You have the freedom to do everything you can to change any of these variables as they affect your business. Our point is you can't look at a customer's one year history and determine what you are willing to spend to acquire that customer. Lifetime value of a customer, discounted by the present value method, is a reasonable way to set the maximum investment you should make to acquire a customer.

Some things you can do to change the results are:

- You can keep customers alive longer through various regeneration programs.
- You can add new products and upgrade customers to increase your average order.
- You can work with your costs to drive up your contribution percentage.

You must make some assumptions based on your situation in order to arrive at the amount you should spend on customer acquisition. In the example above, you can spend $473.41 to acquire a new customer without making any profit on the customer. Anything less than this customer acquisition target number should mean a profit over the next five years.

In the example above, we did not include as a separate expense, the cost to service and promote the customer on an on-going basis. We have assumed these costs to be a part of the overhead expense when calculating the net contribution.

If you spend more than the $473.41 to acquire a customer, you will lose money and unless you can find other ways to generate additional revenue to off-set the acquisition expenses. Perhaps you can borrow money at no cost; streamline operations costs to increase contribution; or create some other form of income (like list rental) to off-set the higher acquisition cost. These are all nice ideas that may or may not work. The most prudent course of action is not to spend more than your customer acquisition cost target.

Acquisition costs are dynamic and should be re-evaluated on a sustained and on-going basis.

Critical Mass

Whether you are just starting your catalog operation or have been in business for years, you should evaluate how large your catalog operations should be. As in all business, growth may resemble an upward sloping curve, but overhead growth occurs in plateaus. To evaluate how large your business can be, you must be realistic in estimating the size of the market opportunity.

Once you have determined the size of the available market, you must determine the resources you are willing to invest to acquire your desired market share. In the case of catalogs, market share is not some abstract number computed by an external research company. Your market share is the number of customers you have.

As we discussed earlier, you should set a target acquisition cost for each new customer. Then, applying the most prudent cost accounting system you can, you should begin the process of new customer acquisition.

The dynamic model you enlist should constantly measure the price you are paying to acquire each new customer. The method we demonstrated earlier is one approach to evaluate acquisition costs.

When you have tested and mailed all of the available lists that you can identify and have not exceeded the acquisition cost objective, you then should examine your operating costs. In this environment, growth consists of reducing costs thereby increasing the catalog's contribution.

If you are satisfied with the size of your catalog operation, it may be time to look at alternatives. Keep in mind that you must evaluate the contribution of a customer over some period to determine the total value of that customer. The method we discussed earlier is one method of determining the value of a customer. If you are uncomfortable with the size of your catalog operation, there are two things you can do:

1. Develop additional product lines and/or catalogs to sell to your existing customers. These new lines could also give you new growth as well as a new customer base for your

existing catalog.

2. Restructure your catalog operations to allocate all overhead to your existing customers. Using this approach you
   could now acquire additional customers using only the
   variable cost of list, production and postage. This would
   lower you acquisition cost and allow you to spend more
   to acquire new customers.

These two approaches are not mutually exclusive. You should under-
take both of these courses of action once you reach you critical mass
and are profitable without new customers.

Be very careful of the never ending growth syndrome. Business catalogs have grown at incredible rates for the last 15 years. Growth is
currently slowing for many business catalogers due to competition
and a slower growing economy. Do not be afraid to call a halt to geo-
metric circulation growth. It is very easy for costs to increase faster
than sales. In direct mail, your costs are sunk in promotion before
you realize the sales are not going to be there. Be willing to stick with
known productive lists that can give you the new customers you need
to maintain your critical mass.

Direct Mail Assets

All good businesses are becoming more sensitive to the needs of customers. Peter Drucker said "that the goal of business is to gain and
keep customers." This philosophy is even more important in the catalog business. The way to determine the value of anything is to sell it.

Assets of any business are represented on its balance sheet and are
normally fairly easy to identify. The most important asset of the
direct mail catalog is not an asset that normally appears on its financial statement . To financial analysts, unfamiliar with mail order marketing methods, the catalogs customer file may appear as a good-will
item. Traditionally they have found it hard to quantify.

In the catalog business, always remember that your main asset is your customer file. Different customers will buy from you at different volumes and different levels of frequency. The concepts used by consumer catalog marketers of Recency, Frequency and Monetary, also apply in the business world.

Consumer catalog marketers long ago identified that the customer that purchased from you most recently has a high tendency to purchase again. Customers that buy from you on a sustained and frequent basis will also continue to buy from you as long as you meet their expectations And, the more money a customer has spent with you, the better the chances that he/she will buy from you again.

As you develop your customer database, you should 'score' or categorize all of your customers using some algorithm that identifies customer levels. For example, one of our clients used the following algorithm:

- 'A' Customer -- any customer who has purchased $1,500 or more in last 12 months.

- 'B' Customer -- any customer who has purchased between $1,000 and $1,499 in the last 12 months.

- 'C' Customer -- any customer who has purchased between $500 and $1,000 in the last 12 months.

- 'D' Customer -- any customer who has purchased less than $500 in the last 12 months.

- 'E' Customer -- any customer who has not been coded by the previous criteria but has purchased in the last 24 months.

Different categories of customers should receive different levels of marketing activity. For example, an 'A' customer may warrant a telemarketing or even a face-to-face contact at least once a quarter or once a year. On the other hand, you can probably only afford to contact the 'D' customers every quarter by mail.

Too frequent contact is sometimes thought to be a problem. The reality is that you cannot contact your customers too frequently. Business catalog marketers that used to mail once a quarter are now mailing as frequently as once a month to a portion of their customer base. Your customers will tell you by their purchasing levels what your schedule should be. Your 'A' customers have bought at a level that generates enough contribution to allow you to contact them as frequently as you desire. On the other hand, your 'E' customers only generate enough contribution to justify one or two mailings per year.

The scoring system above is very basic. You might use a different algorithm that is more comprehensive. We have seen systems that identify each of the elements of RFM; that include product categories in their algorithm; source codes in the code; or combinations of all of these. If you have not already created a scoring algorithm, select something simple to start with. Follow the age old KISS adage, 'keep it simple, stupid'.

The scoring system you select must be dynamic. Don't code a customer an 'A' and never re-score that customer. Some suggestions can prove to be very helpful as time goes on. All require that you completely document and:

- identify the scoring algorithm and review it with everybody involved in the catalog effort.

- identify how, and how frequently, you will re-evaluate the customer file and re-score customers.

- don't force the scoring as an issue. If you have been too stringent in your category selection you may have no 'A' customers. On the other hand, if you have no 'A' customers it may be because your catalog performance is slipping.

All of the other assets within a business can change; they can be purchased, sold and exchanged. All except your customer file. You establish the relationship with your customers. Even if you sell your company, the customers will still continue to think they are doing business with you.

If you are careful in maintaining and utilizing your customer file, it will be your most valuable asset. This customer file can allow you to grow and expand in other product areas and even other markets. The classic example is Sears. Initially only a catalog marketer, they have expanded into retail, insurance, and other financial services. It all starts with the customer base.

Financial Planning

In the chapter on business planning we explained how to develop objectives for lead generation and for selling a single product. The catalog process complicates the issue because, by definition, you are selling more than one product. Your financial controls are therefore based on a different system and cover more than just the marketing issues.

The catalog, or even face-to-face sales, will create a group of prospects who respond to your offer and want to do business with you that you will decline for various reasons. You may have prior experience with the customer and decide that it is not in your best interest to re-establish the relationship. For example:

- Customers who did not pay their bills.
- Customers who continually take advantage of your return policies. They are, in effect, continually trying products but never purchasing.
- People who return the products incomplete.
- Constant customer service problems. This group includes customers who are always complaining in an effort to negotiate better terms and conditions.
- The customer has insufficient credit for you to sell them.

In the catalog environment, other catalog marketers have declined about 20% of their orders for credit and other reasons. From a financial review and planning perspective, these orders should not appear as gross sales. You did not accept the order so therefore it was never sold to the customer.

You must handle your financial reporting in a method that is acceptable to your management. In the model we outline below, we illustrate gross orders received and then allow for returned goods and allowances to arrive at the net sales. Note that we include the gross demand, which includes customers who want to purchase from you that have been rejected.

Item	Description	% of Gross Demand
1	Gross Demand	100%
2	Gross Sales	80%
3	Net Sales	70%

In the above model, the gross demand (1) is the total amount of product that the market would like to buy from you. As we have discussed, you will not want to ship a part of the demand. The gross sales (2) represents the total amount of sales that you have accepted and shipped product. As you can see, there is about a 20% shrinkage from gross demand to gross sales. This shrinkage may be different in your business, but other business-to-business catalog marketers are experiencing about 20%. The net sales (3) are the actual revenues you collect for the sales of product. The difference between the gross and net sales are those orders that are returned.

We use the net sales figure as the basis for our financial model calculations. You may choose to use gross sales for your percentage calculation in your financial model. Either way, consistency is the key. The purpose of the financial model is to give you a management indicator if your catalog operation is running as expected.

Item	Description	% of Net Sales
1	Net Sales	100%
2	Cost of Goods	60%
3	Gross Margin	40%
4	Catalog Production and Mailing	19%
5	Net Margin	21%

6	Variable Expenses		
	6a Salary/Benefits	4.5%	
	6b Toll free phone	1.3%	
	6c Credit Card Fees	2.2%	
	6d Freight Out	3.0%	
	6e Shipping Income	-5.0%	
	6f Packaging Supplies	.9%	
	6g Miscellaneous Postage	.3%	
	6h Bad Debt	2.0%	
	Total Variable Expenses		9.2%
7	Net Contribution		11.8%
8	Fixed Expenses		
	8a Exec Salary/Benefits	4.0%	
	8b Travel/Entertainment	0.3%	
	8c Office Supplies	0.4%	
	8d Prof.Fees	0.5%	
	8e Rent	0.5%	
	8f Utilities	0.2%	
	8g Repair/Maintenance	0.1%	
	8h Insurance	0.2%	
	8i Equip Lease/Maintenance	0.8%	
	8j Telephone	0.5%	
	Total Fixed Expenses		7.5%
9	Net Profit before taxes		4.3%

In our model, net sales equal 100% of the production of the catalog being measured. This model uses all costs and expenses applied as a percentage of the net sale or total revenue of the operation. The percentages in this model are used for illustration only. You must develop your own model using your own conditions. While these numbers are not absolute, they are indicative of the order-of-magnitude of the various costs and expenses as they relate to net sales.

When you subtract your cost of goods (2) from net sales (1) you arrive at your gross margin (3).

Gross margin (3) less the costs you incur as a direct result of being in the catalog business (4) (catalog production and mailing) establishes the net margin (5). Catalog production and mailing expenses are the total cost of creating, printing, list rental, addressing and postage required to mail your catalog. If you are using in-house creative services, and can specifically identify the actual expenses, you can include the costs in this figure. If you are charged an overhead number for the creative services, the costs are really overhead and should not be included as a variable expense.

Net Margin (5) less the variable expenses (6) related to the actual catalog operations will establish the net contribution (7) from catalog operations. We have identified several broad categories of variable expenses. You should work with your accounting department to establish the variable expense items for your operation. The following identifies the items we have included:

6a Wages and benefits are the employee expenses that are directly related to the operation of the catalog.

6b Toll free telephone is your cost to provide free inbound telephone service to your customers.

6c Credit card fees are the cost for your credit card suppliers as a result of customers using charge cards to pay for their purchases.

6d Freight out is your shipping expense to get your products to your customers.

6e Shipping Income is what you charge your customers per order or per item for you to handle and ship your products to them. Shipping income is a contra-expense or an income item. We have chosen to handle this income item under your variable expenses so that the net sales number is not inflated. This allows you to keep an exact accounting of your costs as a percentage of the true net sales.

6f   Packaging supplies are the cartons and packing materials you use to ship your products.

6g   Miscellaneous postage covers items too small to ship economically by other means and also your postage to support customer service.

6h   Bad debt is the expense you incur when customers that keep your products do not pay their bills.

Net contribution (7) less the fixed expenses (8) will establish the net profit before taxes (9) from the catalog operations. The fixed expenses are the costs you would incur no matter what business you are in. Our example does not include:

- interest expense or income
- business taxes
- depreciation.

We are trying to provide a guideline and not a complete financial proforma. Fixed overhead is different in almost every business. They need to be monitored and evaluated on a regular basis. Since individual fixed expenses are often very small as a percentage of sales, they sometimes are allowed to get out of control. Even though they are small, overhead can quickly destroy the profit from your operation. The overhead items we have included are:

8a   Executive salaries and benefits are the costs of the management team and supervisory team not already included as a variable expense. It is not unusual to include only percentages of some peoples' salaries as they have other functions not related to the catalog effort.

8b   Travel and Entertainment are the expenses incurred by the personnel identified in 8a above.

8c   Office supplies.

8d Professional Fees are the charges you receive from your lawyer, accountant and outside consultants you might engage.

8e Rent.

8f Utilities include your heat, electricity, water or other services.

8g Repairs and Maintenance are the expenses you incur to keep you facility in good operating condition.

8h Insurance are costs for the coverages you need to carry by law and as a prudent manager.

8i Equipment Lease and Maintenance is what you pay to lease the machines and equipment necessary to operate your business.

8j Telephone are the costs you incur to operate the business telephones exclusive of the cost for inbound telephone service already identified as a variable expense.

In our example, the pretax profit for this company is 4.3%. Decide what your profit objectives are before you begin, and again as you grow your catalog operation. Review pricing, quantities mailed, variable costs and fixed costs to increase the net profit from your catalog.

One additional income item was not covered in our model: list rental. Some business catalogers rent their lists in order to generate additional income. The income from list rentals can be 6% to 8% of net sales, a very substantial revenue source. Most businesses that are operating a catalog imbedded within their overall operations do not rent lists to others.

If you do not rent your list you will not enjoy this income opportunity. If you do rent your list, we suggest you account for your list rental income as another income item. This would be done after you have accounted for your income from operations. By not including the list income in the net revenue figure from operations, you will have a clearer picture of operating expenses compared to operating income.

Break Even Analysis

You had to make a lot of significant business decisions to create the model of your overall catalog operation. Once this is done you can make some very practical applications of the information created. You can use the percentages to calculate the level of sales you will need to operate your catalog business at a break even level.

The following break even calculation is one method to establish some measurement objectives that can prove invaluable in evaluating the success of your efforts. You can also use this calculation to determine if a given catalog test or venture looks feasible. This formula establishes the break even sales revenue required from each catalog mailed.

$$BE = \frac{CC \div (GM\% - OE\%)}{(1.00 - R/C\%)}$$

BE = Break even *gross* sales per catalog stated in cents per catalog

CC = Catalog cost stated in cents/catalog

GM = Gross Margin stated as a percent of net sales

OE = Operating expenses(fixed + variable) as a percent of net sales

R/C = Refunds/cancellations as a percent of *gross* sales

Using the figures from our model above, assuming a catalog cost of
$ .40; the break even would be:

$$BE = \frac{.40 \div (40\% - 16.7\%)}{(1.00 - 11\%)}$$

$$= \frac{.4 \div (.4 - .167)}{1.00 - .11}$$

$$= \frac{1.72}{.89}$$

= $1.93 gross sales per catalog mailed to break even.

If you do rent your list, the break even formula would be:

$$BE = \frac{CC \div (GM\% - OE\% + LR\%)}{(1.00 - R/C\%)}$$

LR = List rental income as a percent of net sales.

In this calculation (using a 6% list rental figure), the income from list
rental lowers the break even of the necessary gross sales. The gross
sales per catalog would become $1.54 to reach break even.

You could use the gross revenue per catalog figure to determine when
your gross sales reach your break even point. For example, if you
calculate a gross sales per catalog break even of $1.75. If you mail
500,000 catalogs, the gross sales you need in order to reach break
even is;

500,000 x $1.75 = $875,000.00

You can also use the break even calculation to determine the sales
you need per page, per spread and per item on a per catalog basis. If
you use the $1.75 figure for the gross sales per book, you can divide

the pages and products into this number to arrive at some interesting objectives.

- Sales per page (assume a 40 page catalog) =

  $1.75 ÷ 40 = $0.044 sales per page per catalog

- Doubling the per page will give the per spread (you may not be selling off your cover which will change the numbers slightly). The sales per spread per catalog would be $0.088.

- Sales per item (assume 100 items) =

  $1.75 ÷ 100 = $0.0175 sales per item per catalog

These calculations are only intended to provide you with a way to evaluate and analyze the dynamic performance of your catalog. As you change any part of the formula it is fairly easy to recalculate the gross sales needed for you to reach break even.

If you are accustomed to working on a cost per thousand basis, multiply the results by 1,000 to arrive at your objectives. If you calculate that you need $1.75 gross sales per catalog to break even, you will need $1,750.00 per thousand catalogs mailed.

However you do your calculations, establish some type of easy to use objectives. You will continually be measuring the overall financial performance of the catalog operation. The break even analysis gives you a method to review the progress of your catalog on a more dynamic basis. It also allows you to focus on the strength and weakness of each catalog.

Catalogs Summarized

We have covered a lot of ground in this chapter and tried to give you a foundation that you could build on. Virtually every business is in the catalog business in some way. Even if you are only publishing a price list for various manufactured items, you are really preparing a catalog. Whenever you offer you market more than one product choice at a time, you have created a catalog.

Your method you choose to deliver your catalog can range from direct mail to sales representatives delivering them personally. Whatever the method used, your ability to calculate your catalog's profitability does not change.

The performance and sales of catalogs are as varied as there are types of businesses. A manufacturing company making higher priced products can generate hundreds of thousands of dollars of sales per page of the catalog. In fact, in these kinds of situations, the companies use catalogs as a tool for the sales force. On the other hand, an office supply company might only generate $0.10 sales per page and the catalog is the only channel of distribution.

Whatever your strategy, catalog as a sales tool or catalog as a mail order vehicle, your catalog is you sales representative. When you are not present, the catalog will present your products to your prospects and customers. You should review your catalog and ensure that it is representative of you, your company and your products. Don't just reprint your catalog and assume that the market will find it interesting. As we have stressed in other parts of this book, never mail or deliver anything that you wouldn't want to receive yourself.

Glossary

Access Time: The time it takes a computer to locate a piece of information in memory or storage and to take action, i.e., the "read" time. Also, the time it takes a computer to store a piece of information and to complete action, i.e., the "write" time.

Action Devices: Items and techniques used in a mailing to initiate the response desired.

Active Buyer: A buyer whose latest purchase was made within the last twelve months. *(See buyer.)*

Active Customer: A term used interchangeably with "active buyer".

Active Member: Any member who is fulfilling the original commitment or who has fulfilled that commitment and has made one or more purchases in the last 12 months.

Active Subscriber: One who has committed for regular delivery of magazines, books or other goods or services for a period of time still in effect.

Actives: Customers on a list who have made purchases within a prescribed time period, usually not more than one year; subscribers whose subscriptions have not expired.

Additions: New names, either of individuals or companies, added to a mailing list.

Add-On Service: Service of Direct Marketing Association (DMA) which gives consumers an opportunity to request that their names be added to mailing lists.

Address Coding Guide (CG): Contains the actual or potential beginning and ending house numbers, block group and/or enumeration district numbers, ZIP Codes, and other geographic codes for all city delivery service streets served by 3,154 post offices located within 6,601 Zip Codes.

Address Correction Requested: An endorsement which, when printed in the upper left-hand corner of the address portion of the mailing piece (below return address), authorizes the U.S. Postal Service, for a fee, to provide the known new address of a person no longer at the address on the mailing piece.

A.D.I.: (Area of Dominant Influence) Broadcaster's method of defining a market within its reach.

A.I.D.A.: The most popular formula for the preparation of direct mail copy. The letters stand for Get Attention, Arouse Interest, Stimulate Desire, Ask for Action.

Alphanumeric: A contraction of "alphabetic" and "numeric". Applies to any coding system that provides for letters, numbers (digits), and special symbols such as punctuation marks. Synonymous with Alphameric.

Assigned Mailing Dates: The dates on which the list user has the obligation to mail a specific list. No other date is acceptable without specific approval of the list owner.

Average Order Size: A simple arithmetic formula used to establish the average order size. The total revenue generated from a program divided by the total number of orders will establish the average order size.

Audience: The total number of individuals reached by promotion or advertisement.

Audit: Printed report of the counts involved in a particular list or file.

Back End: The activities necessary to complete a mail order transaction once an order has been received and/or the measurement of a buyer's performance after he has ordered the first item in a series offering. Can also be used to define the measurement of prospects who became leads and performance towards purchasing.

Back Test: Often described as a "retest" or "confirming test". For example, a list was tested, the response was within acceptable range but not good enough to order a large quantity. To reconfirm the results the list will be retested.

Bad Pay: Also referred to as "nonpay". Subscription or membership offers which are "bill me" (charge orders) and which subsequently must be cancelled due to nonpayment.

Bangtail: Promotional envelope with a second flap which is perforated and designed for use as an order blank.

Batch Processing: Techniques of executing a set of computer programs/selections in batches as opposed to executing each order/selection as it is received. Batches can be created by computer programming or a manual collection of data into groups.

Batched Job: A job that is grouped with other jobs as input to a computing system, as opposed to a transaction job entry where the job is done singly to completion.

Beat-the-Champ: A process where you establish a base line or best performing promotion as the champ. You then continually test other promotions in hopes of finding a new champ. Also known as Control.

Bill Enclosure: Any promotional piece or notice enclosed with a bill, an invoice or a statement not directed toward the collection of all or part of the bill, invoice or statement.

Binary: Involves a selection, choice or condition in which there are two possibilities such as the use of the symbols "0" or "1" in a numbering system.

Bingo Card: A reply card inserted in a publication and used by readers to request literature from companies whose products and services are either advertised or mentioned in editorial columns.

Bit: A single character or element in a binary number (digit). The smallest element of binary machine language represented by a magnetized spot on a recording surface or a magnetized element of a storage device.

Bounce Back: An offer enclosed with mailing sent to a customer in fulfillment of an offer.

BPI (Bytes per Inch): Characters, represented in bytes, per Inch. Bytes per inch on magnetic tape *(see Tape Density)*.

BRC: Business Reply Card.

BRE: Business Reply Envelope.

Breakeven: The point in a business transaction when income and expenses are equal.

Broadcast Media: A direct response source that includes radio, television and cable TV.

Broadside: A single sheet of paper, printed on one side or two, folded for mailing or direct distribution, and opening into a single, large advertisement.

Brochure: Strictly, a high-quality pamphlet, with especially planned layout, typography and illustrations. Term is also used loosely for any promotional pamphlet or booklet.

Buckslip: A separate slip attached to a printed piece containing instructions to route the material to specified individuals.

Bulk Mail: A category of Third Class Mail involving a large quantity of identical pieces but addressed to different names for mailing before delivery to post office.

Business List: Any compilation or list of individuals or companies based upon a business-associated interest, inquiry, membership, subscription or purchase.

Burst: To separate continuous form paper into discrete sheets.

Buyer: Someone who has purchased from the company.

Buyer (1982-1984): Indicates that these people purchased from the company at one time during one of these years.

Byte: Sequence of adjacent binary digits operated upon as a unit and usually shorter than a computer word. A character is usually considered a byte. (A single byte can contain either two numeric characters or one alphabetic or special character). A group of bits, usually eight, that stores a piece of information. Computer memory is measured in Bytes: 32K means 32,000 bytes.

Carrier Route: Grouping of addresses based on the delivery route of each letter carrier. The average number of stops is 400 but does range from under 100 to 2,500 to 3,000. In total, there are about 180,000 carrier routes in the United States.

Carrier Route Pre-sort: Refers to pre-sorting of mail (usually by a letter shop) to carrier route by ZIP codes and preparing it to specifications established by the U.S. Postal Service. Properly executed, the mailing so prepared receives a discounted postal rate.

Cash Buyer: A buyer who encloses payment with order.

Cash Rider: Also called "cash up" or "cash option" wherein an order form offers install- ment terms, but a postscript offers the option of sending full cash payment with order, usually at some saving over credit price as an incentive.

C/A: Change of Address.

Catalog: Any promotion that offers more than one product. Frequently, a catalog is described as a book or book- let showing merchandise with descriptive details and prices.

Catalog Buyer: A person who has bought products or ser- vices from a catalog.

Catalog Request: (Paid or Unpaid). One who sends for a catalog (prospective buyer). The catalog may be free; there may be a nominal charge for postage and han- dling, or there may be a more substantial charge that is offer refunded or credited on the first order.

Cell(s): In list terminology, a sta- tistical unit or units. A group of individuals selected from the file on a consistent basis.

Census Tract: Small geographi- cal area established by local committees, and approved by the Census Bureau, which contains a population seg- ment with relatively uniform economic and social charac- teristics with clearly identifi- able boundaries averaging approximately 1,200 house- holds.

Cheshire Label: Specially pre- pared paper (rolls, fanfold or accordion fold) used to pro- duce names and addresses to be mechanically affixed, one at a time, to a mailing piece.

Circulars: General term for printed advertisement in any form, including printed mat- ter sent out by direct mail.

Cleaning: The process of cor- recting and/or removing a name and address from a mailing list because it is no longer correct or because the listing is to be shifted from one category to another.

Closed face envelope: An enve- lope that is addressed directly on the face, does not have a die-cut window.

Cluster Selection: A selection routine based upon taking a group of names in a series, skipping a group, taking another group, etc. E.g.-a cluster selection on an nth name basis might be the first 10 out of every 100 or the first 125 out of 175, etc.; a cluster selection using limited ZIP Codes might be the first 200 names in each of the specified ZIP Codes, etc.

COBOL: Computer Business Oriented Language. A procedure-oriented business computer language.

Coding: (1) Identifying devices used on reply devices to identify the mailing list or other source from which the address obtained. (2) A structure of letters and numbers used to classify characteristics of an address on a list.

Collate: (1) To assemble individual elements of a mailing in sequence for inserting into a mailing envelope. (2) A program which combines two or more ordered files to produce a single ordered file. Also the act of combining such files. Synonymous with merges as in Merge/Purge.

Commission: A percentage of sale, by prior agreement, paid to the the list broker, list manager, or other service arm for their part in the list usage.

Compile: The process by which a computer translates a series of instructions written in a programming language into actual machine language.

Compiled List: Name and addresses derived from directories, newspapers, public records, retail sales slips, trade show registrations, etc., to identify groups of people with something in common.

Compiler: Organization which develops lists of names and addresses from directories, newspapers, public records, registrations, and other sources, identifying groups of people, companies, or institutions with something in common.

Completed Cancel: One who has completed a specific commitment to buy products or services before cancelling.

Comprehensive: Complete and detailed layout for a printed piece. Also: "Comp", "Compre".

Computer: Data processor that can perform substantial computation, without intervention by a human.

Computer Compatibility: Ability to interchange the data or programs of one computer system with one or more of other computers.

Computer Language: A generic term for the codes used to give computers instructions. Basic is a computer language.

Computer Letter: Computer-printed message providing personalized, fill-in information from a source file in pre-designated positions. May also be full-printed letter with personalized insertions.

Computer Personalization: Printing of letters or other promotional pieces by a computer using names, addresses, special phrases, or other information based on data appearing in one or more computer records. The objective is to use the information in the computer record to tailor the promotional message to a specific individual.

Computer Program: Series of instructions or statements prepared to achieve a certain result.

Computer Record: All the information about an individual, company, or transaction stored on a specific magnetic tape or disk.

Computer Service Bureau: An internal or external facility providing general or specific data processing services.

Consumer List: A list of names (usually at home addresses) compiled, or resulting, from a common inquiry or buying activity indicating a general or specific buying interest.

Continuation: The next step after a list test. If the test proved responsive within established financial parameters, the list should be reordered.

Continuity Program: Products or services bought as a series of small purchases, rather than all at one time. Generally based on a common theme and shipped at regular or specific time intervals.

Continuous Form: Paper forms designed for computer printing that are folded, and sometimes perforated, at predetermined vertical measurements. These may be letters, vouchers, invoices, cards, etc.

Contribution: is a term that describes the amount of gross profit made by a specific activity. In essence, it is the gross profit of a project after allowing for cost of goods and cost of selling including commissions

C.T.O.: Contribution to overhead (profit).

Contributor List: Names and addresses of persons who

have given to a specific fund raising effort. *(See Donor List.)*

Control: A baseline package or program against which other packages or programs can be measured.

Controlled Circulation: Distribution of a publication at no charge to individuals or companies on the basis of their titles or occupations. Typically, recipients are asked from time to time to verify the information that qualifies them to receive the publication.

Controlled Duplication: A method by which names and addresses from two or more lists are matched (usually by computer) in order to eliminate or limit extra mailings to the same name and address.

Conversion: (1) Process of changing from one method of data processing to another, or from one data processing system to another. Synonymous with Reformatting. (2) To secure specific action such as a purchase or contribution from a name on a mailing list or as a result of an inquiry. (3) First time renewal of a subscriber.

Co-op Mailing.: A mailing of two or more offers included in the same envelope or other carrier, with each participating mailer sharing mailing costs according to some predetermined formula.

Corner card: Most often associated with the return address information in the upper left-hand corner of the mailing envelope.

C.P.I.: (Cost Per Inquiry) A simple arithmetic formula derived by dividing the total cost of a mailing or an advertisement by the number of inquiries received.

Cost per Order: (C.P.O.) A simple arithimetic formula derived by dividing the total cost of a direct marketing campaign by the number of orders received. Similar to Cost per Inquiry, except based on actual orders rather than inquiries.

C.P.O.: (Cost per Order). See Cost per Order.

C.P.M.: (Cost per Thousand). Refers to the total cost-per-thousand pieces of any part or the entire direct mail program.

Coupon: Part of an advertising promotion piece intended to be filled in by the inquirer or customer and returned to the advertiser.

Coupon Clipper: One who has given evidence of responding to free or nominal-cost offers out of curiosity, with little or no serious interest or buying intent.

CRT: Cathode Ray Tube used for display of computer information.

Customer: An individual who has purchased product(s) or service(s) from you.

Data: A representation of facts, concepts or instructions in a formal manner suitable for communication, interpretation, or processing by persons or automatic means.

Database: An integrated body of information. Within Direct Marketing, this will provide a means to contact a group of prospects, a method to measure respondents to the direct marketing effort, a method to measure purchasers and a method to provide continuing communications.

Deadbeat: One who has ordered a product or service and, without just cause, hasn't paid for it.

Decoy: A unique name especially inserted in a mailing list for verifying usage.

Delinquent: One who has fallen behind or has stopped sched-

uled payment for a product or service.

Delivery Date: The date a list user or a designated representative of the list user receives a specific list order from the list owner.

Demographics: Socio-economic characteristics pertaining to geographic unit (county, city, sectional center, ZIP Code, group of households, education, ethnicity, income level, etc.).

Dimensional Mailings: are generally large in a three-dimensional sense; they are packages or fat letters that have a tendency to get put on the top of a a prospect's mail pile

Direct Access: An access mode in which records are obtained from, or placed into, a mass storage file in a non-sequential manner so that any record can be rapidly accessed. Synonymous with Random Access.

Direct Mail Advertising: Any promotional effort using the Postal Service, or other Direct delivery service, for distribution of the advertising message.

Direct Response Advertising: Advertising, through any

medium, designed to generate a response by any means (such as mail, telephone, or telegraph) that is measurable.

Disk Processing: in data processing. data is stored in tracks on a rotating magnetic surface. A movable arm is directed to a specific track location. As the rotating surface passes under the access arm, the required data is read.

DMA: Direct Marketing Association. The primary trade association for direct marketing.

DMA Mail Preference Service: *See Mail Preference Service.*

Donor List: A list of persons who have given money to one or more charitable organizations. *(See Contributor List)*

Doubling Day: A point in time established by previous experience when 50% of all returns to a mailing will be received.

Dummy: (1) A mock-up giving a preview of a printed piece, showing placement and nature of the material to be printed. (2) A fictitious name with a mailable address inserted into a mailing list to check on usage of that list similar to Decoy.

Dupe: (Duplication). Appearance of identical or nearly identical entities more than once.

Duplication Elimination: A specific kind of controlled duplication which provides that: no matter how many times a name and address is on a list, and how many lists contain that name and address, it will be accepted for mailing only once by that mailer. Also referred to as "dupe elimination" or "de-duplication" or "merge/purge".

Editing Rules: Specific rules used in preparing name and address records that treat all elements in the same way at all times. Also, the rules for rearranging, deleting, selecting, or inserting any needed data, symbols and/or characters.

Envelope Stuffer: Any advertising or promotional material enclosed in an envelope with business letters, statements or invoices.

Exchange: An arrangement whereby two mailers exchange equal quantities of mailing list names.

Expire.: A former customer who is no longer an active buyer.

Expiration: A subscription which is not renewed.

Expiration Date: Date a subscription expires.

Field: Reserved area in a computer which services a similar function in all records of the file. Also, location on magnetic tape or disk drive which has definable limitations and meaning: e.g., Position 1-30 is the Name Field.

File Maintenance: The activity of keeping a file up-to-date by adding, changing, or deleting data (all or part). Synonymous with List Maintenance *(See Update)*.

Fill-In: A name, address or other words added to a preprinted letter.

First-Time Buyer: One who buys a product or service from a specific company for the first time.

Fixed Field: A way of laying out, or formatting, list information in a computer file that puts every piece of data in a specific position relative to every other piece of data, and limits the amount of space assigned to that data. If a piece of data is missing from an individual record, or if its assigned space is not completely used, that space is not filled (every record has the same space and the same length). Any data exceeding its assigned space limitation must be abbreviated or contracted.

Former Buyer: One who has bought one or more times from a company with no purchase in the last twelve months.

Fortran: Formula Translation. Computer language usually used to perform mathematical procedures.

Free-Standing Insert: A promotional piece loosely inserted or nested in a newspaper or magazine.

Frequency: The number of times an individual has ordered within a specific period of time. *(See Monetary Value and Recency)*.

Friend-of-a-Friend: (Friend Recommendations) The result of one party sending in the name of someone considered to be interested in a specific advertiser's product or service; a third party inquiry.

Front End: Activities necessary, or the measurement of direct marketing activities, leading to an order or a contribution

F.S.I.: See Free-Standing Insert.

Full Print: is when the addressee and all of the body

copy are generated by the computer printer.

Geo Code: Symbols used or the identification of geographic entities (state, county, ZIP Code, SCF, tract, etc.).

Geographics: Any method or subdividing a list, based on geographic or political subdivisions (ZIP Codes, sectional centers, cities, counties, states, regions).

Gift Buyer: One who buys a product or service for another.

Gimmick.: Attention-getting device, usually dimensional, attached to a direct mail printed piece.

Guarantee: A pledge of satisfaction made by the seller to the buyer and specifying the terms by which the seller will make good his pledge.

Hot-Line List.: The most recent names available on a specific list, but no older than three months. In any event, use of the term "hot-line" should be further modified by "weekly", "monthly", etc.

House List: Any list of names owned by a company as a result of compilation, inquiry or buyer action, or acquisition, that is used to promote that company's products or services.

House-List   Duplicate: Duplication of name-and-address records between the list user's own lists and any list being mailed by him on a one-time use arrangement.

Indicia: Imprint on the outgoing envelope to denote payment of postage.

Influencer: In the business-to-business environment, a person who is involved in the buying decision process but not the decision maker. They can influence the decision but not make it themselves.

Inquiry: One who has asked for literature or other information about a product or service. Unless otherwise stated, it is assumed no payment has been made for the literature or other information. **Insert:** Refers to a promotional piece inserted into an outgoing package or invoice.

Installment Buyer: One who orders goods or services and pays for them in two or more periodic payments after their delivery.

Inter-List   Duplicate: Duplication of name and address records *between* two or more lists, other than house lists, being mailed by a list user.

K: Used in reference to computer storage capacity, generally accepted as 1,000. Analogous to M in the direct marketing industry.

Key: One or more characters within a data group that can be used to identify it or control its use. Synonymous with Key Code in mailing business.

Key Code (Key): A group of letters and/or numbers, colors, or other markings, used to measure the specific effectiveness of media, lists, advertisements, offers, etc., or any parts thereof.

Keyline: Can be any one of many partial or complete descriptions of past buying history coded to include name-and-address information and current status.

KBN: (Kill Bad Name). Action taken with undeliverable addresses, i.e., nixies. You KBN a nixie.

Label: Piece of paper containing the name and address of the recipient which is applied to a mailing for address purposes.

Layout: (1) Artist's sketch showing relative positioning of illustrations, headlines, and copy. (2) Positioning subject matter on a press sheet for most efficient production.

Letterhead: The printing on a letter that identifies the sender.

Lettershop: A business organization that handles the mechanical details of mailings such as addressing, imprinting, collating, etc. Most lettershops offer some printing facilities and many offer some degree of creative direct mail services.

Lifetime Value: A Measurement of the long-term dollar value of a customer, subscriber, donor, etc. This figure is essential when evaluating initial costs to bring in a customer against the lifetime proceeds.

List: (Mailing List). Names and addresses of individuals and/or companies having in common a interest, characteristic or activity.

List Broker: A specialist who makes all necessary arrangements for one company to use the list(s) of another company. A broker's services may include most, or all, of the following: research, selection, recommendation and subsequent evaluation.

List Buyer: Technically, this term should apply only to one who actually buys mailing lists. In practice, however, it is usually used to identify one who orders mailing lists for one-time use: a List User or Mailer.

List Cleaning: The process of correcting and/or removing a name and/or address from a mailing list because it is no longer correct. Term is also used in the identification and elimination of house list duplication

List Compiler: One who develops lists of names and addresses from directories, newspapers, public records, sales slips, trade show registrations and other sources for identifying groups of people or companies with something in common.

List Exchange: A barter arrangement between two companies for the use of mailing list(s). May be: list for list, list for space, or list for comparable value - other than money.

List Maintenance: Any manual, mechanical or electronic system for keeping name-and-address records (with or without other data) up-to-date at any specific point(s) in time.

List Manager: One who, as an employee of a list owner or as an outside agent, is responsible for the use, by others, of a specific mailing list(s). The list manager generally serves the list owner in several or all of the following capacities: list maintenance (or advice thereon), list promotion and marketing, list clearance and record keeping, collecting for use of the list by others.

List Owner: One who, by promotional activity or compilation, has developed a list of names having something in common; or one who has *purchased* (as opposed to rented, reproduced, or used on a one-time basis) such a list from the developer.

List Rental: An arrangement whereby a list owner furnishes names to a mailer, together with the privilege of using the list on a one-time basis only (unless otherwise specified in advance). For this privilege, the list owner is paid a royalty by the mailer. ("List Rental" is the term most often used although "List Reproduction" and "List Usage" more accurately describe the transaction, since "Rental" is not used in the sense of its ordinary meaning of leasing property.)

List Royalty: Payment to list owners for the privilege of using their names on a one-time basis.

List Sample: A group of names selected from a list in order to evaluate the responsiveness of that list.

List Segmentation: *(See List Selection)*

List Selection: Characteristics used to define smaller groups within a list (essentially, lists within a list). Although very small, select groups may be very desirable and may substantially improve response; minimum set-up costs, however, often makes them expensive.

List Sequence: The order in which names and addresses appear in a list. While most lists today are in ZIP Code sequence, some are alphabetical by name within the ZIP Code; others are in carrier sequence (postal delivery); and still others may (or may not) use some other order within the ZIP Code. some lists are still arranged alphabetically by name and chronologically, and in many other variations or combinations.

List Sort: Process of putting a list in specific sequence or no sequence.

List Source: The media used to acquire names: direct mail, space, TV, radio, telephone, etc.

List Test: Part of a list selected to try to determine the effectiveness of the entire list.*(See List Sample.)*

List User: One who uses names and addresses on someone else's list as prospects for the user's product or service; similar to Mailer.

Load Up: Process of offering a buyer the opportunity of buying an entire series at one time after the customer has purchased the first item in that series.

M: Refers to a 1000 measurement unit.

Magnetic Tape: A storage device for electronically recording and reproducing, by use of a computer, defined bits of data. Processing via computer tape is restricted to sequential processing of the information.

Mail Date: Date a list user, by prior agreement with the list owner, is obligated to mail a specific list. No other date is acceptable without specific approval of the list owner.

Mailer: (1) A direct mail advertiser who promotes a product or service using lists of others or house lists or both. (2) A printed direct mail advertising piece. (3) A folding carton, wrapper or tube used to protect materials in the mails.

Mailgram: A combination telegram-letter, with the telegram transmitted to a postal facility close to the addressee and then delivered as first class mail.

Mailing Machine: A machine that attaches labels, address, inserts printed pieces into any style envelope, affixes postage to mailing pieces and otherwise prepares such pieces for deposit in the postal system.

Mail Order Action Line: (MOAL): A service of the Direct Marketing Association which assists consumers in resolving problems with mail order purchases.

Mail Order Buyer: One who orders, and pays for, a product or service through the mail. (Generally, an order telephoned in response to a direct response advertisement is considered a direct substitute for an order sent through postal channels.)

Mail Preference Service: (MPS): A service of the Direct Marketing Association wherein consumers can request to have their names removed from, or added to,

mailing lists. These names are made available to both members and non-members of the association.

Master File: File that is of a permanent nature or regarded in a particular job as authoritative, or one that contains all sub files.

Match: A direct mail term used to refer to the typing of addresses, salutations or inserts onto letters with other copy imprinted by a printing process.

Match Code: A code determined either by the creator or the user of a file for matching records contained in another file.

Match Fill: having the letter body copy typeset and preprinted by a printer then achieving the appearance of a fully personalized letter. The address, salutation and perhaps some specific information in the body of the letter are added during computer printing.

MOAL: Acronym for Mail Order Action Line.

Monetary Value: Total expenditures by a customer during a specific period of time, generally twelve months.

MPS: Abbreviation for Mail Preference Service.

Multimedia: The use of a variety of media in promotional efforts such as direct mail, space, TV, or radio.

Multiple Buyer: One who has bought two or more times (not one who has bought two or more items, one time only); also a Multi-Buyer or Repeat Buyer.

Multiple Regression: Statistical technique used to measure the relationship between responses to a mailing with census demographics and list characteristics of one or more selected mailing lists. Used to determine the best types of people/areas to mail. This technique can also be used to analyze customers, subscribers, etc.

Name: Single Entry on a mailing list.

Name Acquisition: Technique of soliciting a response to obtain names and addresses for a mailing list.

Name-Removal Service: Portion of Mail Preference Service offered by the Direct Marketing Association wherein a consumer is sent a form which, when filled in and returned, constitutes a request to have the individual's name removed from all mailing lists used by partici-

pating members of the Association and other direct mail users.

Negative Option: A buying plan in which a customer or club member agrees to accept and pay for products or services announced in advance at regular intervals unless the individual notifies the company, within a reasonable time after each announcement, not to ship the merchandise.

Nesting: Placing one enclosure within another before inserting into a mailing envelope.

Net Name Arrangement: An agreement, at the time of ordering or before, whereby the list owner agrees to accept adjusted payment for less than the total names shipped to the list user. Such arrangements can be for a percentage of names shipped or names actually mailed (whichever is greater) or for only those names actually mailed (without a percentage limitation). They can provide for a running charge or not.

Nixie: A mailing piece returned to a mailer (under proper authorization) by the Postal Service because of an incorrect, or undeliverable, name and address.

No-Pay: One who has not paid (wholly or in part) for goods or services ordered. "Uncollectable", "Deadbeat", and "Delinquent" are often used to describe the same person.

North/South Labels: Mailing labels that read from top to bottom and can be affixed with Cheshire equipment.

Novelty Format: An attention-getting direct mail format.

Nth Name Selection: A fractional unit that is repeated in sampling a mailing list. For example, in an "every tenth" sample, you would select the 1st, 11th, 21st, 31nd, etc. records-or the 2nd, 12th, 22nd, 32nd, etc., records and so forth.

OCR: (Optical Character Recognition) Machine identification of printed characters through use of light sensitive devices.

Offer: The terms promoting a specific product or service.

One-Time Buyer: A buyer who has not ordered a second time from a given company.

One-Time Use of A List: An intrinsic part of the normal list usage, list reproduction, or list exchange agreement in which it is understood that the mailer will not use the names on the list more than one time without specific prior approval of the list owner.

Open Account: A customer record that, at a specific time, reflects an unpaid balance for goods and services ordered, without delinquency.

Optical Scanner: An input device that optically reads a line of printed characters and converts each character into its electronic equivalent for processing.

Order Blank Envelopes: An order form printed on one side of a sheet, with a mailing address on the reverse. The recipient simply fills in the order, folds and seals like an envelope.

Order Card: A reply card used to initiate an order by mail.

Order Form: A printed form on which a customer can provide information to initiate an order by mail. Designed to be mailed in an envelope.

Package: A term used to describe all of the assembled enclosures (parts or elements) of a mailing effort.

Package Insert: Any promotional piece included in a product shipment. It may be for different products (or refills and replacements) from the same company or for products and services of other companies.

Package Test: A test of part or all of the elements of one mailing piece against another.

Paid Cancel: One who completes a basic buying commitment, or more, before cancelling the commitment. *(See Completed Cancel).*

Paid Circulation: Distribution of a publication to individuals or organizations which have paid for a subscription.

Paid During Service: Term used to describe a method of paying for magazine subscriptions in installments, usually weekly or monthly, and, usually, collected in person by the original sales person or a representative of that company.

Peel-Off Label: A self-adhesive label attached to a backing which is attached to a mailing piece. The label is intended to be removed from the mailing piece and attached to an order blank or card.

Penetration: Relationship of the number of individuals or families on a particular list (by state, ZIP Code, S.I.C., etc) compared to the total number possible.

Personalization: Individualizing

of direct mail pieces by adding the name or other personal information about the recipient.

Phone List: Mailing list compiled from names listed in telephone directories.

P.I.: (Per Inquiry): A payment method in the direct marketing industry. The user contracts with a media vendor and agrees to pay for services on a per lead or per sale basis.

Piggy-Back: An offer that hitches a free ride with another offer.

Poly Bag: Transparent polyethylene bag used in place of envelopes for mailing.

Pop-Up: A printed piece containing a paper construction pasted inside a fold and which, when the fold is opened, "pops up" to form a three-dimensional illustration.

Positive Option: A method of distributing products and services incorporating the same advance notice techniques as Negative Option but requiring a specific order each time from the member or subscriber. Generally, it is more costly and less predictable than Negative Option.

Postal Service Prohibitory Order: A communication

from the Postal Service to a company indicating that a specific person and/or family considers the company's advertising mail to be pandering. The order requires the company to remove from its own mailing list and from any other lists used to promote the company's products or services all names listed on the order. Violation of the Order is subject to fine and imprisonment. Names listed on the Order are to be distinguished from those names removed voluntarily by the list owner at an individual's request.

Post Card: Single sheet self-mailers on card stock.

Post Card Mailers: Booklet containing business reply cards which are individually perforated for selective return, to order products or obtain information.

Premium: An item offered to a buyer, usually free or at a nominal price, as an inducement to purchase or obtain for trial a product or service offered via mail order.

Premium Buyer: One who buys a product or service to get another product or service (usually free or at a special price), or who responds to an offer of a special product (premium) on the package or label (or sometimes in the advertising) of another product.

Preprint: An advertising insert printed in advance and supplied to a newspaper or magazine for insertion.

Private Mail: Mail handled by special arrangement outside of the Postal Service.

Program: (1) A sequence of steps to be executed by the computer to solve a given problem or achieve a certain result. (2) A sequence of direct marketing activities that identify a direct marketing effort to sell products or generate leads.

Programming: Design, writing and testing of a computer program.

Prospect: (1) A name on a mailing list considered to be a potential buyer for a give buyer for a given product or service buy who has not previously made such a purchase. (2) That group of suspects that meets your predetermined qualification criteria and you want to include them in an on-going marketing program.

Prospect: A prospect is a suspect that meets your predeter- .

mined qualification criteria. You might want to include him/her in an ongoing marketing program.

Prospecting: Mailing to get leads for further sales contact rather than to make direct sales.

Protection: The amount of time, before and after the assigned mailing date, a list owner will not allow the same names to be mailed by anyone other than the mailer cleared for that specific date.

Psychographics: Any characteristics or qualities used to denote the lifestyle(s) or attitude(s) of customers and prospective customers.

Publisher's Letter: A second letter enclosed in a mailing package to stress a specific selling point. Also called a buck slip or lift memo.

Purge: The process of eliminating duplicates and/or unwanted names and addresses from one or more lists.

Pyramiding: A method of testing mailing lists, in which one starts with a small quantity and, based on positive indications, follows with increasingly larger quantities of the list balance until the entire list is mailed.

Questionnaire: A printed form to a specified audience to solicit answers to specific questions.

Random Access: An access mode in which records are obtained from, or placed into, a mass storage file in a non-sequential manner so that any record can be rapidly accessed. Synonymous with Direct Access.

Recency: The latest purchase or other activity recorded for an individual or company on a specific customer list. *(See Frequency and Monetary Value.)*

Referral: (1) That group of prospects that is of such high quality that it should be referred for immediate handling by a salesperson or customer support organization. Sometimes called leads. (2) Usually derived form the Friend-get-a-Friend program, where a member is offered a record or book to suggest the names of friends who might be interested in joining the club.

Reformatting: Changing a magnetic tape format from one arrangement to another, more usable format. Synonymous with Conversion (list or tape).

Renewal: A subscription that has been renewed prior to, or at, expiration time or within six months thereafter.

Repeat Buyer: *(See Multiple Buyer.)*

Rental: *(See List Rental.)*

Reply Card: A sender-addressed card included in a mailing on which the recipient may indicate his response to the offer.

Reply-O-Letter: One of a number of patented direct mail formats for facilitating replies from prospects. It features a die-cut opening on the face of the letter and a pocket on the reverse. An addressed reply card is inserted in the pocket and the name and address therein shows through the die-cut opening.

Reproduction Right: Authorization by a list owner for a specific mailer to use that list on a one-time basis.

Response Rate: Percent of returns or inquiries from a mailing.

Return Envelopes: Addressed reply envelopes, either stamped or un-stamped as distinguished from business reply envelopes which carry a postage payment guarantee included with a mailing.

Return on Investment: (ROI): The evaluation of return on invested capital. In direct mail, often loosely described as the return (income) based on the dollars expended in a direct mail campaign.

Return Postage Guaranteed: A legend imprinted on the address face of envelopes or other mailing pieces when the mailer wishes the Postal Service to return undeliverable third class bulk mail. A charge equivalent to the single piece, first class rate will be made for each piece returned. *(See List Cleaning.)*

Return Requested: An indication that a mailer will compensate the Postal Service for return of an undeliverable mailing piece.

Returns: (1) Responses to a direct mail program. (2) Returns of products shipped to customers on free or limited trials that are not purchased.

RFMR: Abbreviation for Recency-Frequency-Monetary Value Ratio, a formula used to evaluate the sales potential of names on a mailing list.

Rollout: To mail the remaining portion of a mailing list after successfully testing a portion of that list.

R.O.P.: (Run of Paper or Run of Press): Usually refers to ads which can be placed on any page of a newspaper or magazine by the publisher.

Rough: Dummy or layout in sketchy form with a minimum of detail.

Royalties: Sum paid per unit mailed or sold for the use of a list, imprimatur, patent, etc.

Running Charge: The price a list owner charges for names run or passed, but not used by a specific mailer. When such a charge is made, it is usually to cover extra processing costs. However, some list owners set the price without regard to actual cost.

Salting: Deliberate placing of decoy or dummy names in a list to trace list usage and delivery. *(See Decoy or Dummy.)*

Sample Buyer: One who sends for a sample product, usually at a special price or for a small handling charge, but sometimes free.

Sample Package: (Mailing Piece): An example of the package to be mailed by the list user to a particular list. Such a mailing piece is submitted to the list owner for approval prior to commitment for one-time use of the list. Although a sample package may, due to time pressure, differ slightly from the actual package used, the list owner agreement usually requires the user to reveal any material differences when submitting the sample package.

Scented Inks: Printing inks to which a fragrance has been added.

SCF: (Sectional Center Facility) See Sectional Center.

Sectional Center: (SCF or SCF Center): A Postal Service distribution unit comprising different Post Offices whose ZIP Codes start with the same first three digits.

Selection Criteria: Definition of characteristics that identify segments or sub-groups within a list.

Self-Cover: A cover of the same paper as the inside text pages.

Self-Mailer: A direct mail piece mailed without an envelope.

Sequence: An arrangement of items according to a specified set of rules or instructions. Refers generally to ZIP Codes or customer number sequence.

Sequential Processing: Type of information storage, reading one item at a time, having to move through all the preceding records to get the next record in sequential order.

Sheet-fed forms: During computer printing using a standard cut form as opposed to continuous form. Also referred to as cut-sheet forms.

S.I.C.: (Standard Industrial C l a s s i f i c a t i o n) : Classification of businesses, as defined by the U.S. Department of Commerce.

SMSA: (Standard Metropolitan Statistical Area) Major metropolitan areas as set forth by the government used by the print publications to define and compare markets. See also A.D.I..

Software: A set of programs, procedures and associated documentation concerned with operation of a data processing system.

Solo Mailing: A mailing promoting a single product or a limited group of related products. Usually it consists of a letter, brochure and reply device enclosed in an envelope.

Source Code: Unique alphabetic and/or numeric identification for distinguishing one list or media source from another. *(See Key Code.)*

Source Count: The number of names and addresses, in any given list, for the media (or list sources) from which the names and addresses were derived.

Split Test: Two or more samples from the same list - each considered to be representative of the entire list - used for package tests or to test the homogeneity of the list.

State Count: The number of names and addresses, in a given list, for each state.

Statement Stuffer: A small, printed piece designed to be inserted in an envelope carrying a customer's statement of account.

Step Up: The use of special premiums to get a mail order buyer to increase his unit of purchase.

Stock Art: Art sold for use by a number of advertisers. Also called clip art.

Stock Cut: Printing engravings kept in stock by the printer or publisher for occasional use.

Stock Formats: Direct mail formats with pre-printed illustrations and/or headings to which an advertiser adds his own copy.

Stopper: Advertising slang for a striking headline or illustration intended to attract immediate attention.

Stuffer: Advertising enclosures placed in other media - i.e., newspapers, merchandise packages, mailings for other products, etc.

Strategic: Use of direct marketing relating to the long term efforts and results that will be experienced.

Subscriber: Individual who has paid or has qualified to receive a periodical.

Suspect: The name of a business in business-to-business direct marketing.

Swatching: Attaching samples of material to a printed piece.

Syndicated Mailing: Mailing prepared for distribution by firms other than the manufacturer or syndicator.

Syndicator: One who makes available prepared direct mail promotions for specific products or services to a list owner for mailing to his own list. Most syndicators also offer product fulfillment services.

Tabloid: A preprinted advertising insert of four or more pages, usually about half the size of a regular newspaper page, designed for inserting into a newspaper.

Tactical: use of direct marketing;

how you will implement direct marketing with the current approach to selling.

Tag: To mark a record with definitive criteria which allows for subsequent selection or suppression.

Tape Density: The number of bits of information (bytes) that can be included in each of a specific magnetic tape - e.g., 556 BPI, 800 BPI, 1600 BPI, etc.

Tape Dump: A printout of data on a magnetic tape to be edited and checked for correctness, readability, consistency, etc.

Tape Layout: A simple "map" of the data included in each record and its relative, or specific location.

Tape Record: All of the information about an individual or company contained on a specific magnetic tape.

Teaser: An advertisement or promotion planned to elicit curiosity about a later advertisement or promotion.

Telecommunications: (1) Data transmission between a computer system and remotely located devices via a unit that performs the necessary format conversion and controls the rate of transmission over telephone lines, microwaves, etc. Synonymous with Transceive. (2) The management and control of the routing that a voice or data communication takes when leaving one location and traveling to another.

Telephone Preference Service (TPS): A service of the Direct Marketing Association for consumers who wish to have their names removed from national telemarketing lists. The name-removal file is made available to subscribers on a quarterly basis.

Telephone Switch: A computer designed to control the telephone activity within a business. Phone calls are receive or routed automatically. Often referred to as a PBX - private branch exchange or CBX - computerized branch exchange.

Terminal: Any mechanism which can transmit and/or receive data through a system or communications network.

Test Panel: A term used to identify each of the parts or samples in a split test.

Test Tape: A selection of representative records within a mailing list that enables a list user or service bureau to prepare for reformatting or converting the list to a form more efficient for the user.

Throwaway: An advertisement or promotional piece intended for widespread free distribution. Generally printed on inexpensive paper stock, it is most often distributed by hand to passers-by or from house-to-house.

Tie-In: Cooperative mailing effort involving two or more advertisers.

Til Forbid: An order for continuing service which is to continue until specifically cancelled by the buyer. Also "TF".

Title: A designation before (prefix) or after (suffix) a name to more accurately identify an individual. (Prefixes - Mr., Mrs., Dr., Sister, etc.; Suffixes - M.D., Jr., President, Sales Manager, etc.)

Title Addressing: Usually refers to functional titles used in compiling business lists, where there is no individual name.

Time Sharing: Multiple utilization of available computer time, often via terminals, usually shared by different organizations.

Tip-On: An item glued to printed piece.

Token: An involvement device, often consisting of a perforated portion of an order card designed to be removed from its original position and placed in another designated area on the order card, to signify a desire to purchase the product or service.

Town Marker: A symbol used to identify the end of mailing list's geographical unit. (Originated for "towns" but now used for ZIP Codes, Sectional Centers, etc.).

Traffic Builder: A direct mail piece intended primarily to attract recipients to the mailer's place of business.

Trial Buyer: One who buys a short-term supply of a product, or buys th product with the understanding that it may be examined, used, or tested for a specified time before deciding whether to pay for it or to return it.

Trial Subscriber: A person ordering a publication or service on a conditional basis. The condition may relate to: delaying payment, the right to cancel, a shorter than normal term and/or a special introductory price.

Uncollectable: One who hasn't paid for goods and services at the end of a normal series of collection efforts.

Unit Of Sale: Description of the average dollar amount spent by customers on a mailing list.

Universe: Total number of individuals that might be included on a mailing list; all of those fitting a single set of specifications.

Update: Recent transactions and current information added to the Master (main) list to reflect the current status of each record on the list.

Up Front: Securing payment for a product offered by mail order before the product is sent.

UPS: Acronym for United Parcel Service.

Variable Field: A way of laying out for formatting list information that assigns a specific sequence to the data, but doesn't assign it specific positions. While this method conserves space, on magnetic tape or disk, it is generally more difficult to work with.

Verification: The process of determining the validity of an order by sending a questionnaire to the customer.

WATS: Acronym for Wide Area Telephone Service. A service providing a special line allowing calls within certain areas to be called a significantly lower rates.

White Mail: Incoming mail that is not on a form sent out by the advertiser. All mail other than orders or payments.

Window Envelope: Envelope with a die-cut portion on the front that permits viewing the address printed on an enclosure. The "die-cut window" may or may not be covered with a transparent material.

Wing Mailer: Label-affixing device that uses strips of paper on which addresses have been printed.

ZIP Code: A group of five digits used by the U.S. Postal Service to designate specific post offices, stations, branches, buildings or large companies.

ZIP Code Count: The number of names and addresses in a list, within each ZIP Code.

ZIP Code Sequence: Arranging names and addresses in a list according to the numeric progression of the ZIP Code in each record. This form of list formatting is mandatory for mailing at bulk third class mail rates, based on the sorting requirements of Postal Service regulations.

Bibliography

The following books are excellent reference sources that can be very helpful in learning more about all facets of direct marketing.

Baier, Martin Elements of Direct Marketing
New York, NY: McGraw-Hill Book Co., 1983

Barton, Roger, Editor Handbook of Advertising Management
New York, NY: McGraw-Hill, 1970.

Bettger, Frank How I Raised Myself From Failure to Success in Selling
Englewood Cliffs, NJ: Prentice-Hall, Inc., 1949.

Bonoma, Thomas V. and Shapiro, Benson P. Segmenting The Industrial Market
New York, IL: Lexington Books, 1983.

DMA Business/Industrial Direct Marketing Monograph Volume 5
New York, NY: DMA Publications Division, 1982.

DMA   1986 Fact Book on Direct Marketing
                        New York, NY: DMA Publications Division,
                        1987.

Dodge, Robert H.   Industrial Marketing
                        New York, NY: McGraw-Hill, 1970

Elling, Karl A.   Introduction to Modern Marketing
                        New York, NY: Macmillan Co., 1969

Fox, Edward and Wheatley, Edward   Modern Marketing
                        Chicago, IL: Scott, Foreman, and Co., 1974

Gosden, Freeman F., Jr. Direct Marketing Success
                        New York, NY: John Wiley & Sons, 1985.

Haas, Robert, W.   Industrial Marketing Management
                        New York, NY: Litton Educational
                        Publishing, Inc., 1976.

Harper, Rose   Mailing List Strategies A Guide to Direct
                        Mail Success
                        New York, NY: McGraw-Hill Book Co.,
                        1986.

Hodgson, Richard S.   Direct Mail and Mail Order Handbook
                        Chicago, IL: The Dartnell Corp, 1977.

Kobs, Jim   Profitable Direct Marketing
                        Chicago, IL: Crain Books, 1979.

Lavin, Henry   How to Get and Keep! Good Industrial
                        Customers Through Effective Direct Mail
                        New York, NY: Exposition Press, 1980.

Mayer, Edward N., Jr. and Ljungven, Roy G., Editors The Handbook
        of Industrial Direct Mail Advertising
        New York, NY: Association of Industrial
        Advertisers, Inc., 1972.

Messner, Fred R.   Industrial Advertising
        New York, NY: McGraw-Hill, 1963.

Nash, Edward, L.   D i r e c t   M a r k e t i n g :
        Strategy/Planning/Execution
        New York, NY: McGraw-Hill Book Co.,
        1982.

Nash, Edward, L.   The Direct Marketing Handbook
        New York, NY: McGraw-Hill Book Co.,
        1984.

Ogilvy, David   Ogilvy on Advertising
        New York, NY: Crown Publishers, Inc.,
        1983.

Posch, Robert J., Jr. The Direct Marketer's Legal Adviser
        New York, NY: McGraw-Hill Book Co.,
        1983.

Rand McNally   Rand McNally Zip Code Atlas
        Chicago, IL: Rand McNally & Company,
        1983.

Roman, Murray   How to Build Your Business By Telephone -
        Telephone Marketing
        New York, NY: McGraw-Hill Book Co.,
        1976.

Roman, Murray   Telemarketing Campaigns That Work!
        New York, NY: McGraw-Hill Book Co.,
        1983.

Sawyer, Howard G. Business-To-Business Advertising: How to
                    Compete for a $1-trillion-plus Market.
                    Chicago, IL: Crain Books, 1978.

Steckel, Robert C.   Profitable Telephone Sales Operations
                        New York, NY: Arco Publishing Company,
                        Inc., 1977

Stone, Bob   Successful Direct Marketing Methods, Third
                        Edition
                        Lincolnwood, IL: Crain Books, An Imprint
                        of National Textbook Company, 1986.

Strunk, William, Jr. and White, E. B. The Elements of Style
                        New York, NY: Macmillan Publishing Co.,
                        Inc., 1979.

U. S. Department of Commerce   Standard Industrial Classification
                        Manual
                        Washington, DC: US Government Printing
                        Office, 1972

Wademan, Victor   Risk-Free Advertising; How to Come Close
                        to It
                        New York, NY: John Wiley & Sons, 1977.

Webster, Frederick E., Jr. Industrial Marketing Strategy
                        New York, NY: Ronald Press, 1979.